An Introduction to the Philosophy of Religion

An Introduction to the Philosophy of Religion provides a broad overview of the topics which are at the forefront of discussion in contemporary philosophy of religion. Prominent views and arguments from both historical and contemporary authors are discussed and analyzed. The book treats all of the central topics in the field, including the coherence of the divine attributes, theistic and atheistic arguments, faith and reason, religion and ethics, miracles, human freedom and divine providence, science and religion, and immortality. In addition it addresses topics of significant importance that similar books often ignore, including the argument for atheism from hiddenness, the coherence of the doctrines of the Trinity and the Incarnation, and the relationship between religion and politics. It will be a valuable accompaniment to undergraduate and introductory graduate-level courses.

MICHAEL J. MURRAY is Arthur and Katherine Shadek Professor in the Humanities and Philosophy, Department of Philosophy, Franklin and Marshall College.

MICHAEL C. REA is Associate Professor and Associate Director, Center for Philosophy of Religion, Department of Philosophy, University of Notre Dame.

An Introduction to the Philosophy of Religion

MICHAEL J. MURRAY
Franklin and Marshall College

and

MICHAEL C. REA
University of Notre Dame

CAMBRIDGE
UNIVERSITY PRESS

CAMBRIDGE UNIVERSITY PRESS

Cambridge, New York, Melbourne, Madrid, Cape Town, Singapore, São Paulo, Delhi

Cambridge University Press
The Edinburgh Building, Cambridge CB2 8RU, UK

Published in the United States of America by Cambridge University Press, New York

www.cambridge.org
Information on this title: www.cambridge.org/9780521619554

First published 2008

Printed in the United Kingdom at the University Press, Cambridge

A catalogue record for this publication is available from the British Library

ISBN 978-0-521-85369-9 hardback
ISBN 978-0-521-61955-4 paperback

To our families
Kirsten, Samuel, Elise, and Julia
and
Chris, Aaron, and Kris

Contents

Preface

Anyone going to a major university library and searching for books on "philosophy of religion" would think that this area of philosophy was quite new. By all appearances, it would seem that the philosophy of religion emerged sometime in the middle of the twentieth century, and then blossomed rapidly over the period between then and now. Yet this appearance would be deceiving. Philosophical reflection on religious themes has been a central part of philosophy from the time of its origin to the present. In the Western philosophical tradition this is due at least in part to the fact that most philosophers in the West either have been theists themselves or have written in intellectual climates dominated by theistic presuppositions. Yet while philosophy of religion is not itself new, what is new is the attempt to tease out some of the questions that philosophers raise when discussing religion and to treat them together under a single heading. That is what contemporary philosophers of religion do, and it is what this book aims to do as well.

Some of the issues that philosophers raise when discussing religion are of perennial interest: Is there a God? How could God permit evil? Does morality depend on God in some fashion? And so on. Other questions become more or less important as the discipline of philosophy itself changes and the culture in which this philosophical reflection goes on changes. In this book we try to balance discussion of those central, perennial questions with ones that are just beginning to appear over the horizon. In this way, the text aims to give students access to the long tradition of philosophical reflection in religion, while also acquainting them with where the discipline now stands, and where it seems to be going.

This book opens with a section discussing the nature and attributes of God. We then move to consider questions about the rationality of belief in such a God, as well as a variety of questions about what philosophers in the major religious traditions oriented around belief in this sort of God have said (or ought to say) about science, morality, politics, mind, and immortality. Readers will notice that the focus throughout is on theistic belief – that is, belief in the God of the Western monotheistic traditions. Those unaware of the way in which contemporary philosophy of religion in the English-speaking world has developed over the past several decades might find this focus puzzling, or even objectionable. Thus, a few words of explanation are in order.

Religious beliefs and practices have proliferated in virtually every human culture; and the supernatural entities that figure in these religious beliefs (if any) are highly variegated. Some religions hypothesize no supernatural beings at all, either because those things that are the objects of religious devotion, attention, or fear are parts of the natural order itself, or because God is identified with the totality of the natural order, the latter view being known as pantheism. Other religious traditions instead propose that God is a larger whole consisting of a body – the physical cosmos – in addition to a divine soul that is intimately joined with this cosmic body. This view is known as panentheism. In addition there are myriad versions of polytheism in the history of religion. More familiar to those in the West, however, are religions which argue that there are many supernatural beings (among them, angels and demons) only one of whom counts as God, a supremely perfect or ultimate being who creates and controls all that there is. And there are still more variations. In light of this, it seems that any attempt to provide (in the space that we have been given) a suitably inclusive or comprehensive introduction to philosophical problems associated with the concept of divinity will come at the price of objectionable superficiality.

The best way forward, then, is to restrict our focus somehow. Since the primary goal of this book is to provide a properly representative introduction to the field of philosophy of religion as it has developed in English-speaking countries over the past fifty years, and since that field has been overwhelmingly dominated by questions arising in connection with theism in general and particular doctrines of the three major theistic religions (Judaism, Christianity, and Islam), we have elected to restrict our focus largely to these questions.

Some might regard that choice as unfortunate, thinking that more attention should be devoted to non-Western, non-theistic religious traditions. We agree that more reflection should be devoted to these traditions and, indeed, philosophical work on these topics in English-language philosophy departments is on the rise. But space limitations preclude giving these traditions the full and careful treatment that they would merit. Note, however, that there will be times throughout this book where we will make reference to non-monotheistic religious alternatives when they bear directly on one of the issues we are discussing. Monotheists have, for example, often argued for the truth of monotheism by arguing that it is the only way of making sense of some important evident fact or widely held belief. Sometimes these monotheists seem only to have in view two alternatives: monotheism and atheistic naturalism. But there are going to be many cases where alternative religious traditions would equally well or better explain or make sense of the facts or beliefs in question. In cases like these, we will discuss the relevant alternatives as a way of helping us assess claims that theists make.

How shall we approach the questions that we propose to discuss? Here a few words about disciplinary differences are in order. There are various disciplinary approaches one can take when considering questions concerning the nature of God. For example, one can take a strictly theological approach. Some theologians aim to develop theologies based entirely on the data of purported revelations within particular religious traditions. Islamic theologians, especially those adhering to the Asharite tradition, thus try to piece together a conception of God from the way in which God is described and characterized in the Koran. Theology of this sort is known as revealed or sacred theology. Other theologians look to see what can be known about God by drawing inferences from various facts about the world. The fact that the world began to be, or that its existence is contingent, or that it exhibits special types of design, are invoked in an attempt to show that God exists and has certain characteristics or properties. Such reasoning is known as natural theology.

Alternatively, one can approach questions about the nature of God from within the disciplines of religion or religious studies. Scholars within these disciplines typically seek to explain the concept of God as it is developed and used by various constituencies within a specific tradition. They might thus elucidate and study the emergence of novel Vedic theological traditions in thirteenth-century Hinduism or the differences between Western and Eastern Christianity. Some will take a more fine-grained approach by seeking to describe the concept of God as it is developed by particular theological figures, like Augustine or John Calvin, or might instead take a wider angle approach, looking to plot the course of theological development over long spans of time. Scholars in these fields also examine the relationship between various conceptions of God and their impact on the behavior and practice of adherents of those traditions.

Philosophers approach theological or religious questions with their own aims and questions. Within the discipline of philosophy there are many sub-disciplines, a number of which seek to use the tools and methods of philosophical inquiry to ask distinctively philosophical questions about other disciplines. Thus there is, within philosophy itself, the philosophy of art, the philosophy of science, the philosophy of law, the philosophy of psychology, and so on. There is also the philosophy of religion. What questions do philosophers of psychology or philosophers of art or philosophers of religion consider that are different from the questions considered by psychologists or artists or theologians? When doing philosophy of this sort, philosophers are usually engaged in one or both of two activities that we can call "conceptual clarification" and "propositional justification." These two activities look at the methodologies, presuppositions and outputs of the disciplines in question and ask the following two questions: what do those within the discipline mean when they affirm the claims they do, and why do they think those affirmations are true? In one sense every discipline asks these questions within their own domain. When philosophers ask these questions, however, they are typically directed towards claims or practices that are regarded as fundamental or are perhaps merely presupposed within the discipline. Thus while adherents of a religious tradition will typically assume a certain body of doctrine to be true – doctrines about God, for example – the philosopher of religion wants to explore what exactly is meant by the word "God," whether the meanings are coherent, and whether or not one should even accept the reality of God in the first place. These questions, and others related to them, will be the subject of this book.

In closing, we would like to express our gratitude for comments on earlier partial drafts of various chapters to Robert Audi, Jeff Brower, Fred Crossan, Tom Flint, Dennis Monokroussos, Sam Ochstein, Dan Speak, and Lea Schweitz. We owe a special debt of thanks to Michael Bergmann, who provided detailed comments and advice on several chapters of the penultimate manuscript. Chapter 3 includes material from "Understanding the

Trinity" (*Logos* 8 (2005), 145, no. 57) by Jeffrey Brower and Michael Rea; and chapter 6 includes material from Michael Murray's "Theodicy," forthcoming in Thomas Flint and Michael Rea (eds.), *The Oxford Handbook for Philosophical Theology* (Oxford: Oxford University Press, 2008). We are grateful to the respective publishers for permission to use this material.

Part I

The Nature of God

1 Attributes of God: independence, goodness, and power

In the preface, we explained and defended our decision to focus our attention in this book primarily on the Western monotheistic religious traditions. Those traditions claim, in some rough sense, to share a common concept of God; and one of the most important enterprises in theistic philosophy of religion has been the task of analyzing that concept and exploring some of its more puzzling and problematic aspects. In this and the following two chapters we too shall take up this task, paying special attention to those attributes of God that have traditionally been regarded as most important and of the greatest philosophical interest.

Before turning to our discussion of the attributes of God, it will be helpful first to say a few words both about what we mean when we talk about "the" concept of God and about how we might go about unpacking that concept.

The concept of God

Theologians in the Western tradition have characterized "the concept of God" in a variety of different ways. For some, the concept of God is just the concept of the ultimate reality, or the source and ground of all else; for others it is the concept of a maximally perfect being. Still others would say that to be God is to be the one and only being worthy of worship, so that analyzing the concept of God would involve coming to a full understanding of worship-worthiness. Alternatively, one might think that the concept of God is just the concept of whatever being happens to be revealed in one's favored sacred text as the supreme ruler of all. And so on. Which concept, then, are we concerned with?

Before answering this question, a few preliminary clarifications are in order. First, note that there are two different ways of using the word "God." It can be used as a proper name or as a title. To illustrate the distinction, consider the difference between the name "Ronald Reagan" and the title "The President of the United States." The term "Ronald Reagan" names a specific individual and being Ronald Reagan is just a matter of being identical to that specific individual. You can't be elected to the position of being Ronald Reagan; nobody other than the man who was in fact Ronald Reagan could have been or could come to be Ronald Reagan; and if all you knew about the man was that he was named Ronald Reagan, you wouldn't be able to draw any conclusions about what he was like or about what offices he held. Referring to Ronald Reagan by his name leaves open all questions about what Reagan was actually like. Of course, the term "the President of the United States" also can be (and often is) used to pick out a specific individual. But it is not always used this way. For example, it would be perfectly true to say that the President of the United States is the commander-in-chief of the United States military even at a time when the office of president was vacant – i.e. even at a time when there was no such person as the President of the United States. By contrast with what is expressed by the term "Ronald Reagan," being president is a matter of fulfilling a certain office, not of being identical to some specific individual. You can be elected to the position of president; people other than the current president have been and will be president; and if all you knew about someone was that he or she was President of the United States, you would be able to infer quite a lot about that person – for example, that the person is over thirty-five years old, that he or she is a United States citizen, that he or she is commander-in-chief of the US military, and so on. Referring to a person by his or her title tells you (sometimes, anyway) quite a lot about the person.

Likewise, when "God" is used as a name, it is being used simply to refer to a specific individual, leaving open questions about what that individual is like. Being God is just a matter of being that individual; and to find out what God is like, we have to acquire information about that specific individual. On the other hand, if and when "God" is used as a title, we can learn quite a lot about what God is or would be like simply by unpacking our concept of the role associated with the term "God."

Thus, corresponding to this difference in ways of using the term "God," there is a distinction to be made between two ways in which the monotheistic traditions have fleshed out or developed their concept of God. We can, following a long tradition, call these the *a posteriori* and the *a priori* ways. The *a posteriori* approach begins with data that people believe put them in direct contact with the individual referred to by the name "God" – data coming from revealed texts, religious experiences, mediums or prophets, and the like – and then builds the concept of God out of those data (just as you might develop your concept of Ronald Reagan out of data gathered from a written biography, videotapes of speeches and interviews, and so on). When people speak of the God of the Bible, or the God who speaks to them in mystical experience, or the God of Abraham or Mohammed, they are referring to some particular individual with whom they are in direct or indirect contact through these different media. They are also using the term "God" and its relatives (like "the God of so-and-so") as proper names.

The second or *a priori* way begins with some basic characteristic, property, or feature that people take to belong to anyone or anything that might count as God. Those taking this approach are likely to say things like: "For something to count as God, that thing must be the creator of all that is" or "For something to count as God, it must be worthy of worship" or "For something to be God it must be the ground of morality," and so on. Those who treat the concept of God this way start with the idea that for something to "count as" God, it must play a certain role or satisfy some description. Then they ask what a being must be like in order to play that role.

There is some reason to think that these various starting points will not all converge on the same entity. A Pure Land Buddhist and a charismatic Protestant might both claim to have had repeated religious experiences of God. But the concepts of Amida Buddha and Jesus are vastly different and seem not to pick out the same thing. Furthermore, someone who thinks of God primarily as the greatest possible being might well arrive at a concept of God very different from what would be arrived at by someone taking as her guiding notion the idea that God is the entity that acts as the ground of morality.

In the Western theistic tradition, the concept of God has arisen from a careful negotiation between these two methods. In many respects this dual approach makes perfectly good sense. It makes sense to think of the word "God" as a proper name since theists do think that there is some unique individual entity or person that they are acquainted with – through religious experience or revelation or the mediation of prophets, and so on. But it is also true that revelation or reason sometimes describes God as an entity that plays a certain role. So when the Hebrew Scriptures describe God as the creator, or when someone takes a "first cause" argument to show that the universe was brought into existence by something distinct from itself, we have reason to think that these two approaches are, or at least can be, converging on a description of the same thing.

The Western theistic traditions tighten the connection between these two approaches in that, whereas they acknowledge that the term "God" often functions both as a proper name and as a title, they also usually agree that (unlike the office of President) whatever person fills the "God-role" cannot fail to fill it. It is odd to use the term "President of the United States" as a name (though one can do so: just imagine naming your dog or your child "President of the United States"). The reason is that, in normal use, the term is associated with a role that is fulfilled at different times by different people. But if the term were associated with a role that could only be filled by the person who in fact fills it, it would be quite natural to use the term as a name. For example, suppose we tell you that Paul is the Galactic Emperor and that, furthermore (strangely), Paul necessarily holds that office. The word "Paul," then, functions as a proper name; but the title "Galactic Emperor" might also function the same way. In other words, since Paul necessarily holds the office of Galactic Emperor – since nothing can possibly be Paul without being the Galactic Emperor, and vice versa – the term "Galactic Emperor" can function either as a name or as a title according to our preference. And the same is true, according to many theists, of the term "God."

This is important because it helps to explain why we naturally vacillate between the *a priori* and *a posteriori* ways of fleshing out our concept of God (whereas we don't vacillate between these approaches in fleshing out the concepts associated with terms like "Ronald Reagan" or "President of the United States"). Thus, if someone were to ask us to tell them about the Galactic Emperor, we might do so simply by talking about whatever information – from news reports, telescopic observations, media appearances, personal correspondence, or whatever – we have about Paul. In this way, we develop our concept of the Galactic Emperor via the *a posteriori* route. Alternatively, we might do so by talking about the role of Galactic Emperor – explaining what is involved in that role and what sorts of beings could or could not be qualified to hold it (ignoring for the moment the fact that Paul holds it of necessity). In doing this, we would provide something like an *a priori* analysis of the concept of Galactic Emperor. And, again, likewise in the case of God.

If we think about approaching the concept of God in these two ways, what concept of God emerges? We might first take note of the fact that theistic traditions almost all agree on the following basic claims about God;

(C1) Nothing made God, and God is the source or ground of everything other than God.

(C2) God rules all that is not God.

(C3) God is the most perfect being.

These three points of agreement correspond to three distinct starting points for developing a richer, more detailed concept of divinity. We can label these three starting points: creation theology, providential theology, and perfect-being theology. According to creation theology God is not made or caused but is rather the cause or maker of everything else. Can we learn anything further about God by conceiving of God in this way? Yes. We can learn, first, that God is a being with causal power. If the created universe exhibits signs that its cause was a rational agent, we can learn that God is a being with intelligence or rationality. When we turn to consider various arguments for the existence of God in chapter 5 we will see that some theists claim that indeed much more can be known about the character of God by thinking of God as the creator.

Similarly, from providential theology, we can infer that God is supreme among all existing things because God rules over and superintends those things. If the universe exhibits continuing signs of divine providential activity, either because God must continue to sustain the world in existence or because we have reason to think that God has miraculously intervened in the world, then we might infer even more about the character of God from this sustaining activity or the nature of the purported miracles. Again, we will consider these potential sources of information in chapter 5 and in chapter 7 when we examine the topic of miracles.

Perfect-being theology

The most important conceptual foundation for the monotheistic notion of God derives from the third starting point: perfect-being theology. Perfect-being theology plays an important role in all three of the major Western theistic traditions: Judaism, Christianity, and Islam. Within philosophy, perfect-being theology traces its roots at least as far back as Plato, who identifies God with the supreme reality, which he labels "the Good," and Aristotle, who characterizes God as "the best substance." These traditions converged in powerful ways to inform the writing of some of the most important theologians in each tradition: Philo of Alexandria and Maimonidies in Judaism, Al-Kindi and Avicenna in Islam, and Augustine, Anselm, and St. Thomas Aquinas in Christianity.

Although perfect-being theology has a very long history, it emerges as an explicit driving consideration first in the writings of the eleventh-century philosopher Anselm of Canterbury. Anselm explicitly characterized God as "that than which none greater can be conceived." Contemporary perfect-being theologians understand Anselm to be affirming that God is the greatest possible being, that is, an individual displaying maximal perfection. This conception of divinity does not provide us with much in the way of specifics. But it does provide us with a rule or a recipe for developing a more specific conception of God. Perfect-being theology is thus the attempt to unpack the concept of God by way of this recipe.

To begin exploring the implications of perfect-being theology in more detail we first need a succinct characterization of it. The core of perfect-being theology is the claim that:

> (GPB) Something is God only if it has the greatest possible array of great-making properties.[1]

GPB invites us to think about two critical questions: what are "great-making properties," and how does one specify a greatest possible array of them? We will look at these problems in turn.

What are great-making properties? An obvious answer is that great-making properties are properties that make something great. But this leads to immediate problems. The first is that some properties are great-making in some contexts but not in others. Being tall is a great-making property for basketball players, but not for horse-racing jockeys. Does this mean that the idea of a great-making property makes sense only relative to a certain kind or context – that, for example, we should speak only of properties that are great-making-for-a-jockey or great-making-for-a-basketball-player rather than of properties that are simply great-making, period?

---

[1] Thomas Morris, *The Concept of God* (New York: Oxford University Press, 1987), p. 35.

Thomas Morris argues that while some great-making qualities should be seen as good only relative to a kind of thing, other great-making qualities are good in a non-relative way. On this view there are two broad types of goodness: intrinsic and extrinsic. An object or property is extrinsically good if that object or property is instrumental for bringing about something else that is good. For example, being tall is good for a basketball player because it allows him to shoot unhindered, rebound, and so on. There is nothing about being tall that is good all by itself. Shooting unhindered is a good, but it is merely an extrinsic good too: it is good because it allows the player to score more points, which in turn allows the team to win games, which in turn helps him secure a living, and so on.

But not all goods can be (merely) extrinsic. At some point, extrinsically good things must be good because they bring about something which is good just in itself. Earning a living is good because it is instrumental to, perhaps, being happy. And why is being happy a good thing? One might think that there is no answer to this question: being happy isn't good because it allows us to secure something else; happiness is good just all on its own. That's it. Goods of that sort are intrinsic goods.

Morris avoids the charge that the notion of great-making properties used in perfect-being theology is incoherent by claiming that they are ones that it is intrinsically good for a being to have. As a result, we can say that God is personal, or has wisdom, knowledge, causal power, moral excellence, and so on, not because having these is good for something else but simply because having them is intrinsically good.

The second problem that arises when thinking about great-making properties is that the process of deciding which properties count as great-making seems subjectively or culturally biased. Are there really objective grounds for taking some property or other to be intrinsically good or great-making? Defenders of perfect-being theology respond that such judgments require appeal to our fundamental intuitions about value. Generally and roughly speaking, intuitions are judgments that are based neither on linguistic conventions nor on other evidence but rather on what seems to us (even if not to others) to be obviously and necessarily true. Importantly, philosophical intuitions are different from mere hunches or gut feelings. They are, rather, beliefs about what seems to us to be self-evident or necessary. Beliefs like "two objects can't occupy exactly the same region of space at the same time" or "no human being could survive being transformed into a rock" are examples of beliefs based on intuition. If someone were to ask you why you hold these beliefs, you would be hard pressed to answer.

Beliefs based on intuitions, then, are fundamental or bedrock beliefs; and we use them to help us judge the plausibility of other claims. Among our intuitions are intuitions concerning value. For example, we think (typically on the basis of intuition) that human beings have intrinsic moral worth, that it is wrong to torture someone for fun, that it is good to help others in need, and so on. Like other intuitively held beliefs, these are fundamental, not based on or inferred from independent evidence; and, again, we use them to judge the adequacy of other beliefs, including abstract moral theories and principles. Advocates of perfect-being theology argue that we are just as entitled to appeal to intuitions in analyzing our concept of God as we are in the context of moral theorizing.

In making appeals to value intuitions, however, a few cautions are in order. First, one must realize that appeals to intuitions – value or otherwise – are defeasible or subject to correction. Further inquiry might show us that something we initially believed on the basis of intuition is in fact false. Second, appeals to value intuition are only capable of taking us so far in filling out the concept of God. This is true in part because God may have some characteristics that are not relevant to an assessment of God's greatness. For example, if there is a God, and if contemporary scientific estimates about the age of the cosmos are correct, then God has the property of having created the cosmos approximately 14 billion years ago. However, this property could not be derived from the recipe proposed in perfect-being theology, since (as far as we can discern) it is not better to have this property than to lack it. According to Christians, God exists as a Trinity consisting of three persons with one nature. Could this be derived from perfect-being theology? It hardly seems so (though as we will see in chapter 3, some disagree).

In addition, there may be some deep and perhaps intractable disagreements that lie at the very root of our intuitive judgments in this area. For example, within perfect-being theology generally there is a tension between those who think of perfection in terms of the qualities of beings and others who think of perfection in terms of the qualities of persons. Perfection conceived in terms of mere being tends to lead perfect-being theologians to describe God in terms of attributes such as timelessness, unchangeability, causal independence, and the like. Perfection conceived of in a way that prioritizes personhood tends to lead perfect-being theologians to focus on distinctively personal attributes like knowledge, wisdom, power, goodness, loving providential concern, mercy, and so on. And it is not immediately obvious that perfect-being theology and perfect-person theology yield the same results. Can a loving, providentially concerned person truly be unchangeable? Can a being who exercises knowledge and power be outside of time and causally independent? These are hard questions. And the tension between these ways of thinking about perfection is evident within the mono-theistic religious tradition. In Islam, the Mu'tazili tend to characterize God in terms of the categories of perfect being, while their critics view divine perfection in personal terms, as God is revealed in the Koran. A similar distinction can be found between, for example, medieval Roman Catholic and Reformation-era Protestant theologians.

The second feature of GPB that requires explaining is the claim that God is the being with the greatest possible array of great-making qualities. One question that immediately arises is this: why not simply define God as the being possessing all great-making properties? The answer is that it may turn out that not all great-making qualities are compossible. An array of proper-ties is compossible when it is possible for a being to have them at the same time. It is not possible for something to be both married and a bachelor, and so those two properties are not compossible. Are any pairs or sets of great-making properties also not compossible? Certainly pairs like omniscience and benevolence, or omnipotence and eternality, seem unproblematic. But as we will see, some have argued that other pairs are more troublesome. For example, there is at least an apparent conflict between omnipotence and perfect goodness. An omnipotent being can, it seems, do anything possible. A perfectly good being, it seems, would never be able to do something morally wrong. Does this mean that omnipotence and perfect goodness are not compossible? We will look at this question in detail below. For now it will suffice for us to see that there might be such conflicts and that, if there are, then no being can have all great-making qualities. The greatest possible being would thus have all of the properties that belong to the greatest possible set of compossible great-making properties.

But now another worry arises. Perhaps multiple sets of great-making properties are tied for the title "greatest possible array of great-making properties." Suppose it turns out that some pairs of great-making properties are not compossible. Is there really any reason for thinking that a being who possesses (say) omnipotence, omniscience, and great-but-not-perfect goodness is better overall than a being who possesses (say) great-but-not-maximal power, omniscience, and perfect goodness? If not, then at least two packages of properties might equally deserve the label "greatest possible array of great-making properties." Determining whether this worry is genuine, however, must await a more detailed analysis of alleged great-making properties, their compossibility, and the relative goodness of packages of properties like those just described.

So much, then, for preliminary remarks about the concept of God and the various ways of unpacking it. In the remainder of this chapter and the following two, we turn our attention to the task of exploring the concept of God as it is found in the Western monotheistic tradition, focusing in particular on those attributes that have been taken to be both most central and of greatest philosophical interest.

Self-existence and necessity

Anselm argued that everything that exists falls into one of three categories:

(a) things that are explained by another,
(b) things that are self-explaining, and
(c) things that are explained by nothing.

According to Anselm, it is not possible for anything to fall into category (c) since for anything that exists there must be some reason why it exists rather than not. We will have an opportunity to examine the claim later in our discussion of the Cosmological Argument for the existence of God. For now we can simply note that this principle accords well with our ordinary way of thinking about objects and their explanations.

If Anselm is right, God is either self-explaining or explained by another. Classical theists have uniformly held that God is self-explaining. The reason for this is that things that are explained by another are dependent on other things for their existence in a way that makes their existence fragile. The Grand Canyon would not exist were it not for the fact that there is liquid water on the planet in sufficient quantities to create rivers, and which lasts long enough to cause widespread erosion, and so on. Were any of these conditions to fail to hold, the Grand Canyon would not exist. Having the sort of existence that leaves a thing at the mercy of so many contingencies seems to detract significantly from a thing's greatness. This divine attribute is commonly labeled aseity, a word that derives from the Latin phrase "*a se*" meaning "deriving from oneself."

Initially the idea of being self-explaining seems to border on the incoherent for it might seem that one thing, A, explains the existence of another, B, only when A causes B. But for A to cause B, A has to pre-exist B. This entails that nothing can explain itself, since to do so would require that a thing pre-exist itself, and this is clearly impossible. Moreover, it is hard to see how something might cause itself, even if pre-existence weren't an issue.

Fortunately, this is not the only way such explanatory relations can work. There are many cases in which one thing explains another thing without causing it and without preceding it in time. The fact that a triangle is a closed figure with three sides seems to explain why the triangle has three angles. The fact of your reading a book seems to explain its being true that you are reading a book. But, of course, you don't read the book before it becomes true that you are reading a book; and a triangle's being a closed figure with three sides doesn't cause it to have three angles.

Is there a way in which we can conceive of God as being a simultaneous or non-causal explanation of God's own existence? Classical theists have offered two accounts of God's aseity along these lines.

On the first account, God explains his own existence because it is part of the very essence or nature of God to exist. Consider, by way of contrast, something like elven-nature – i.e. the nature that something would have if it were an elf. If there is such a thing as elven nature, it is the sort of thing that may or may not be instantiated: it is possible that there be instances of that nature in the world, and it is possible that there not be. Being instantiated, we might say, is not part of the nature. It might be that elven nature exists, and yet there simply are no elves. According to this first account of God's aseity, however, the divine nature is not like that. Necessarily, the divine nature exists if and only if something having that nature exists. Indeed, proponents of this view typically go a step further: God is identical to his nature. Thus there can't be more than one thing with the divine nature; and so, necessarily, the divine nature exists if and only if God exists. If all of this is right, then the following propositions are logically equivalent (that is, the truth of G1 logically entails the truth of G2, and vice versa):

(G1)   God exists.

(G2)   The divine nature exists.

And now it is much easier to see a sense in which God is self-explaining. If you ask, "Why does Legolas exist?", the (metaphysical) answer will be something like this: "Because elven nature exists, and ...", where the ellipsis is filled in by some story about how elven nature came to be instantiated in the person of Legolas. But, if you ask, "Why does God exist?", the complete metaphysical answer will be simply "Because the divine nature exists." But that, as we have seen, is logically equivalent to "Because God exists."

Note too that if, as many are inclined to think, natures (whatever they are) are necessary beings, then either the divine nature is impossible or it exists necessarily. To say that something is (or would be, if it existed) a necessary being is just to say that it exists and, furthermore, cannot fail to exist. So if natures are necessary beings, then it is possible for the divine nature to exist only if it actually exists and, furthermore, could not fail to exist. And if that is right, then this first account of God's aseity implies that either God is impossible or God exists necessarily. For, again, the truth of G1 logically entails the truth of G2, and vice versa; so if G2 is impossible, then G1 is impossible, and if G2 is a necessary truth, then G1 is a necessary truth. Thus, it looks as if it is in principle possible to reason from the mere possibility of God's existence to the necessity – and therefore actuality – of God's existence. We shall return to this way of arguing for God's existence later, in chapter 5.

The second account is developed by way of an analogy. Thomas Morris and Christopher Menzel ask us to imagine a clock-radio-sized "materialization machine" which has the power to create material objects out of nothing, and to sustain those material objects in existence as long as the machine itself exists and is turned on. One could use this magical machine to replace food in the refrigerator, worn out batteries, broken dishes, you name it. However, if the machine is destroyed, or if someone turns the machine off, all of the things that were made with it instantly cease to exist.

Such a machine would, of course, get a great deal of use and, over time, the parts of the materialization machine would undoubtedly begin to wear down themselves. Now imagine that we use the machine itself to generate its own replacement parts. If this process happens enough times, we will eventually reach a point where all of the parts of the machine have been replaced with parts we have made using the machine. We can now ask this question: once all the parts have been replaced in this way, what explains the existence of the machine? The answer would be: the machine itself – it explains its own existence. It is both the source of its own parts and the source of its own continuing existence.

In our story the machine was at some time made by some other entity and only later came to be composed of parts of its own making. But imagine a machine that is and has always been the cause of its own parts in this way. If we can coherently imagine such a machine then we can imagine something which is eternally self-explaining and self-dependent. This model thus provides another way of thinking about divine aseity.

Omnipotence: perfect power

Central to all theistic conceptions of God is the notion that God has maximal power or omnipotence. Such great power is thought to follow not only from the fact that power is itself a perfection, but also from God's pre-eminent place among existing things. God's power explains and entails that God creates all that there is, sustains it in existence, and confers on those things the powers and limitations that they have. Power of this sort entails that God is in complete control of what things there are, and of what those things do (though, of course, it doesn't by itself entail that God determines what everything or everybody does).

The paradox of the stone

Some object that the very idea of omnipotence or maximal power makes no sense. Defenders of this claim argue that the incoherence of the concept of omnipotence can be demonstrated by considering paradoxes that follow from it. The most famous of these is the paradox of the stone. Many of us have heard someone quip: "Can God make a rock so big that he cannot lift it?" and assumed it was nothing more than philosophical silliness. Yet behind the apparently silly question lurks a paradox that threatens to undermine the coherence of omnipotence itself.

The question invites us to notice that no answer to it could be satisfactory. If we say that God cannot make rock of this sort, then we have identified something that God cannot do, thus undermining his omnipotence. Yet if we say that God can make such a rock, we are admitting that God's power is potentially limited, since God could make a rock which would reveal such a limitation – a limitation in his lifting powers. The point is that no matter which way we answer the question, omnipotence would be undermined, and this is supposed to show that there is something problematic with the notion of omnipotence itself.

Some have replied that the paradox results from an incoherent notion that is smuggled into the paradox but that has nothing to do with God. The smuggled incoherence concerns the rock. What sort of rock is this? It is, we would have to say, a rock that has a mass so large (i.e. is so big) that a being who can lift any mass cannot lift it (i.e. that God cannot lift it). Is such a rock possible? It seems not. After all, if God can lift a rock of any mass, there is no mass so great that it outstrips the lifting power of an omnipotent being. So the hypothesized rock is impossible.

One might find this response unconvincing. For example, some think that they can imagine a rock that is unliftable, not because it has a mass that exceeds God's lifting power, but because it has the property of being "essentially unliftable" or "essentially immobile." If a rock with such a property is coherent, God could make it, but could not lift it. However, even if this is true, note that the power that God supposedly lacks is a power that is itself impossible. If the rock has the property of being essentially immobile, then it is as impossible for God to have the power to lift it, as it is for God to have the power to make a triangle with four sides. Since neither of these is logically possible, the notion of having the power to do these things is incoherent, and shows no limitation on divine power.

Finally, some have argued that the paradox rests on an ambiguity. To see this, we might consider God's making and lifting powers separately. Can God make a rock so big that he cannot lift it? If the answer is no, there are two possible reasons for this. One reason is that God has unlimited lifting powers, but limited making powers, that is, God can't make such a rock because he can't make very big rocks in the first place. On this way of answering, God's inability would indeed imply a lack of power.

But we might also justify a "no" answer by pointing out that if God's lifting ability is unbounded, and if his rock-making ability is also unbounded, then none of the rocks he can make would outstrip his lifting power. This does not indicate any lack of power on God's part since both his making and lifting powers are, on this answer, completely unlimited. As a result nothing paradoxical about omnipotence would follow if we give the "no" answer and understand it this way.

Defining omnipotence

In addressing the paradox of the stone, however, we have conspicuously avoided giving any definition or characterization of omnipotence. And providing such a characterization is more difficult than one might initially expect. Ordinarily we might say that omnipotence is just the ability to "do anything." Such a claim is, however, so imprecise that it is of little value. Critics of this simple characterization are quick to note that without some qualification, there seem to be a number of "things" God cannot do. For instance, in the previous section we took it for granted that an omnipotent being cannot move essentially unmovable things, or create married bachelors, or round squares, or cause necessarily existing beings not to exist. These things cannot be done because they are logical impossibilities. More precisely, we can say that these things cannot be done because the description of the seemingly impossible task fails to describe a task at all. To speak of creating a bachelor is to speak of creating someone who is, among other things, unmarried. To create a married bachelor would be to create an unmarried person who is married. Obviously, that is incoherent.

Some philosophers and theologians have resisted the idea that God cannot do the logically impossible. The seventeenth-century philosopher René Descartes seems to fall into this camp, and this view is thus often described as the Cartesian view of omnipotence. One of the main motivations for the Cartesian view, especially in the popular mind, is just the reverent idea that God is not limited by anything – not even by the laws of logic. Most contemporary philosophers and theologians, however, reject the Cartesian view; and they justify the rejection in part by pointing out that the laws of logic aren't really genuine limitations at all. Creating a married bachelor isn't a task that God cannot perform due to some logical impediment. Rather, it simply isn't a task to be performed at all. Since we are inclined to take our stand with the contemporary (near-)consensus on this topic, we shall, in the remainder of this section, ignore the Cartesian position.

A more careful definition of omnipotence, then, would hold that omnipotence is the power to do anything it is logically possible to do. However, one might think that even this more cautious definition will not do. In 1912 the Titanic hit an iceberg and sank in the icy waters of the North Atlantic. While this event really happened, it was possible for it not to happen. Had the iceberg not been where it was, had the captain steered a different course, had the hull been a little thicker, the ship would have avoided its tragic fate. So, the "Titanic never sank" is logically possible. Can God bring this state of affairs about? Of course, God could have done so in the past. But God can no longer bring this about. It is too late – the ship has sailed, and has sunk. As a result, one might argue, not even all things that are logically possible are such that God can bring them about. (On the other hand, one might doubt that there really is a logically possible state of affairs here after all. For, one might argue, the task at issue isn't exactly bringing it about that the Titanic never sank, but rather bringing it about that, though it was the case that the Titanic sank, it is also the case that the Titanic never sank. But describing the task this way seems to reveal an internal contradiction. Exploring this response in detail, however, would take us too far afield.)

In addition, there are certain other logically possible things that it looks as if God cannot do. For example, God cannot do those things done by agents other than God. Consider this logically possible occurrence:

(T) Gordon Brown running a mile in six minutes.

While God could (if incarnate, say) run a mile in six minutes, God can't do T since T describes something that Gordon Brown does, not God. And God cannot do something not done by God.

But perhaps that seems like a trick. After all, we can imagine someone replying to this supposed limitation on God's power by saying that while God might not be able to do T, God can bring it about that T by creating a world with Tony Blair running the mile in six minutes. This might lead us to reconceive of divine power not in terms of what God can do but in terms of what God can bring about or actualize, as follows:

(OMNIP) O is omnipotent if and only if O can actualize any logically possible state of affairs.

Defining omnipotence this way avoids any concerns about God being unable to "do" the actions of agents other than God.

Unfortunately, this characterization is not satisfactory either. If there are creatures with genuine free choice, that is, with the ability to choose between multiple courses of action, then there will be many logically possible states of affairs that God cannot actualize. It is fairly easy to see why. Earlier today Sally was at a coffee shop faced with a choice between having coffee or not. In fact, she chose not to have coffee. At that moment of choice, we might say, two possible worlds lay before her: the coffee world and the non-coffee world. These two different worlds were identical up to the moment of choice, but at that moment they diverged. Let W be a complete description of the world up to the time at which she chose. Now consider two possibilities:

(W1)   W is actual and then Sally freely chooses to have coffee.
(W2)   W is actual and then Sally freely chooses not to have coffee.

If Sally was genuinely free, each of these was possibly true. But, of course, only one was in fact true. Suppose, as it happens, (2) was true. Now consider this: what if God had wanted to actualize W but have Sally choose coffee? It looks as if God would have been out of luck. Sally did not freely choose coffee; and the only way God could have guaranteed that she do otherwise would have been to override her freedom.

Why does this matter? Because according to OMNIP, omnipotence is the power to actualize any logically possible state of affairs. But the state of affairs "W is actual and then Sally freely chooses to have coffee" is one that God cannot bring about. Thus, it looks as if there are some logically possible states of affairs that even an omnipotent being cannot bring about.

Maximal power and divine goodness

If one is convinced by the example involving Sally, then what it shows us is that putting omnipotence in terms of the number or types of things the omnipotent being can do or bring about is not the most promising strategy for defining omnipotence. To remedy this, we might try characterizing it in terms of the maximal amount of power that a possible being could have. If God had as much power as any being could have, God would at least have maximal power if not omnipotence. We might thus characterize God's power in this way: O is maximally powerful if and only if there is no possible being whose powers exceed O's.

While this characterization is better than earlier ones, some have argued that this account will be inconsistent with other divine attributes. For example, classical theists hold that God is perfectly morally good. What does it mean to be perfectly morally good? One thing it could mean is: never in fact acting immorally or falling short of the standards of perfect moral behavior. On this view, God is perfectly morally good if God never in fact falls short of whatever the relevant moral standards might be. However, most classical theists have argued that perfect goodness requires something more. Perfect moral goodness requires not merely that God never in fact falls short of the moral mark, but rather that God cannot possibly fall short of that mark. Necessary moral perfection of this sort is known as impeccability. To deny impeccability to God is to imply that it is indeed possible for God to do wrong, even if he never does. But a being who can do wrong seems less good than a being whose goodness precludes the possibility of doing wrong altogether. As a result, it seems that the greatest possible being would be impeccable.

We can now see the problem. If God is impeccable there are some things that God cannot do: murder, lie, break promises, and so on. Because of this, we can at least imagine a being who has all of the creative and causal powers that God has and who also can do those things God cannot: murder, lie, break promises, and so on. If such a being is possible, then that being would have powers exceeding God's, and so God would not be maximally powerful.

Short of denying that God has either perfect goodness or maximal power, there are two ways to avoid this apparent incompatibility. The first way is just to deny that perfect goodness requires impeccability. One reason for denying this is that it is reasonable to think that someone cannot be praiseworthy (or blameworthy for that matter) unless that person can perform both good and evil actions. If someone unavoidably performs an evil action (because she was brainwashed or drugged, for example) she is not morally accountable for her action because she could not have avoided it. The same seems to be true for praiseworthiness: if the reason that you did some good action was that you were under the influence of a drug that made doing the good action unavoidable, then you are not praiseworthy for doing it. If God is similarly unable to avoid doing evil in virtue of his impeccability, then it seems that God is not praiseworthy either. As a result, we should deny impeccability.

Many will be inclined to reject this solution, however. Many, perhaps most, philosophers in the theistic tradition have found the following proposition to be strongly intuitive:

(IMPEC)   A being who is impeccable is morally better (and thus deserving of greater moral praise) than one who is not.

Thus, when faced with a tension between this proposition and the following

(PRAISE)   A being is morally praiseworthy only if it has the ability to sin – i.e. only if it is not impeccable

many of these philosophers have preferred to give up PRAISE to resolve the tension rather than to give up IMPEC. Some of these philosophers have argued that moral praise and blame are justified wherever freedom is present, but that freedom is compatible with various kinds of determinism. If they are right, then there is no obvious reason to doubt that we could be justified in morally praising a being who is determined by its very nature always and necessarily to do what is good. Relatedly, some have argued that it is a mistake to think that true moral freedom requires both the ability to sin and the ability to refrain from sin. Rather, true freedom consists just in the ability to do the good. The more one is able to do this – the more one is free from influences that lead one to stray from the good – the freer and more deserving of praise one is. On this view, then, a being who was literally incapable of sin would be maximally free and maximally praiseworthy. And isn't there something rather intuitive about this? Consider two people, A and B: A considers homicide and finds himself genuinely torn; he faces moral struggle over whether to commit the crime, and finally decides not to. B, on the other hand, finds homicide unthinkable. Other things being equal, don't we think that B is more deserving of praise? And doesn't our moral estimation of B go up rather than down the more it seems to us that B simply couldn't commit such a horrible crime? If so, then we have the beginnings of a case for the conclusion that PRAISE, rather than IMPEC, is false.

The second way of avoiding the apparent conflict between maximal power and perfect goodness is to say that the "power to do evil" is not really a "power" at all. The mere fact that we can form the phrase "power to do evil" is not enough to show that there is a distinct power to which the phrase corresponds. You have the power to hail a cab and the power to hail a waiter. But these are not distinct powers. In both cases, you do these things by exercising a more fundamental power: the power to wave your hand.

There is nothing more to those other powers than the power to wave your hand.

Now consider the power to raise one of your fingers. You exercise it when you signal a play to your basketball team or when you bid at an auction. You would also exercise it were you to make a certain insulting gesture. But let's imagine that you have resolved never to make that gesture. In fact, imagine that you are such a good person that you are incapable of making that gesture. Does this incapacity entail that you lack a power? There is good reason to think not. There is nothing more to the power to make the gesture than the power to raise a finger. And you have that power. What you don't have is the capacity to raise it in a way that constitutes an insulting gesture. Since this is not a distinct power, there is no power you thereby lack. If God's inability to do evil is understood this way, it would imply no lack of power after all.

Creation, conservation, and providence

However we define the exact extent of divine power, classical theists have always agreed that God's power is great enough to confer on him the capacity to create and providentially superintend the existence of everything distinct from God. How are we to understand these characteristics of God as creator and providential superintender? Some theists suppose that God's creating activity consists merely of rearranging already existing entities. For example, Plato's divine Demiurge engages in the act of creation by imparting specific sorts of order on a pre-existing reality. Yet most theists hold that God creates and fashions the world out of no pre-existing materials at all. Creation of this sort is typically designated by the phrase "creation *ex nihilo*." Strictly speaking, theists have taken the doctrine of divine creation *ex nihilo* to entail that the universe came into existence at some time in the finite past. And such a view corresponds to the best cosmological theories that scientists currently accept. But this has not always been the case. At numerous times throughout scientific and philosophical history it has seemed that the best evidence available pointed to a universe that is infinitely old. Would a beginningless universe imply that God is not its creator?

Not necessarily. In addition to holding that God is the originating cause of the universe, theists have also traditionally held that God must sustain the universe in existence from moment to moment. Descartes, for example, gave a striking argument for this claim, arguing that since no instant of the universe contains within itself anything which would explain or guarantee its existence at the next moment of time, something else must guarantee this. And that thing, Descartes argued, is God. This form of divine activity, commonly called divine conservation (springing from the Latin "*conservare*" which means "to maintain or preserve"), implies that, even if the universe were beginningless, God would be its creator in the sense that his existence is metaphysically or explanatorily prior to the existence of the universe. This is so because God's existence and causal activity is required to sustain the universe in existence from moment to moment.

In addition to creating and conserving, most classical theists have held that God is also involved in the occurrence of each and every event, or the exercise of every causal power by creatures. Thus, when the cue ball strikes the eight-ball, God is in some sense involved in bringing it about that the collision causes the eight-ball to move. This exercise of divine power, called divine concurrence, supposes that God is intimately involved not only in preserving the world in existence, but in the activity of created things as well. Why do theists hypothesize the reality of divine concurrence? Some do so because they take it to be revealed in scriptural texts. Christian thinkers in the Middle Ages commonly cited St. Paul's claim that "In God we live, and move, and have our being" as evidence for such divine activity. As they saw it, "having our being" refers to creation, "living" refers to conservation, and "moving" refers to God's concurrence.

There are, in addition, three important philosophical motivations for supposing that God concurs with creaturely action in this way. First, some theists, such as Thomas Aquinas, contend that it is through divine concurrence that God is able to know what creatures will do when they act. Since God makes a causal contribution to the creature's act, God can know the outcome by knowing his own action. Second, others have argued that divine concurrence is necessary, since without it creatures would have, and would be able to exercise, causal powers in a way that is completely independent of divine control. Such abilities, it is argued, undermine God's ability to providentially superintend every event that happens in creation. Finally, some have argued that every instance of causation involves one substance causing some new thing to come into existence (either another thing or some property in an already existing thing). However, since God is the only true source or cause of being, no created thing could be a true cause all by itself. Thus God must be involved in every causal event in nature.

Such motivations raise some serious difficulties, however. Consider the first. If God is able to know what a creature would or will do simply by knowing God's own causal contribution to the creature's action, it follows that God's contribution is sufficient for the creaturely action to occur. But if God's concurring contribution is sufficient in this way, then the creature cannot have any genuine control over its action since what God does determines what the creature will do. Such an account is especially worrisome when we consider free creaturely action. If the actions of creatures are determined by a causal contribution by God, it is hard to see how these actions can count as genuinely free. What is more, such an account makes it acutely difficult to explain the reality of evil. If God can prevent creatures from freely choosing evil by simply causing them to refrain from it, why would God not do so?

The second motivation leads to a different problem. If theists who accept concurrence do so because they are reluctant to give creatures any sort of independent causal powers, they will have to provide an account of how the causal contributions of God and creatures collaborate to produce causal effects. Perhaps God and creatures cooperate in causing events in the way that two horses pulling a wagon do. In that case, each horse contributes its causal powers so that they together produce the motion. If this were the model for divine concurrence, some important questions must be answered. For example, is the causal contribution of each agent necessary for the effect to obtain, or is one or the other of the causal contributions sufficient on its own? If the first, then it appears that God is merely a partial cause, and that the creature is providing some real causal contribution quite independently of any causal contribution on God's part. That might seem unproblematic, until we remember that we were motivated to adopt the notion of divine concurrence as a way of denying that creatures make independent causal contributions to events obtaining in the world. If, on the other hand, one of the concurring causes would be sufficient on its own, that contributing cause would have to be God. After all, the whole point of introducing concurrence was that creaturely causal contributions could not alone suffice for the effects. Yet if God's causal contribution were sufficient, then it is hard to see how the creature's contribution helps bring about the effect at all. The creature would be like a little child standing behind a car and pushing on the bumper as the car accelerates forward. In that case, the child might think she caused the car to move, even though she didn't.

The third motivation is problematic for similar reasons. It holds that objects or events that come to exist through some sort of creaturely causal activity get their existence or being directly from God. However, if God causes the existence of the effects of creaturely action in this way, it appears that it is God, and not the creature, who brings these things about. As a result, the creature once again seems to play no real role in causation after all.

Because of these difficulties, some theists have adopted an even more radical account of divine action in the world. If it is important that God has a role in bringing about effects in the world, and yet all models of concurrence fail, it must be the case that God is the sole cause of all effects that come to pass. This view, known as occasionalism, has been most famously defended by the seventeenth-century French philosopher Nicholas Malebranche. According to the occasionalist, while it might appear to us that the collision of the cue-ball and the eight-ball causes the eight-ball to move, the collision instead provides merely an occasion on which God alone will cause the eight-ball to move as it does. On this view, the laws of nature are not descriptions of the causal powers had by created things, but rather descriptions of how God has committed himself to act when certain events occur in the world.

In light of the problems generated by the notion of divine concurrence, occasionalism may seem to be an attractive alternative. Note, however, that it actually faces some of the same difficulties that divine concurrence does. Two difficulties are especially noteworthy. First, if occasionalism is true, it seems that genuine free action by creatures is ruled out. When a creature makes a free choice or forms a free act of will, the creature must be, in some crucial way, the root and cause of the action. If occasionalism is true, however, there appears to be no way for the creature to be such a cause. Second, if occasionalism is true, every event in the universe is brought about directly by God. If this is right, however, one would expect the world to contain no evil. Of course, all varieties of theism must confront the problem of evil. But most theists are insistent, as we will see in chapter 6, that God does not cause evil but rather merely (justifiably) permits it. Seeing God as merely permitting evil provides a moral buffer that would be unavailable if God were the full and direct cause of evil as is the case with occasionalism. This view thus makes God "the author of sin," a position that has been almost universally rejected by theists.

We were led to consider the possible truth of occasionalism because, first, it seemed that the greatest possible being would have some sort of direct involvement with the occurrence of every event in nature in a way that transcended mere conservation, and second, because the model of involvement through concurrence faced potent objections. Perhaps these assumptions are mistaken. Perhaps, that is, the greatest possible being need only be regularly causally connected to the world as its creator and sustainer. This view is commonly known as deism. How does this view fare?

To answer this question we must go back and consider the reasons why theists think that God's causal involvement in creation must go beyond creation and conservation alone. The first reason was that such additional causal involvement would be needed for God to have knowledge of how creatures would or will act and, as a result, would be needed for God to exercise providential control. As we have seen, and will see in greater detail in chapter 2, this claim is highly contentious. There are other models of divine knowledge and providence which do not involve divine concurrence at all. The second and third reasons involved the claim that, absent concurrence, creatures would be objectionably causally independent, either because they could act independently of God, or could produce being (the being of objects or events as the effects of their actions). However, these objections are not especially forceful. First, as we saw earlier in our discussion of divine power, if some creatures have free choice, it seems that their actions must indeed have a very strong sort of causal independence in any case. Second, while some accounts of causation hypothesize that causes bring about new instances of being in their effects, this view is highly controversial.

Goodness

Theists hold that God is absolutely and perfectly good. They commonly take divine goodness to involve much more than moral faultlessness or impeccability. In addition, God's goodness entails that he is maximally loving and benevolent towards every created thing. Because of this, God is taken to be not merely morally faultless, but morally unsurpassable. It is this aspect of divine goodness which figures most centrally in the theist's conception of

God as a being distinctively worthy of worship. Worship-worthiness is a central divine attribute – indeed for some theists it is the central divine attribute – and it signals God's unique status as that being who merits our complete devotion and adoration. Worship of God is sometimes portrayed by cynics as springing from radical divine egomania. But on classical theism God is to be worshipped not primarily out of motives of fear or divine command, but rather because God is good and God manifests goodness in a way that no other thing does or can.

We have already considered some philosophical issues that arise for God's moral faultlessness or impeccability when considering its compatibility with omnipotence or maximal power. Recently, philosophers of religion have turned their attention to some arguments which aim to show that there is something objectionable about moral unsurpassability. We will consider those arguments here.

The first tension

From very early on in the theistic tradition, theists have recognized various tensions between the doctrines of divine freedom in creation and divine moral unsurpassibility. The first tension can be put in the form of an argument as follows:

1.1. God is omniscient and is thus aware of all of the possible worlds that he can create.
1.2. God is perfectly and unsurpassibly good and is thus unfailingly drawn to do that which is best.
1.3. Free agents can will an action that is less than the best only if they either fail to understand what is genuinely best, or fall prey to a weakness of will, thus choosing contrary to what they know to be best.
1.4. God is susceptible neither to ignorance of the best nor weakness of will.
1.5. Therefore, God cannot do anything less than the best.
1.6. Since our world exists, either it is the best world, or it is one among other worlds that are tied for best.
1.7. To have morally significant freedom, one must be able to choose among alternatives of differing moral quality.
1.8. If our world is best, God could not refrain from creating it and is thus not free in creating it.

1.9. If our world is tied for best, God could not choose among worlds of differing moral quality and thus would lack morally significant freedom in creating.

1.10. Thus God lacked morally significant freedom in creating.

As we saw above, some theists hold that God is not impeccable because such an inability to sin is inconsistent with moral responsibility. Theists in that camp would reject premise 1.4 since they would claim that God can be susceptible to weakness of will.

However, most theists object either to premises 1.6 or 1.7. Let's consider 1.7 first. Philosophers generally are divided on whether or not freedom requires that one can do otherwise than what one actually does. However, many theists have been content to accept this condition on freedom. Much more contentious is the claim of premise 1.7, namely that morally significant freedom requires "an ability to choose between alternatives of differing moral quality." Why would someone accept this? There are two reasons. The first reason is an argument that we discussed earlier, according to which God's good acts could not be praiseworthy unless God could just as well perform evil acts. Since we have examined this argument already we will not pursue it further here.

The second reason is that if a free agent is positioned so that it can only choose among alternatives that are equivalent, free will seems to be robbed of much of its importance or gravity. One wouldn't place much value on freedom that allows one to choose among, for example, 300 identical Campbell's tomato soup cans.

That seems fair enough. But this line of reasoning comes up short if it is meant as a defense of premise 1.7. Premise 1.7 does not say that our morally significant freedom is disabled when all of our alternatives are utterly identical (which would be true), but rather when the alternatives are of the same moral quality (which is not at all clearly true). More apt analogies might be these:

(Case 1) You have goods to donate to charity. Several charities present themselves as equally worthy and equally in need of your donation. However, you can choose just one of them to receive your donation.

(Case 2) Ten people are badly in need of rescue. You, and only you, can help; helping is very easy for you (you need only push a button, at no risk or cost to yourself); but you can help only one, or none at all. Each person is equally deserving of your help. You choose one.

(CASE 3) You wish to adopt a child from an orphanage. You are able to adopt only one child, or none at all. All of the children in the orphanage are equally in need. Some are nicer than others; some are more talented than others; but you choose one without regard to these qualities, decide to love the child, and adopt her.

In each of these cases, it seems that your choices are significant and meaningful. Thus, if God's choice among worlds is like that, it seems that there is good reason to think that God's choice is significant and meaningful as well.

Some critics have also noted that premise 1.6 does not exhaust all of the possibilities. In fact, it leaves out at least two important ones. To understand the first, imagine a genie appears before you and tells you that you can choose one of three alternative gifts that he is willing to give you. First, the genie can instantaneously make you fluent in any foreign language you choose. Second, the genie can make you a virtuoso at any musical instrument you choose. Third, the genie can make you a world-class athlete in any sport you desire. Which would you choose? Perhaps you obviously prefer one of these over the others. But many would, undoubtedly, be hard pressed to choose. How do we compare such very different options? Each of them is very good indeed. But they are so different from one another in kind that it is hard to know how to compare them. Philosophers call goods like these – goods that do not seem comparable to one another – incommensurable goods.

In light of this, we should amend premise 1.6 to say that our world is the best world, or it is tied for the best, or it is one among many worlds that is the best of its kind and incommensurable with other worlds that are the best of their kind. If this is right, God can choose among worlds of variable moral quality in the sense that they are all good and yet also as incommensurable as the goods of knowing a foreign language and being a world class sumo wrestler. If these are the sorts of choices God confronts in creating, the choices seem strikingly rich and significant. Moreover, the choices seem morally significant, especially if, as many theists will suppose, the decision to create our world was relevantly like the decision in CASE 3 – i.e. a decision to choose (by actualizing an antecedently known set of possibilities) and to love the (resulting) inhabitants of a particular world.

The second missing alternative in premise 1.6 has been recognized by theists from at least the time of St. Thomas Aquinas in the thirteenth century. On this view, there is no single best world, nor a set of equally best worlds, nor a set of incommensurable worlds that are best in their kind. How could this be? The answer is that the worlds available for creating form a series of increasingly better worlds to infinity. What constraints would God face if confronted with this choice?

The seventeenth-century German philosopher Gottfried Leibniz argued that if confronted with such a choice God would be unable to choose, since there would be no sufficient reason for choosing one world over any other. Most have denied the need for a sufficient reason for God's creative choice, arguing that it would be perfectly permissible for God to create any world that exceeds a certain minimum threshold of acceptability. There are, for example, some possible worlds in which the quantity of evil, lack of good, or imbalance of goods and evils render those worlds ineligible for creation by a perfectly good God. Setting aside worlds like that, God still faces a choice among a range of worlds which increase in goodness *ad infinitum*, and thus God still has an enormous range of freedom in choosing to create.

The second tension

In light of the foregoing, the first tension concerning divine freedom and moral goodness seems to be resolved. However, resolving this first tension leads to a second one. It is this: if God chooses from among an infinite spectrum of increasingly better worlds, then no matter which world God creates, there is a better world that could have been created. This doesn't imply that God does something wrong or objectionable in creating one of these not-maximally-good worlds. But it does imply that it is possible that there exist a creator who creates a world that is better than the world God actually created. Why is this a problem? The answer is that when this fact is conjoined with a certain superficially plausible principle, it entails that God is (and must be) morally surpassable in character, no matter what world God creates. The principle is this:

(P) If an all-knowing and all-powerful being, B, were to create a world when there is a better world that B could have created, then it is possible that there exists a being that is morally better than B.

William Rowe concludes on the basis of this principle that if our world is one in a spectrum of possible worlds that increase in goodness to infinity, then God does not exist, since the creator of our world is possibly morally surpassable, a characteristic God cannot have. As a result, this argument is, in the end, an argument for atheism.[2]

The crucial assumption in the argument is Principle (P). What should we think of it? Daniel and Frances Howard-Snyder have argued that the principle is false by way of a series of thought experiments. Consider first two creators, Jove and Juno, facing the decision of which world to create from among the infinite array of increasingly better worlds. Since every world is surpassably good, Jove decides to use a randomizing device which arbitrarily selects one of those worlds. We can imagine all of these worlds being ordered in increasing goodness, with each one being assigned a number starting with 1. Jove activates the device, and it selects world 777. Now consider Juno who, facing the same choice, decides to use the same randomizing device. In Juno's case, the randomizer selects world 999. If Principle (P) is correct, we ought to conclude that Juno is morally better than Jove. But this is surely wrong. Both chose to use a randomizing device which arbitrarily led to differing outcomes. Why would we then judge one creator to be better than the other?[3]

Can Rowe modify (P) in such a way that his argument can be salvaged? Perhaps. To see how, consider another example raised by the Howard-Snyders, the case of Thor. Thor, seeing the outcomes of Jove and Juno's randomizing machine, decides to try a different strategy. Thor decides that if one is going to create, getting stuck with worlds numbered less than 1,000, as they did, is a pretty lousy outcome. As a result, he resolves to use the randomizing machine, but he modifies it so that it can only select worlds with numbers greater than 1,000. Thor activates his modified machine and it selects world 3,016. Is Thor morally superior to Juno and Jove? Rowe thinks so. While all three used the randomizing device to create, Thor is distinctive because he was unwilling to settle for the outcomes that Juno and Jove were willing to settle for. For Rowe, this is enough reason to think that Thor is indeed morally better.

---

[2] William Rowe, "The Problem of Divine Perfection and Freedom," in Eleonore Stump (ed.), *Reasoned Faith* (Ithaca, NY: Cornell University Press, 1993).

[3] Daniel and Frances Howard-Snyder, "How an Unsurpassable Being Can Create a Surpassable World," in *Faith and Philosophy* 11:2, pp. 260–8.

The example of Thor might suggest the following substitute for Principle (P):

(P*)   If an all-knowing and all-powerful being, B, were to create a world by employing a lower standard than B might have used, then it is possible that there exists a being that is morally better than B (one using a higher standard).

Both Juno and Jove used the same standard (any world with a number of 1 or higher). We thus rightly judge them to be morally equivalent. But because Thor has higher standards than either of them, Thor is to be judged morally better. We can now generate an argument similar to the one based on (P). Since for any standard one might mention a higher standard could have been used, whatever standard a creator actually uses could have been higher than it is. As a result, any creator would be morally surpassable, including God.

Two observations are in order concerning this argument based on (P*). First, if Rowe is correct, the argument shows that, if there are an infinite number of increasingly better worlds to choose from in creating, being morally unsurpassable is not possible for any creator. But, the theist might argue, if it is logically impossible for a creator to have such a property, then this argument doesn't show the non-existence of God. Instead, since God is the greatest possible being, the argument would merely show that God does not (and could not) have this property.

One might think that this is enough to defang Rowe's criticism. It is not. Rowe is emphatic that the problem is not that God lacks the impossible property of being morally unsurpassable, but rather that God has the property of moral surpassability. Since God has this property, God cannot be the greatest possible being.

Second, the argument will not succeed unless (P*) is true. Is it? There is surely some plausibility to the claim that having higher standards is a sign of moral superiority. And in considering the example of Thor, one is initially tempted to wonder: if Juno and Jove are really on a par, morally speaking, with Thor, how could they have been willing to settle for such lousy worlds given the infinite spectrum of better worlds available to them?

In fact, however, it seems that a little reflection provides a fairly easy answer to this question. Maybe Juno and Jove chose worlds in the way in which you, in CASE 3, were supposed to have chosen a child for adoption:

they surveyed the range of possible creatures and decided, without regard for "merit," to actualize these rather than those to be objects of their love and attention. Since the worlds from which they selected are all morally permissible, they can't be morally faulted for choosing the worlds they chose (as even Rowe will agree). So there is nothing wrong with their choice. Why then should it follow that they could have been morally better if only, like Thor, they had created something better? Why must we agree that creating something better makes one a better person? Why can't a perfectly good person create something (out of love, or aesthetic preference, or even sheer arbitrary choice) that is less good than he or she could have created? Rowe doesn't really tell us; rather, his main support for principles like (P*) consists simply in an invitation to inspect them and find them obviously to be true. But, of course, if that is all that can be said for such principles, then the theist might easily be forgiven for not being persuaded. For the theist will already be committed to divine perfection; and so once she sees that if there is no best world then God must create something less good than he could have created if he creates at all, the most natural (and, to our minds, sensible) move will be to conclude that principles like (P*) are simply false.

Conclusion

As the foregoing makes clear, the topic of the concept of God is a philosophically rich and fascinating one. In engaging the concept philosophically we must first decide which concept of God is salient, and then consider the various puzzles that arise for the divine attributes that follow from that concept. Our attention has been focused on the concept of God that arises from perfect-being theology. On that concept God is, among other things, self-existent (or necessarily existing), a creator and providential superintender, and perfectly good. While these attributes initially seem straightforward, more careful scrutiny shows us that interesting puzzles lie just beneath the surface. Do these puzzles show that there is something incoherent about the concept of God found in perfect-being theology? It is not at all clear that they do. However, it is also not clear that they don't. As we have seen, resolving this question requires taking stands on controversial claims which are currently at the forefront of the discussion in the field. For this reason, discussion on these topics will be vigorous and ongoing.

Further reading

Davis, Stephen T., *Logic and the Nature of God* (Grand Rapids, MI: Eerdmans, 1983). *Christian Philosophical Theology* (Oxford: Oxford University Press, 2006).

MacDonald, Scott (ed.), *Being and Goodness* (Ithaca, NY: Cornell University Press, 1991).

Morris, Thomas, *Our Idea of God: An Introduction to Philosophical Theology* (Downers Grove, IL: InterVarsity Press, 1994).

Plantinga, Alvin, *Does God Have a Nature?* (Milwaukee, WI: Marquette University Press, 1980).

Rowe, William, *Can God Be Free?* (Oxford: Clarendon Press, 2004).

Swinburne, Richard, *The Coherence of Theism* revised edn. (Oxford: Oxford University Press, 1993).

Weirenga, Edward, *The Nature of God* (Ithaca, NY: Cornell University Press. 1989).

2 Attributes of God: eternity, knowledge, and providence

Many take comfort in the thought that God knows, down to the smallest detail, everything that the future holds. Nothing takes God by surprise. So we can be assured that whatever happens was foreseen by him and has a role to play in his sovereign, perfect plan. For some, the thought that God foresees but still permits the myriad causes of human pain and misery is troubling at best, morally repugnant at worst. But for many others, the belief that God has foreseen the disasters that befall us and the evils wrought against us is precisely what makes those things bearable.

Still, whatever comforts it may bring, the belief that God knows the future in full and fine-grained detail raises difficult philosophical problems. For example, we are accustomed to thinking of the future as open – which is just to say that future events do not exist, and facts about the future are not "fixed" in advance. Indeed, many of our attitudes toward daily decisions seem to presuppose that the future is open in this sense. You agonize today about whether to accept a job, or about whether to decline a marriage proposal. But would you agonize in the same way if you knew that the outcome was already fixed – that there was already a definite fact about what you would or would not do? Deliberating, weighing costs and benefits in an effort to determine the best course of action, and worrying about making the wrong choices seem all to reflect a belief that the future is not yet settled. But if the future is knowable – by God, or by anyone else – then it is settled. If God knows today that you will decline the marriage proposal tomorrow, then the fact of your declining is now fixed. Indeed, it is tempting to say that, given God's knowledge of what you will do, you simply can't do other than accept the proposal – in which case, God's foreknowledge would seem to preclude your being free.

For these and other reasons, many philosophers and theologians are inclined to give up belief in divine foreknowledge. But difficulties lurk here as well. You are now reading a book. Surely, then, it was true yesterday that you would today be reading a book. Suppose someone had said yesterday, "You will read a book tomorrow." Given that you are reading a book, what they would have said certainly wouldn't have been false. And it is hard to take seriously the idea that their statement might have been neither true nor false. So it would have been true. Thus, it was true yesterday that you would read a book today. But if that was true yesterday, then God, being omniscient, must have known it. So it would appear that, if God is omniscient, he knew yesterday that you would read a book today, which is just to say that God has foreknowledge. To deny his foreknowledge, you would apparently have to deny his omniscience – not a happy prospect.

The question of whether God has exhaustive, thoroughly detailed knowledge of the future is one of the central questions in the great debates about the nature of divine providence. One reason for this is that, as we shall see, the degree of control that God exercises over events in the world may partly constrain, or be constrained by, the extent to which God knows the future. And, as the foregoing considerations make clear, questions about God's foreknowledge are intimately connected both with questions about time and God's relationship to time (Does the future exist? Is it somehow settled, and present to God?), and with questions about the nature of omniscience (What exactly is omniscience? Is it possible to be omniscient without knowing the future?). It is for this reason that we have chosen to discuss God's eternity, omniscience, and providence together in one chapter.

Past, present, and future

"Scientific people," says the Time Traveler in H. G. Wells's *The Time Machine*, "know very well that Time is only a kind of Space." In the story, this remark comes toward the end of a brief parlor lecture wherein the Time Traveler argues that reality is extended in four dimensions, not three, and that the so-called temporal dimension is not fundamentally different from the so-called spatial dimensions. The point of the lecture is to help prepare the Time Traveler's friends for the unveiling of his grand invention: a machine that can travel backward and forward in time. But, whatever we think about the possibility of time travel, the story about time that the Time Traveler tells is one that merits serious reflection.

According to the Time Traveler, and, indeed, according to the standard interpretations of some of our best scientific theories, everything that ever did exist or ever will exist does exist – not here and now, of course, but at some spatio-temporal distance from here and now. So dinosaurs exist; outposts on Mars (if there will be such things) exist; your birth and your death exist; and the reality these things enjoy is no less than and no different from the reality you yourself, here and now, enjoy. Other times and the objects and events that exist at them are like distant places and things: fully real and, in principle, capable of being visited if only one had the right sort of device. This view of time is called eternalism, and it is one among several versions of four-dimensionalism, the view that reality exists as a sort of four-dimensionally extended block.[1]

The main rival to eternalism is presentism, the view that only present things exist. According to presentism, there are no merely past or merely future things. Dinosaurs did exist, outposts on Mars (if there will be such things) will exist; but there is no sense in which these things do exist. Yesterday's sins are quite literally gone; what tomorrow may bring is in no way actual.

Presentism is often heralded as the "common-sense" view of time. This is largely because presentism respects both the common intuition that the past is gone and the future is in some sense open, as well as the related intuition that the passage of time is an objectively real phenomenon. Though some eternalists believe in the passage of time (they believe that the property of presentness is like a "moving spotlight" that moves along the temporal dimension, highlighting one time after another and giving each time a privileged status for as long as it is highlighted), most eternalists do not. There is no "moving now," and the familiar subjective experience of the flow of time, the transition from one moment to the next, is mere illusion. Likewise, eternalism leaves no room for the idea that the past is gone or that the future is open and unsettled. All of this might sound highly counterintuitive – not at all in accord with what we ordinarily think about time. But a great many fictional stories (mostly time-travel stories) seem to embody the view that other times are like distant places; so perhaps common sense is somewhat divided on the question of the reality of other times.

---

[1] Among the other versions of four-dimensionalism are the "growing block" view, according to which only the past and the present exist, and the block of reality just continues to grow as new times come into existence and existing times move from being present to being past, and the "shrinking block" view, according to which only the present and the future exist, and the block of reality continues to shrink as times cease to exist.

This is not the place to discuss at length the relative merits of eternalism and presentism. But it is worth mentioning that both views have serious considerations in their favor. On behalf of presentism are the two common-sense intuitions just mentioned, together with the fact that it is hard to see how there could be real change in the world if, as the typical eternalist envisions, time does not flow and objects and events do not really come into or pass out of existence. On the other hand, some of our best physical theories (in particular, Einstein's special and general theories of relativity) speak strongly in favor of eternalism. Moreover, presentism seems, at least initially, to face some rather difficult problems that eternalism easily avoids.

One problem arises in connection with one of the very features of presentism that makes it attractive: its ability to accommodate the passage of time. The problem is that it is hard to see what the passage of time could possibly amount to. Time passes only if propositions like "t is present" change their truth value. But it is quite natural to suppose that a proposition p changes its truth value only if there is a time at which it is true and another time at which it is false. If that is right, though, then time passes only if something like the following is true:

(PASS)   There is a time T_1 at which "t is present" is true and another time T_2 at which "t is present" is false.

But now what are these times T_1 and T_2? It seems obvious that the only time "at which" t is present is t itself. But if that is right, then T_1 must just be t; and T_2 must be any other time. But the problem here is that even the eternalist who doesn't believe in the passage of time can say that t is present at itself and not present at any other time. So it seems that we must either insist that T_1 and T_2 refer to other times, or else we must deny that the passage of time requires the truth of something like PASS. Taking the former option, we seem to be stuck. What could these "other times" possibly be? Taking the latter option, we seem to be left without any understanding of what the passage of time amounts to. Thus, it is hard to see how to make sense of temporal passage.

Another problem is what philosophers sometimes refer to as the "grounding" problem: if there are no past or future things, it is hard to see what grounds or explains the truth of particular claims about the past. Intuitively, present-tense truths are made true by presently occurring events. What makes it true that you are reading right now, for example, is just the occurrence of a particular event – the event of your reading. But what makes it true, say, that Fred ate apples for breakfast yesterday? The eternalist can say that a claim like this is made true by the occurrence of another event – the event of Fred's eating apples for breakfast – at a time located within the boundaries of yesterday. But the presentist cannot say this, for the presentist does not believe in merely past events. For the presentist, there simply is no such thing as the event of Fred's eating apples for breakfast (unless he happens to be doing so right now). A presentist might say that what makes it true that Fred ate apples for breakfast yesterday is just the fact that some such apple-eating event occurred yesterday. But what are we to make of such a fact? If there is such a fact, it seems not to be grounded in anything happening in the world, for, on presentism, the world now doesn't include any event involving Fred eating apples for breakfast.

The considerations just mentioned (on both sides of the debate) are far from decisive; and the lists of pros and cons associated with each of these two views are far from complete. But the dispute is pertinent to our present discussion because what one thinks about the reality of other times (and about the reality of past and future objects and events) will make a difference to how one thinks about divine providence and God's knowledge of the future. If eternalism is true and God is omniscient, then it is hard to resist the idea that God knows the future in exhaustive detail. Because the entire future is out there, so to speak, an omniscient being could hardly avoid knowing about it. On the other hand, if presentism is true, the door is open to denying that God knows the future. Presentists aren't clearly forced to deny that God knows the future. They might try to accommodate divine knowledge of the future in the same way that they accommodate divine knowledge of the past (for example, by supposing that, at any given time, there is a wide range of brute, irreducibly tensed facts like its having been the case that there are dinosaurs, or its being true that Fred will eat oranges for breakfast tomorrow). But, in any case, rejecting divine foreknowledge is more clearly an option for presentists than for their eternalist counterparts.

Eternal or everlasting?

There are two main questions about how God relates to time. One of these is the question of whether God is eternal or everlasting. Christians sometimes speak alternately of their hope for everlasting life or their hope for eternal life as if the two were one and the same thing. This way of speaking is perfectly legitimate; but it embodies a way of using the terms "eternal" and "everlasting" that is different from the way those terms are used in the philosophical literature on God's relationship to time. In this literature, God is said to be everlasting if and only if God is temporal and there is no time at which God does not exist. God is said to be eternal, on the other hand, if and only if (to use the oft-quoted words of Boethius) God enjoys "the complete possession all at once of illimitable life."[2] As the phrase indicates, God is eternal only if his life is not marked by temporal succession. Thus, God is eternal only if he is atemporal, or timeless. But eternity, as it is usually conceived, includes more than mere atemporality, as will emerge when the notion is discussed in more detail below.

The second main question about how God relates to time is the question whether God is in our spacetime – i.e. the spacetime investigated and described by modern physics. People sometimes speak as if this second question is identical to the first because they assume that God is located in time if and only if God is everlasting, and that God is not located in time if and only if God is eternal. But it is by no means clear that these connections hold. It seems at least possible to suppose that an eternal being is omnipresent throughout physical spacetime; and so, it seems, there is no logical obstacle to the supposition that an eternal being could be *located at* every spacetime point. In this way, God would be both eternal and in time. Nor is there any clear obstacle to believing that a being that existed wholly outside of our physical spacetime could nonetheless be in time in a different respect, for example, by experiencing a changing succession of mental states. But if that is so, then God is temporal, despite having no location in our spacetime. The upshot of all of this is simply that the question whether God is somehow located in physical spacetime is different from the question whether God is eternal or everlasting.

In the remainder of this section, we will leave aside questions about God's relationship to physical spacetime and focus exclusively on the question of whether God is everlasting or eternal. We'll begin by explaining the

---

[2] E. K. Rand, in H. F. Stewart, E. K. Rand, and S. J. Tester, *Boethius: The Theological Tractates and the Consolation of Philosophy* (London: Heinemann; Cambridge, MA: Harvard; 1973) p. 400. The translation here is from Eleonore Stump and Norman Kretzmann's "Eternity," *Journal of Philosophy* 78 (1981), pp. 429–58.

notion of eternity in a bit more detail, and then we'll turn to some common arguments for and against the doctrine of divine eternity (that is, the doctrine that God is eternal rather than everlasting).

As we have seen, the Boethian understanding of eternity has it that eternity consists in the complete possession of illimitable life all at once. Eleonore Stump and Norman Kretzmann, two of the most well known contemporary defenders of the doctrine of divine eternity, note that this conception was hardly original with Boethius, and was, indeed, widely held among ancient and medieval philosophers and theologians. They go on to note four ingredients in this understanding of eternity.

First, an eternal being possesses life. Thus, numbers, sets, and other abstracta, if there are such things at all, do not count as eternal, despite the fact that they would surely be atemporal.

Second, the life possessed by an eternal being is without limit. That is to say, it has no beginning and it has no end.

Thus, third, the life of an eternal being is of infinite duration.[3] This might seem puzzling at first: how could an atemporal life have duration? Isn't duration just persistence through time? But here perhaps we can be helped by attending to a distinction between the metaphysical present and what some have called the "specious" present. The metaphysical present is a durationless instant, an infinitesimal moment in time. But our experience of the present isn't nearly so small. What we would describe in experience as "the present moment" has some temporal thickness. For example, your friend speaks to you and, though your experience of her action is surely divisible into experiences of parts of her action – bits of sound and perceived movement on her part and so on – it is not at all divisible into experiences of *infinitesimal* parts of her actions. The smallest units of your experience are, again, temporally thick. They have duration, even though all of their parts are, as it were, present to you all at once. This sort of temporally thick experience of the present is what people refer to as (experience of) the

---

[3] Stump and Kretzmann note that one might think that a life of *zero* duration – a life that occupies a mere point in time, as it were – might also qualify as "beginningless and endless." But, though it is possible to find some textual support for the claim that Boethius took eternal life to be life without duration, in the end Stump and Kretzmann conclude that the balance of reasons favors the claim that, on the Boethian conception – and, indeed, on the standard Christian conception – eternal life is life of infinite duration.

"specious present." And the idea underlying the doctrine of divine eternity is that God's life is sort of like an infinitely thick specious present.

Fourth, and finally, an eternal being possesses its entire life all at once: it experiences no succession; there is no temporal ordering to the events in its life; its life is not marked by gain, loss, or any other sort of change.

Such is the conception of eternity. But why believe that God is eternal? Not surprisingly, the master argument for the doctrine of divine eternity is just that which arises out of perfect-being theology. Thus:

(i) God is a perfect being.
(ii) Being eternal is a more perfect mode of existence than being non-eternal; therefore
(iii) God is eternal.

The question, though, is why we should believe premise (ii). Why think that being eternal is a more perfect mode of existence than the alternative?

Let us begin by setting aside one clearly spurious reason for believing the doctrine of divine eternity. Suppose, as was suggested above, the notion of temporal passage is incoherent. One might think that this clinches the case in favor of divine eternity. After all, it would seem that the main distinction between temporal life and eternal life is just the presence or absence of a "moving now." Thus, if there are strong arguments against the possibility of a moving now, it would seem that those same arguments speak just as strongly in favor of the doctrine of divine eternity.

The trouble, however, is that, regardless of whether temporal passage is possible, it is absolutely clear that our lives are not eternal. We do not completely possess illimitable life all at once. Those who reject temporal passage recognize this, of course. They simply claim that our experience of a moving now is illusory: it seems to us that time flows, but it really doesn't. But to say that it "seems to us that time flows" is just to say that we experience the events in our lives sequentially – one at a time – rather than all at once. Thus, one who rejects temporal passage is forced by our own experience – our own experience of the illusion of temporal passage – to admit that it is possible for a being to experience its life sequentially (and thus fail to be eternal) even if there is no temporal passage. Perhaps some will see this as evidence against the claim that temporal passage is impossible. But, be that as it may, the point is just that the doctrine of divine eternity doesn't seem to follow just from the claim that temporal passage is impossible.

A more powerful consideration in favor of divine eternity is the fact, also mentioned above, that the life of an eternal being is not marked by gain or loss. There is a fullness to the life of an eternal being that is lacking in the lives of temporal beings. Temporal beings have to wait for events in their future; and they experience the genuine loss of things in their past. They are, therefore, vulnerable to the ravages of time in a way that eternal beings are not. For an eternal being, however, every aspect of its life is always immediately present. Thus, it is tempting to think that eternity is a much better mode of existence than temporality.

Moreover, many philosophers have been captivated by the thought that mutability is somehow an imperfection. The phenomenon of change has given rise to some of the most enduring and difficult philosophical problems in the history of philosophy; and one common response to philosophically problematic phenomena is just to deny that the relevant phenomena are genuine. Thus, for example, generations of philosophers – particularly ancient Greek philosophers whose views seem to have played a significant role in shaping the development of traditional theism – have been convinced that change is simply impossible: real things do not change; the world of change that we seem to experience is, in fact, a sort of illusion. If this is right, then to say that God changes is to say that he is somehow less than entirely real – either entirely non-existent, or enjoying only a degenerate grade of reality. The former is, of course, unacceptable to theists; the latter is incompatible with God's perfection. Thus, many philosophers have been led to the conclusion that God simply doesn't change. And if he doesn't change at all, then his life cannot include temporal succession.

So two historically important reasons for believing in the doctrine of divine eternity are (a) the belief that the life of a perfect being could not be marked by gain or loss, and (b) the belief that the life of a perfect being could not be characterized by any sort of change whatsoever. Two further reasons for believing the doctrine are (c) that it helps us to make sense of God's knowledge of creaturely free actions that lie in our future, and (d) it provides a sense in which God is more perfectly and intimately present in the lives of his creatures since, on the doctrine of divine eternity (and only on that doctrine), there can never be a moment in God's life when God fails to be in the presence of any of his creatures.

Reasons (c) and (d) are closely related. Both exploit the fact that, according to the doctrine of divine eternity, everything that God experiences is present to God all at once. Since God is omnipresent throughout space and time, God's experience includes being in the presence of everything in space and time. Thus, it follows that everything that ever has been or ever will be in space and time is present to God all at once. So, for example, God is present with you here and now, and he will be present with you an hour from now as well (assuming you will still exist an hour from now). But since the doctrine of divine eternity entails that God possesses all of his life at once, it follows from this that whatever you are doing an hour from now has, from God's point of view, always been present. And so too for any moment in your life, or in the life of any other creature. Moreover, since God's life consists of no "moments" other than the eternal now, it is simply impossible for there to be moments in his life at which he fails to be in the presence of his creatures.

If the preceding remarks about options (c) and (d) seem to induce a sense of vertigo, it is probably because it is hard to know what, if anything, they presuppose about the reality of past and future times. On the one hand, it is hard to see how events in your past or future could possibly be present to God if those events are not real. Thus, it would seem that (d) is true only if eternalism is true. Moreover, as we'll see below, it is very hard to see how future free actions could be known if they are not already real; thus, it is not at all clear that (c) is true unless eternalism is true. But if eternalism is true, the doctrine of divine eternity isn't needed to make sense of God's knowl-edge of future free actions. The reason is that, on eternalism, future events exist in just the same way that present events do; and so they ought to be knowable by God in just the way that present events are, regardless of whether God's life includes succession. Furthermore, eternalism together with the claim that (i) God is omnipresent throughout spacetime, and (ii) there is no time in God's life at which he fails to be omnipresent throughout spacetime will suffice to guarantee that every moment in the lives of his (physical) creatures is always present to God. Thus, in short, if eternalism is false, then (c) and (d) are at least doubtful, if not clearly false; and if eternalism is true, then (c) and (d) seem to be false. Thus, absent more sustained discussion about what exactly (c), (d), and the doctrine of divine eternity presuppose about the reality of past and future times, it is hard to take (c) and (d) seriously as motivations for belief in divine eternity.

Of course, nothing said so far even so much as suggests that the con-siderations arising out of perfect-being theology fail to motivate the doctrine of divine eternity. But it is precisely at this point in the dialectic that we are forced to come to grips with reasons for thinking that God is everlasting. Though it is indeed tempting to think that atemporal existence is a more perfect mode of existence than temporal existence, the fact is that there are also strong reasons for thinking that a perfect being would have to be temporal. This is because certain perfections seem to require *change*.

Being personal, being an agent, and being omniscient all seem to be perfections. Intuitively, something cannot count as a perfect being without having each of these properties. But, as we will shortly explain, each of the first two seems inherently to involve change; and, plausibly, the third property will as well, at least for any being who happens to be accompanied by a temporal world. If that is right, and if these three properties are indeed perfections, then either being eternal is not a perfection, or else the very notion of a perfect being is incoherent.

Why think that each of these three properties really require change? Consider first the property of being personal. Sometimes those who argue that personality requires change do so on the grounds that having a mental life seems to require change. One motivation for this sort of claim comes from introspection: our own mental lives involve change; and so it is tempting to think that any mental life would have to involve change. As many defenders of the doctrine of eternity have pointed out, however, there is no obvious obstacle to an eternal being having mental states – i.e. beliefs, desires, emotions, intentions, and the like. Nor is there any obstacle to an eternal being having mental states that are in some sense reactive to features of a changing world. For example, an eternal God might be eternally pleased with the Virgin Mary's obedience, eternally displeased with Cain's sacrifice, eternally grieved over the circumstances leading to the Noachian Flood and the destruction of Sodom and Gomorrah, and so on. It's just that for an eternal being all of these various mental states would be possessed at once instead of unfolding over time. But it is hard to see why that difference alone should preclude such a rich set of mental states from counting as a mental life. Thus, one might think, atemporality is in fact no obstacle to possessing a mental life.

Alternatively, one might insist that personality requires change on the grounds that nothing counts as personal unless it possesses dispositions to alter its mental states in response to external stimuli. On this view, part of what it is to be a person is to be a *responder*. But, of course, an eternal being could not possibly be a responder in this sense. For, being incapable of alteration, an eternal being could not possibly have dispositions to alter its mental states in response to anything. Moreover, one might insist that God's being eternally pleased with Mary's obedience, eternally displeased with Cain's sacrifice, and so on, isn't sufficient for God's being a responder since there is no clear sense in which God's attitudes toward those events are caused by, or generated in response to, those events. Defenders of the doctrine of eternity will surely reject this sort of requirement on personality. But to the extent that one finds it intuitive, the requirement will have to be weighed against intuitions that speak in favor of eternity as a more perfect mode of existence.

Similar moves might be made with respect to the claim that *agency* essentially involves change. Reflecting on our own agency, we find ourselves disinclined to regard behaviors not preceded in time by deliberation, choice, or intention as (direct) products of our own agency; and this makes it tempting to think that divine agency must be temporal as well. Moreover, all of our acts have effects – if nothing else, the generation of the event that is the act. So it is very tempting to think that, for any sort of act (divine or otherwise), there must have been a time before the act. But here, as before, the defender of eternity might simply insist that our own case is not representative. Though all of our acts are in time, why not think it is possible for an eternal being to act intentionally without having the intention *temporally precede* the act? Of course, it will be important to say that the intention *explains* the act; but it is not obvious that explanatory priority requires temporal priority. Likewise, there is no obvious obstacle to supposing that God's eternal act timelessly produces its effects. One might insist that there is no time before God acts. The acts of God simply are; and God simply acts. Moreover, on this view, just as God might be eternally pleased with Mary and displeased with Cain, so too he might be eternally parting the Red Sea, eternally igniting Elijah's fire in his showdown with the prophets of Baal, and so on. Here too the moves made by the defender of eternity seem to result in a coherent view. They come at a price – the price of either giving up whatever intuitions one has to the effect that there is no "order of explanation" without temporal ordering, or giving up the view that real agency requires that one's behaviors be genuinely explained by, rather than merely accompanied by, one's intentions, choices, and rationalizations. But it is far from obvious that believers in eternity need to regard this price as objectionably high.

Matters are somewhat more complicated with the question of whether omniscience is compatible with eternity. The basic worry can be put like this: If, as believers in temporal passage maintain, there is always an absolute, objective fact about what time is present, then an omniscient being would always have to know what time is present. But if time passes, then the answer to the question "What time is present?" is constantly changing. Thus, if time passes, an omniscient being would have to be constantly updating its beliefs about what time is present. Thus, an omniscient being accompanied by a temporal world would have to undergo change. Of course, a defender of eternity might respond to this worry by abandoning belief in temporal passage. But many believers in eternity do not want to give up on temporal passage. Moreover, it seems to be bad methodology to allow one's intuitions about the requirements of perfection to determine one's views about the ontology of time. Hence the complication: sorting out the import of this consideration against the doctrine of eternity requires a foray into the philosophy of time in an effort to determine the relative merits and demerits of the view that there is a genuine flow of time. We will not make that foray here. But, as noted in the preceding section, there is at least some *prima facie* reason to doubt that the claim that time passes is even coherent, much less rationally required.

Omniscience

So far in this chapter our focus has been on questions pertaining to God's relation to time. In the course of that discussion, it became clear that our views about what God knows will depend to some extent on our answers to questions about the ontology of time. Moreover, as noted toward the beginning of this chapter, our views about what God knows also depend to some extent on our views about human freedom. Questions about the relations between divine foreknowledge and human freedom will loom large throughout the remainder of this chapter – both in the present section, which focuses on omniscience, as well as in the next section, which focuses on divine providence. Before turning to these issues, however, we will begin with some reflection on the nature of omniscience and some initial concerns with what seems to be the most natural characterization of it.

Characterizing omniscience: initial concerns

According to the common-sense conception of omniscience, an omniscient being knows everything. A bit more precisely: an omniscient being knows every truth and, furthermore, does not have any false beliefs. Assuming that what it is to know something is the same for God as it is for human beings, this common-sense conception implies, at the very least, that God believes every truth and God is warranted in believing every truth (where warrant is just whatever it is that makes the difference between mere true belief and knowledge).

It is important to note, however, that different philosophical theories threaten to force modifications in the common-sense conception of omniscience. So, for example, there are set-theoretical reasons for thinking that it makes no sense to talk about "every proposition." For example, one might think that it makes sense to talk about every proposition only if there is a set of all propositions; but there are good reasons for thinking that there can't be a set of all propositions. Here's why: let P be the set of all propositions. Now consider the conjunction, C of all of the members of P. C won't be a member of P, since no conjunction has itself as a conjunct. Thus, P can't be the set of all propositions. But by hypothesis it was; so we have a contradiction. Hence, it looks like there is no set of all propositions; and so it looks as if we can't say things like "God believes every proposition." If this argument is sound, then, the common-sense definition of omniscience will have to be modified.

Likewise, some philosophers believe that contradictions can be true. For example, consider the liar sentence:

(Liar)   Liar is false.

Notoriously, Liar is true if and only if it is false. Some insist, for one reason or another, that Liar doesn't have a truth value. But some have argued – rather persuasively – that the best solution to the Liar Paradox is to admit that sentences like Liar are both true and false. Suppose that solution is correct. Then God will believe Liar, and God will also believe the proposition that Liar is false. So God will have contradictory beliefs. But can an omniscient being have contradictory beliefs? The common-sense definition doesn't specify. If we say "no," then theism conflicts with dialethism (the view that contradictions can be true). But it seems odd to think that one could rule out the dialethist solution to the Liar paradox simply by appeal to one's own theistic beliefs. On the other hand, if we say "yes," then we apparently leave open the door for the possibility of an omniscient being who believes literally every proposition (which would seem to be bad news).

To rule out this possibility, we would have to say what sorts of contra-dictions can be believed by an omniscient being. But doing this would seem to be a rather difficult task.

Neither of these problems is obviously fatal to the common-sense char-acterization of omniscience. For example, one might doubt the inference from the claim that we cannot speak of a set of all propositions to the claim that we cannot sensibly talk about "every" proposition; or one might doubt that omniscience has to be characterized in terms that presuppose the possibility of talking about "every" proposition. And one might also doubt that the motivations for dialethism pose problems. For, one might think, the plausibility of dialethism stands or falls with the dialethist's ability to specify which sorts of contradictions can be true; and once this specification has been made, then perhaps we also have an answer to the question of which sorts of contradictions can be believed by an omniscient being. Whether these responses or different ones are successful, however, is a matter we shall not pursue further.

The problem of freedom and divine foreknowledge

Perhaps the most commonly suggested refinement to the common-sense characterization of omniscience is one aimed at accommodating the view that God does not know the future. For reasons to be explored in the next section, many philosophers believe that it is impossible for God to know what his creatures will freely do in the future. Many of these same philoso-phers also believe that there are, nevertheless, facts about what free crea-tures will freely do. If they are right, then there are facts that God cannot know. But, they argue, God's inability to know what can't be known shouldn't count against his omniscience. Thus, they typically recommend a modification of the account of omniscience: a being is omniscient if and only if (roughly) it knows everything that it is logically possible to know.

But is it really logically impossible for facts about future free acts to be known? At first blush, it seems that the answer is "yes." At the outset of this chapter, we offered a quick informal argument for the conclusion that freedom and foreknowledge are incompatible. Let us now make that argu-ment more rigorous.

Suppose that Sally is now reading a book. Let t be the present time; let t* be a time 1,000 years before now; and let P_S be the proposition that Sally will read a book 1,000 years hence. Furthermore, let us assume (as seems obviously true) that one is free with respect to an action only if one has a choice about whether one performs it. Then, it seems, we may reason as follows:

2.1. P_S was true at t^*.

2.2. God is omniscient.

2.3. An omniscient being believes every true proposition and has no false beliefs.

2.4. Therefore: at t^*, God believed that P_S was true. [From 2.1, 2.2, 2.3]

2.5. Premise 2.4 entails that Sally reads a book at t. (That is, it is impossible that premise 2.4 be true and Sally not read a book at t.)

2.6. No human being has ever had a choice about the truth of premise 2.4.

2.7. For any propositions p and q, if p is true and if p entails q, and if no human being has ever had a choice about the truth of p, then no human being has ever had a choice about the truth of q.

2.8. No human being – and so not even Sally – has ever had a choice about whether Sally reads a book at t. [From 2.5, 2.6, 2.7]

2.9. A person is free with respect to an action only if that person has a choice about whether or not to perform the action.

2.10. Therefore: though Sally reads a book at t, she does not do so freely. [From 2.8, 2.9]

This argument is specified to a particular action of Sally's, but it should be obvious that the argument generalizes to every action of every creature. So, if it is sound, no genuinely free act could possibly have been foreknown by God.

Premises 2.4 and 2.8 are sub-conclusions that follow logically from the premises mentioned in parentheses at the end of each, so those steps in the argument are unassailable. Premise 2.5 is obvious. Premise 2.7 is not exactly incontestable, but it is very hard to see how it could be false. Even upon close inspection, it seems to be free from counter-examples. Moreover, most theists are unwilling to give up either premise 2.2 or 2.9. That leaves premises 2.1, 2.3, and 2.6 as the most natural places to resist the argument.

Before examining which line of resistance is best, it will be helpful to attend to another, similar argument against human freedom. The argument we have just seen is often described as an argument for *theological fatalism*.

This is because the argument depends in part on assumptions about God and God's beliefs in reaching its conclusion. But it is possible to dispense with the theological assumptions and argue directly from the past truth of P_S to the conclusion that Sally's reading is not free. That sort of argument is commonly referred to as an argument for *logical fatalism*. The argument proceeds as follows:

2.11. P_S was true at t^*.
2.12. Premise 2.11 entails that Sally reads a book at t. (That is, it is impossible that premise 2.11 be true and Sally not read a book at t.) [Trivial]
2.13. Nobody alive now has, had, or ever will have a choice about the truth of premise 2.11.
2.14. For any propositions p and q, if p is true and if p entails q, and if nobody alive now has, had, or ever will have a choice about the truth of p, then nobody alive now has, had, or ever will have a choice about the truth of q.
2.15. Nobody alive now – and so not even Sally – has, had, or ever will have a choice about whether Sally reads a book at t. [From 2.12, 2.13, 2.14]

From 2.15 it is a short step (by way of 2.9) to the conclusion that Sally does not read freely at t. Note that the only real difference between this argument and the argument for theological fatalism is the omission of premises 2.2–2.4 and the replacement of premise 2.5 with premise 2.12. This suggests that it is bad strategy to resist the theological fatalist by rejecting premise 2.3. Some theists do resist the theological fatalist in this way. They do so by rejecting the common-sense account of omniscience in favor of an account according to which an omniscient being need not know every single truth, but only those truths which it is logically possible to know. But the reason that this sort of move seems to be bad strategy is that, even if premise 2.3 is false, one will still have to find a way of resisting the logical fatalist if one wants to believe in human freedom; and it looks as if whatever strategy one employs against the logical fatalist will carry over as a way of also resisting the theological fatalist. In our view, then, the most sensible lines of resistance involve either a rejection of premise 2.1 (and premise 2.11) or of premise 2.6 (and premise 2.13).

To give up premise 2.1, one must say that P_S either was false or had no truth value at t^*. Given that Sally is now reading a book, it is hard to see how P_S could have been false. But perhaps it simply had no truth value – perhaps, in other words, there simply were no facts about Sally's future free acts until

Sally existed and performed those acts. If so, then God's inability to know the future free acts of his creatures is perfectly consistent with his being omniscient and with omniscience being understood in the commonsensical way as involving knowledge of all true propositions. As we mentioned in the introduction to this chapter, many philosophers do not like this sort of view because it is hard to see what it would mean for a proposition to be neither true nor false. Moreover, another potential cost of this view is that it conflicts with eternalism. If eternalism is true, then the event of Sally's reading a book now has always existed. Thus, P_S would have been true 1,000 years ago after all. Of course, one might not care about preserving eternalism; but for those who do, this sort of move will be unpalatable.

Alternatively, one might try to give up premise 2.6. Initially, it appears that to reject premise 2.6 is to say that we somehow have the power to change God's past beliefs. And the ascription of that sort of power seems absurd. After all, given that God did in fact believe 1,000 years ago that Sally would read a book now, how could Sally possibly do anything to make it the case that God didn't believe that she would read a book now? Answer: she can't. One of the hard lessons of growing up is that it is absolutely impossible to change the past.

But one might very well reject premise 2.6 without ascribing to agents any sort of absurd "power to change the past." Here is how. One might think that, though we can't change the past, certain facts about the past are what they are because of how things are in the present. Suppose you own a coin that was given to you long ago by a time traveler; and suppose that very time traveler is, at this very moment, pocketing the coin that she will give you and stepping into the time machine that will take her back to the time of her meeting with you. The time traveler's present actions partially explain a fact about the past – namely, the fact that you were given that coin so long ago. According to this story, then, the past is the way that it is in part because of what the time traveler is doing now.

Can the time traveler be free? Suppose she is. If she is free, then she has the power to do things – namely, refrain from pocketing the coin or refrain from stepping into the time machine – such that, if she were to do one of them, the past would have been different from what it in fact is. The question is whether there is anything incoherent about this supposition. So far as we can tell, there is not. We know that the time traveler *won't* refrain from pocketing the coin or refrain from stepping into the time machine. The past is what it is, and it is that way at least in part because of what the time traveler in fact does. But that doesn't at all mean that the time traveler *can't* do those things. Granted, she can't change the past. But why think that if (say) she were to refrain from pocketing the coin, the past would be changed?

Think of it this way: the actual history of the world is, in effect, a story according to which the time traveler pockets a coin, steps into a time machine, goes back to visit you, and hands you the coin. But what would the story be like if (in the story) she were to refrain from pocketing the coin? The story wouldn't say that, up until now, it was true that you received a coin long ago from a time traveler but now – oops – thanks to the time traveler's refusal to pocket the coin, it is suddenly no longer true that you received a coin long ago from a time traveler. That is a story according to which the past changes, and that sort of story makes no sense. Rather, the story would simply be one in which you never received a coin from a time traveler long ago (though perhaps you met the time traveler and had a nice chat with her). In other words, the story would be one according to which the past was different, not one according to which the past was changed.

How does all of this shed light on the fatalism debate? As follows: past future-tense facts and God's past beliefs are both reasonably thought of as features of the past that depend on the present. God's past beliefs do not determine our present actions; they are *explained by* our present actions. The same is true of past future-tense facts about our present actions. So long as we think that having a choice about these features of the past requires the ability to change the past, we will be strongly tempted to go along with premises 2.6 and 2.13 in the fatalistic arguments above. But if the line of reasoning just offered is sound, we needn't think this way. Rather, we might think that having a choice about those past facts requires only that we have the power to do something such that, had we done it, the past would have been different. This sort of power is often referred to as "counterfactual power" over the past.[4]

---

[4] The term *counterfactual* refers to conditionals like the following: "If Fred were to propose to Wilma, Wilma would accept." The name derives from the fact that, in the paradigm cases anyway, the antecedent of the conditional describes *non-actual* – or "contrary to fact" – circumstances. However, the term now commonly applies to "if…would…" conditionals with true antecedents as well. Counterfactual power over the past, then, is just power to do something that one didn't in fact do, such that had one exercised that power, the past *would have been* different.

What could possibly lead us to think that we have counterfactual power over the past? Here two lines of argument are available. Some philosophers believe both that we are free and that all of our actions are determined. These philosophers are called compatibilists because they think that freedom is compatible with determinism. Moreover, determinism is standardly characterized as the view that a description of the total state of the world at any instant plus the laws of nature logically entails a description of the total state of the world at any other instant. Thus, if determinism is true, all of our power to do anything other than what we actually do is counterfactual power. For, on determinism, the only way for us to do anything different from what we actually do is for the past to be different or for the laws to be different. Compatibilists typically do not want to say that we can change the past or the laws. What they say instead is that we have the power to do things such that, had we done them, the past and the laws would have been different.

But one need not be a compatibilist to think that we have counterfactual power over the past. One might just think, like William of Ockham, that compatibilism is false but that, nevertheless, some facts about the past depend on the present actions of free creatures and other facts do not. Facts of the former kind are often called "soft facts"; facts of the latter kind are called "hard facts." It is notoriously difficult to draw the hard-fact/soft-fact distinction with both precision and plausibility; but the point here is that, so long as one thinks that there is such a distinction to be drawn, one will be committed even apart from compatibilism to thinking that some features of the past are such that, had we acted differently, those facts would have been different.

It is, of course, very tempting to think that there is no meaningful hard-fact/soft-fact distinction, and that counterfactual power over the past is impossible. For this reason many philosophers will have trouble accepting Ockham's way out of the fatalist's clutches. Nevertheless, Ockhamism is very popular among incompatibilists as a way of resisting both kinds of fatalist and, so far as we can tell, there is nothing incoherent about it.

Four views of divine providence

In the last section we explored in some detail the question of whether divine foreknowledge was possible given human freedom. In the present and closing section we turn to the topic of divine providence.

To speak of God's providence is to speak of the nature and extent of God's control over and loving care for his creation. Everyone agrees that God is sovereign in some sense over creation, and that God sees to it that creation unfolds according to a plan. But there is much disagreement about just what sort of control God exercises over creation and also about the depth of detail included in God's plan. Theories of providence fall along a spectrum. At one end lie views according to which God leaves a great deal to chance and to the decisions of free creatures. At the other end lie views according to which absolutely every matter of fact is the product of some divine decree. For purposes here, we will focus on just four of these views: what, for lack of better labels, we will call Openism, Responsivism, Molinism, and Calvinism.

Openism

The term Open Theism, or Openism, is of recent coinage and refers to a family of views about God that bucks the "Classical" conception of God as simple, eternal, impassable, and immutable. Central to Openism is a theory of providence according to which, at least from God's perspective, and maybe objectively as well, the future is in many respects open. In other words: Openists hold that a great many facts about the future – in particular, facts about future free acts and their consequences – are unknown to God; and many Openists also hold that propositions about future free acts and their consequences are indeterminate, or lacking in truth value.

On this view of providence, God is a risk-taker. Openists insist that God is not an irresponsible risk-taker. He is powerful enough and knowledgeable enough to ensure that, whatever decisions his free creatures might happen to make, he can ultimately work all things together for good and accomplish his purposes in the universe. God is, with respect to his creation, like a grand chessmaster playing against a novice. He knows his game so well that he can anticipate the moves of his opponent far in advance; he can very likely lead the novice down a path that ensures his own victory; and even if the novice behaves in unexpected ways, no matter what position he finds himself confronted with, he will know how to turn it to his advantage.

Openism will obviously be attractive to those who believe both that human beings are free and that freedom is incompatible with divine foreknowledge. But many also find it attractive because they think it offers some help with the problem of evil. As we mentioned at the outset of this chapter, many find it unsettling – indeed, downright repugnant – to think that God knew about all of the particular instances of horrible suffering that would take place in the world and yet chose to permit each and every one of them. It is more comforting, they suggest, to think that God is in some sense as surprised as we are by the evils that befall us (and by the evils we ourselves commit), but that, owing to his infinite resourcefulness, tremendous power, and otherwise vast range of knowledge, he is able to turn even the worst of events to the service of good.

Still, hard questions remain. For example, once the German *Wehrmacht* was underway, even the most dense among us could have predicted that, absent divine intervention, a great deal more suffering was on its way. Why is it repugnant to think that God knew millions of years ago that many would suffer at the hands of Hitler but chose to permit that suffering anyway, but not repugnant to think that God knew in (say) 1941 that many (more) would suffer at the hands of Hitler but chose to permit that suffering anyway? In short, the Openist view, like its rivals, is committed to acknowledging the existence of preventable suffering that was both foreseen and permitted by God. Given this, it is hard to see why the limitations on God's foresight imposed by the Openist view should be regarded as especially advantageous.

Indeed, one might press this point even further. Given that God is omnipotent, it seems that there is nothing that anyone could possibly do that God could not foresee and prevent; for presumably there will always be time between a free act of will and the physical effects of that free act, and God could surely foresee the physical effects once the act of will has occurred, even if he could not have foreseen the act of will itself. Thus God can never be surprised by the physical effects of evil choices, and any misery that results from human action could have been prevented by him. Thus, again, it is hard to see why Openism offers any particular advantage, given that it doesn't remove God's foresight of suffering that results from human action but only shortens it.

Moreover, one might find it morally objectionable that God takes the sorts of risks that he takes if the Openist view is true. In the Hebrew Bible book of Deuteronomy, for example, God commands the death penalty for any prophet whose prophecies fail to come true. But, at least on traditional readings of Hebrew prophecy, some of the Hebrew Testament prophets foretold on God's behalf events that came to pass within their own lifetimes and that depended crucially upon the free actions of human agents in order to come to pass. But if God doesn't know what free creatures will do in the future, then it is at least possible for the predictions put in the mouths of his prophets to be proven wrong; and if that is even so much as possible, it is hard to see how God can justifiably command the death penalty for any prophet who happens to be proven wrong. The command reflects either a degree of confidence or a willingness to risk the lives of others that is unseemly for a being who does not ultimately know what the future has in store.

Lastly, there is the very serious concern that (as Peter van Inwagen has recently pointed out), if Openism is true, some of God's promises could prove false. Here the chessmaster analogy is again useful. Given the nature of chess, it is always at least possible (even if massively unlikely) that, simply by moving randomly, a novice will beat a chessmaster. An indeterministic world with free creatures might similarly thwart victory for God – at least if "victory" means ensuring that there is at least one creature who ends up in heaven in part as a result of exercising his or her own free will. In so far as God has promised that heaven will be populated, at least one of God's promises could therefore prove false – at least if God refrains from coercing people into heaven. A price of Openism, then, is belief in a God who is willing to make promises that he knows he might not be able to keep – a high price indeed.

Responsivism

The view that we are calling Responsivism is sometimes referred to as the Simple Foreknowledge theory of providence. On this view, human beings are free, but the future is not open in either of the senses mentioned in our discussion of Openism. There are facts about what will happen in the future, and God knows those facts. Moreover, according to the Responsivist, many of God's providential decisions are made in response to his knowledge of the future.

To illustrate: suppose that God has known from the beginning of time that the flight for which you are now purchasing a ticket is bound to crash. And suppose God wants you not to die in the crash. God might decide, as a result of his knowledge of the destiny of your flight, to take steps to prevent you from making your flight. So, on the fateful day, you find yourself stuck in a providentially orchestrated traffic jam that delays you just long enough to save your life. According to the Responsivist, much of providence works in this way.

The trouble with Responsivism, however, is that it is hard to see how God's knowledge of the future can form the basis for his providential decisions unless (a) God's knowledge of the future is incomplete, or (b) his knowledge of the future and his providential decisions are caught in an explanatory loop. Here's why. Suppose God has complete knowledge of the future. Suppose further (as the Responsivist will agree) that God's knowledge of the future is somehow prior – at least in "order of explanation" – to his providential decisions. If God's knowledge of the future is (always) complete, then as soon as God knows the destiny of your flight, he also knows whether you will be on the flight and, furthermore, he knows whether it will be as a result of his own intervention that you either make or miss the flight. In other words, if God's knowledge of the future is complete, then by the time God knows what will happen, the facts about what providential decisions and interventions he will make are already fixed. Thus, if Responsivism is true and God's foreknowledge really is explanatorily prior to his providential decisions, then one of the following must be true: either God's knowledge of the future is incomplete, or else his knowledge of the future both explains and is explained by his providential decisions. The former makes Responsivism into a version of Openism, a view that no Responsivist has yet been content with. The latter implies that God's knowledge of the future and his providential decisions are caught in an explanatory loop: each explains and is explained by the other. This is impossible if explanation is an asymmetric relation, as many think that it is. But even if it is not incoherent, it is at least rather odd to say that providence is loopy in this way. It would be preferable to have a theory that didn't have this consequence.

Molinism

Molinism is named for the sixteenth-century Spanish Jesuit Luis de Molina, who was the first to defend something like the theory of providence about to be described. Molinists agree with Responsivists in denying that the future is open in either of the senses identified by Openists. But unlike Responsivists, Molinists do not think that God's providential decisions are ultimately explained by his knowledge of the future. Providence, according to Molinists, depends on a rather different kind of knowledge – what is often referred to as "middle knowledge."

Medieval philosophers prior to Molina distinguished between God's natural knowledge, which comprises his knowledge of truths that are both necessary and independent of God's will (such as truths of logic and mathematics), and God's free knowledge, which comprises his knowledge of truths that are contingent and dependent on his will (for example, ordinary truths about what objects and events exist in the world). Molina, however, identified a third kind of knowledge – knowledge of truths that are contingent (like the objects of God's free knowledge), but nevertheless independent of God's will (like the objects of his natural knowledge). Since this sort of knowledge stands, in a way, "in between" God's natural and free knowledge, it was referred to as middle knowledge. The primary examples of truths that are objects of God's middle knowledge are truths about what free creatures would do in circumstances that are not actual. In other words, God's middle knowledge consists primarily of his knowledge of counterfactuals of freedom – claims like "If Fred were to propose to Wilma, Wilma would freely accept." According to the Molinist, such truths are contingent – the counterfactuals true in the actual world might have been false. But they are nevertheless independent of God's will. It is, in other words, not up to God which counterfactuals are true.

The idea, then, is that, in making decisions about what sorts of creative acts to perform and about what sorts of providential interventions in the course of nature, if any, are called for, God relies in part upon his middle knowledge – his awareness of what his creatures would freely do if he were to put them in various different kinds of circumstances. In this way, God exercises a great deal of control over his creation. To see why, just imagine what it would be like if you knew with certitude what your friends would do in response to anything – anything at all – that you might do. It would not be difficult, in that sort of situation, to manipulate them like puppets. And yet they would not *be* your puppets, for all of their responses to you would still be free. Of course, it might be that there are some things that you could not get them to do no matter what you did. Perhaps, sadly for you, the man or woman you want to marry is such that there is absolutely nothing you can do that would result in that person freely agreeing to marry you. So your control would be limited – and limited precisely by the freedom of those around you. But it would, nevertheless, be extensive; and even where you lacked control, you would at least be able perfectly to predict what your friends will do (since, as soon as you knew what you were going to do, your knowledge of what they would do in response to your acts would then tell you what they will do once your acts have been completed).

Likewise, then, with God. If God has exhaustive middle knowledge, his middle knowledge will give him a great deal of control over the universe, and, together with his own knowledge of everything that he himself will do in the future, it will give him infallible and complete knowledge of the future. Since, by hypothesis, some of God's creatures are free, there may be some outcomes that God simply cannot secure. For example, some people might be such that, no matter what God were to do, they would not freely choose to have a relationship with him. Nevertheless, God could at least guarantee that everyone who would, under some possible set of circumstances, freely choose a relationship with him finds themselves in just such circumstances. And he could control a great many other outcomes as well.

Molinism is a powerful view with a great deal of theoretical utility. The fact that, on Molinism, God has extensive but not complete control of his creation allows Molinists to affirm a fairly strong view of divine sovereignty while also offering some explanation for the existence of evil. (Perhaps, Molinists say, evil was simply unavoidable given God's desire to create free creatures and given the hand of counterfactuals of freedom that was dealt to him.) It also supports explanations for why hell might be populated. (Perhaps, for example, there are some people whom it was valuable to create but who were simply such that nothing God could have done would have resulted in their freely choosing a relationship with him.) It has also been invoked in the service of defending particular views about the inspiration of Scripture, developing and buttressing theories about the incarnation and about petitionary prayer, defending the traditional doctrine of original sin, and explaining the nature of predestination and election in a way that reconciles both with a robust (incompatibilist) view of human freedom.

That said, Molinism also faces some serious objections. Central to Molinism is the supposition that there are true counterfactuals of freedom. Many philosophers, however, are inclined to reject this supposition on the grounds that, in the case of counterfactuals of freedom with false antecedents, it is hard to see what could possibly ground their truth. For example: Suppose Wilma is free and would remain free if Fred were to propose to her.

Suppose further that it is true that if Fred were to propose, Wilma would accept. What makes this true? Nothing about Wilma guarantees that she would accept. She is, after all, free – which is just to say that she might or might not accept if Fred were to propose. And if nothing about Wilma guarantees that she would accept, it is hard to see what else might guarantee this without interfering with her freedom. And so, again, it is hard to see what could possibly make it true that she would accept. One might insist – and, indeed, some have insisted – that counterfactuals of freedom don't have to be made true by anything. They might just be true. The worry, however, is that if there is nothing that makes them true, then it is hard to see what in the world explains their truth.

Calvinism

The view that we are calling Calvinism here could also reasonably bear the label Thomism or perhaps even Augustinianism. The view has been attributed to, among others, St. Augustine, St. Thomas Aquinas, and John Calvin; and there is no question that it has been endorsed by Jonathan Edwards and a host of followers of both Aquinas and Calvin. Proponents of this view maintain, contrary to all three of the views described above, both that all contingent matters of fact are completely determined by the will of God and that human freedom is compatible with determinism. Like Openists, Responsivists, and Molinists, then, Calvinists will affirm that human beings are free; but it is important to note that their conception of freedom – compatibilist rather than incompatibilist – is very different.

Calvinism offers the strongest possible conception of divine providence. God's control over his creation is absolute and, as some put it, meticulous. Calvinists take quite literally the Biblical claims that not a sparrow falls to the ground apart from the will of God (Matthew 10:29), and that when the lot is cast, its every result is from God (Proverbs 16:33). Nothing is left to chance; every movement of every particle is subject to the will of God, a product of divine decree. For those unsettled by the possibility of God taking risks or leaving important matters like the destinies of our eternal souls in the hands of fallible free creatures, Calvinism is maximally comforting. Moreover, many find Calvinism attractive because it seems to be implied by perfect-being theology. Unless something like Calvinism is true, it is at least in principle possible for God's will to be thwarted, for creatures to prevent God from getting what God wants, and for God to be disappointed by his creation. Apart from Calvinism, then, God is at least to some extent at the mercy of his creation. Many think that such a state of affairs would be unseemly. A God with more control is better than a God with less; and so if God is perfect, he must have perfect – i.e. absolute – control over what happens in the universe.

But perfect-being theology does not speak unequivocally in favor of Calvinism. The reason is simple: the world contains evil; and so if God exercises absolute control over everything that happens in the world – if, in other words, every event is a product of divine decree – it is hard to resist the appearance that blame for everything that happens ultimately rests with God. Indeed, it is hard even to make sense of the idea that God hates evil; for, after all, it is a consequence of Calvinism that every single horrendous act that takes place in the world was ultimately ordained by God. Moreover, if all our acts are ultimately determined by God, it is also hard to see how we could possibly be guilty of our sins or deserving of God's anger and punishment for them (as the Bible says we are). Imagine a craftsman who designs a small army of robots, programs the army to destroy everything in his living room, and then becomes angry with and "punishes" the robots for doing precisely that. The scenario is absurd. Yet if Calvinism is true, it would appear that God is just like that craftsman if he becomes angry with us and punishes us for our sins.

These objections to Calvinism are so intuitively powerful, it might seem hard to understand why so many great philosophers and theologians have been attracted to it. But here it might help to note that all of the objections to Calvinism could be avoided if only we could understand one thing about it: namely, how it is possible to be morally accountable for acts that we have been determined to do. If we could understand this, then we would also be able to understand why God is not accountable for our bad actions. And if we could understand why God is not accountable for our bad acts, then we would probably also be able to understand why it makes sense to say that he hates evil, and also why it can be both sensible and just for him to become angry with us and punish us for our sins. But how can we make intelligible the claim that we are morally accountable for acts that we have been determined to do? What can be said on behalf of such a *prima facie* implausible claim?

In our view, nobody has yet succeeded in helping us to understand how one could be accountable for acts that one has been determined to do.

However, that does not mean that there is nothing at all to be said for the claim. For example, Jonathan Edwards defended that claim in part by appeal to the doctrine of original guilt. The doctrine of original guilt maintains that human beings are guilty from birth for the sin of Adam. But, of course, none of us could have prevented Adam's sin. Thus, if we accept the doctrine of original guilt (which Edwards seemed to think all right-thinking Christians would – Calvinists or not), we are already committed to thinking that we can be morally accountable for something that we could not prevent. And if we can be morally accountable for something we were unable to prevent, then that opens the door at least a crack to saying that we can be morally accountable for something we were determined to do. Again, this does not help us to understand how we could be accountable for what we were determined to do. But for those who embrace original guilt, it might make an otherwise bitter pill go down a bit more easily.

Of course, there is much more that might be said here both for and against Calvinism and its rivals. But hopefully this brief sketch provides at least a rough sense of the considerations that motivate these various views about divine providence.

Further reading

Craig, William Lane, *The Only Wise God* (Grand Rapids, MI: Baker Book House, 1987).

Time and Eternity (Wheaton, IL: Crossway Books, 2001).

Flint, Thomas, *Divine Providence* (Ithaca, NY: Cornell University Press, 1998).

Ganssle, Greg and David Woodruff (eds.), *God and Time* (New York, NY: Oxford University Press, 2002).

Fischer, John Martin (ed.), *God, Foreknowledge, and Freedom* (Stanford, CA: Stanford University Press, 1989).

Hasker, William, *God, Time, and Knowledge* (Ithaca, NY: Cornell University Press, 1989).

Helm, Paul, *Eternal God* (Oxford: Clarendon Press, 1988).

Kvanvig, Jonathan, *The Possibility of an All-Knowing God* (New York, NY: St Martin's Press, 1986).

Leftow, Brian, *Time and Eternity* (Ithaca, NY: Cornell University Press, 1991).

Rea, Michael (ed.), *Oxford Readings in Philosophical Theology* (Oxford: Oxford University Press, 2008).

3   God triune and incarnate

Thus far in our discussion of the nature of God, we have focused on attributes that Jews, Christians, and Muslims alike have traditionally included in their concept of God. In the Christian tradition, however, God is characterized in two further ways that raise a host of philosophical problems in their own right. First, God is held to be *triune*. That is, Christians believe that, though there is but one God, God nevertheless exists somehow as three distinct divine persons: Father, Son, and Holy Spirit. Second, Christians believe that God became incarnate in the person of Jesus of Nazareth, and that Jesus himself was therefore somehow both fully God and fully human.

These features of Christianity might seem peculiar to say the least. Who would have thought that God had a tri-personal character? Who would have imagined that God would, or even could, become *fully* human? Nevertheless, it has been argued that the truth of the doctrine of the Trinity can be established by philosophical argument alone, wholly apart from divine revelation. On this view, perfect-person theology leads directly to one of the central and distinctive doctrines of the Christian faith, and constitutes an outright refutation of Jewish and Muslim conceptions of deity. (A strong claim indeed!) Moreover, many Christians think that certain historically grounded arguments can make it very reasonable to believe the doctrine of the incarnation.

Still, both doctrines are fraught with philosophical difficulty. For reasons to be explained below, the doctrine of the Trinity appears, on the surface, to be logically contradictory. If this is right, then, since the doctrine is absolutely central to Christian belief, Christianity itself is demonstrably false. (Also a strong claim!) Likewise, there are at least initially persuasive reasons for thinking that no being could possibly be both fully human and fully divine, as well as reasons for thinking that the doctrine of the incarnation as it is traditionally understood is logically untenable.

Before we begin discussing these difficulties, however, some brief remarks about our methodology are in order. In addressing the philosophical concerns that arise in connection with these doctrines, we shall be aiming to do so in a way that avoids falling into the so-called "heresies" associated with each doctrine. In discussing each doctrine, we will identify the most well-known and widely discussed heresies associated with each; and in so doing, we will be characterizing what most of Christendom has traditionally regarded as constraints on a properly orthodox understanding of the Trinity and the Incarnation. But one might wonder *why* we do this. Why should we care about "orthodoxy," and why should we care to avoid "heresy"? Isn't the concern about orthodoxy and heresy more of a medieval obsession – something one cares about mainly just to avoid being tortured on a rack or burned at the stake – rather than something that we moderns (with substantial religious freedom and policies of tolerance) ought to take seriously?

Toward answering these questions, it is important first to notice that Christianity has traditionally been regarded as a *doctrinal religion*. What that means, roughly, is that (in contrast to non-doctrinal religions like, say, Hinduism or the various forms of ancient Egyptian religion) there is a particular set of doctrines to which one must (at least mostly) subscribe if one wishes to be viewed as a member-in-good-standing of the Christian community. The doctrines in this set we can consider to be the *core* of Christian belief.

If this view of Christianity is right (and, admittedly, it is now controversial) – if, that is, Christianity is a doctrinal religion in the sense just described – then a proper assessment of Christianity will require attention to a proper understanding of the core doctrines. And here is where the notions of orthodoxy and heresy become important. To say that a view is orthodox is, roughly, just to say that it is consistent with what has been officially regarded as a proper understanding of Christian doctrines by those who have the power and authority to define how Christian doctrines are to be understood. To say that a view is heretical, on the other hand, is to say that it has been officially recognized as inconsistent with a proper understanding of Christian doctrine.

Of course, there is a great deal of controversy within Christendom about who has the power and authority to define "the" proper understanding of the core Christian doctrines and there is, likewise, a great deal of controversy over the extent to which individual believers ought to be concerned about avoiding heresy (as it has just been characterized). For present purposes, however, we don't need to worry about such controversies. For however they are resolved, there will be widespread agreement at least on this much: regardless of the religious significance of the heresies discussed below, the question of whether there are coherent interpretations of Christian doctrine that avoid those heresies is at least of serious *philosophical* interest. For the creeds and Church councils that have rejected those positions are widely looked to throughout Christendom as sources for a correct understanding of Christian doctrine. So if it turns out that Christian doctrine as interpreted by those creeds and councils is *incoherent*, then, at the very least, large segments of Christendom will be forced to revise their religious views and also, perhaps, to revise their views about the authority and reliability of the relevant creeds and councils.

The Trinity

The Christian doctrine of the Trinity says that there is exactly one God, but that God exists in three persons – Father, Son, and Holy Spirit. The central elements of the doctrine are neatly summarized in a passage of the Athanasian Creed, one of the most widely respected summaries of the Christian faith:

> We worship one God in Trinity and Trinity in unity, neither confusing the Persons, nor dividing the substance. For there is one person for the Father, another for the Son, and yet another for the Holy Spirit. But the divinity of the Father, Son, and Holy Spirit is one ... Thus, the Father is God, the Son is God, and the Holy Spirit is God; and yet there are not three Gods, but there is one God.[1]

To say that this doctrine is mysterious is an understatement. It looks to be outright contradictory. For, intuitively, "is God" either means "is identical to the one and only God" or else it means something like "is divine." Suppose it means "is identical to the one and only God." Then the doctrine says that three numerically distinct persons are each identical to one and the same being, which is a contradiction. Suppose, on the other hand, it

---

[1] Translation by Jeffrey Brower; quoted from Jeffrey Brower and Michael Rea, "Understanding the Trinity," *Logos* 8 (2005), pp. 145–57.

means "is divine." Then the doctrine seems to say both that there are three distinct divine beings (and so, presumably, three Gods), and also that there are not three Gods, which is a contradiction. Contradiction either way, then.

How can Christians resolve these apparent contradictions? And why would anyone think that the nature of God is tri-personal in the first place? These are the questions we shall address in the present section.

The threeness-oneness problem

The central philosophical difficulty with the doctrine of the Trinity – the fact that it appears contradictory, as explained above – is typically referred to by philosophers as the "logical problem of the Trinity" and by theologians as the "threeness-oneness problem." The problem is compounded by the fact that certain rather obvious ways of avoiding contradiction have been explicitly ruled out by the Athanasian Creed – which, again, is the one creed of Christendom that has had the most to say about the doctrine of the Trinity.

The chief errors that we must avoid are the two mentioned in the first line, and a third mentioned in the last line, of the passage quoted above. Those three errors are: confounding the persons (an error known as the heresy of *modalism*), dividing the substance (polytheism), and denying the divinity of one or more of the persons (a view known as *subordinationism*). To fall into modalism is, roughly, to say that the persons of the Trinity are related like Superman and Clark Kent – just different manifestations, or appearances, of one and the same individual. The error of polytheism is, of course, the view that there are three gods – a view that is outright inconsistent with traditional Judeo-Christian monotheism. Finally, subordinationists typically deny that the Son and the Holy Spirit are divine – removing the contradiction, but at the cost of explicitly rejecting the claim that the Son is God and the Holy Spirit is God. Given that the doctrine of the Trinity must be understood in a way that avoids all three of these errors, while also avoiding internal contradiction, it is easy to see why St. Augustine said of the doctrine, "In no other subject is error more dangerous, inquiry more difficult, or the discovery of truth more rewarding."[2]

---

[2] *De Trinitate* I.5, translated by Jeffrey Brower; quoted from Brower & Rea, *ibid*.

The challenge, then, is to explain how it is that there can be *three* divine persons but only *one* God. Sprinkled throughout the history of reflection on the doctrine of the Trinity are various analogies aimed at meeting this challenge. Unfortunately, however, most of these break down at precisely the point where they are supposed to be helpful, suggesting heretical views rather than illuminating the orthodox view.

Among the most popular contemporary analogies for the Trinity, two in particular stand out; and most of the others resemble one or the other of them. These two analogies are the "water" analogy and the "egg" analogy. According to the first, just as water takes three forms (liquid, vapor, and ice), so too God takes the form of Father, Son, and Holy Spirit. According to the second, just as an egg consists of three things (shell, yolk, and albumen), so God consists of three persons. The problem with these analogies is that instead of explaining the orthodox view, they actually lead one *away* from it. Liquid, vapor, and ice are three *states* or *manifestations* of a single substance, water; thus to say that the persons of the Trinity are like them is to fall into modalism. On the other hand, shell, yolk, and albumen are three parts of an egg; but neither shell, yolk, nor albumen is an egg. So this analogy suggests that neither Father, Son, nor Holy Spirit is God – they are merely parts of God. Other popular analogies that are problematic in similar ways are the "man" analogy (God is Father, Son, and Holy Spirit just as a man might be a father, son, and husband), C. S. Lewis's "cube" analogy (God is three persons just as a cube "is" six squares), and the so-called shamrock analogy (just as a shamrock is one shamrock, though three petals, so too God is one God, though three persons).

The phenomenon of light has also inspired a variety of analogies. Justin Martyr, one of the early church Fathers, suggested that Father, Son, and Holy Spirit might be related like the sun and the rays of light that emanate from it: distinct, but nevertheless inseparable. More recently, physics-minded theologians like John Polkinghorne have suggested that just as light is dual (both particulate and wave-like) in a way that nobody can understand, so too God is tri-personal in a way that nobody can understand. But the trouble here, of course, is that neither of these analogies tells us what we want to know. Justin's analogy seems to miss the point entirely since, even if we grant that the sun and its rays are somehow inseparable, there seems to be no sense in which they are "one." And Polkinghorne's analogy, in the end, just points us to another phenomenon we don't understand and says that the Trinity is like *that*: something we perhaps ought to believe but can't yet find intelligible.

Over the past four decades, however, various philosophers and theologians have developed some more promising analogies, or models, for understanding inter-Trinitarian relations. These models are not original; they all have historical roots. But the treatment they are now receiving builds on, and in some important ways extends, the treatment they have received from their historical proponents. The analogies we have in mind are the *social* analogy, a variety of *psychological* analogies, and the *statue–lump* analogy.

The social analogy

Throughout the gospels, the first two persons of the Trinity are referred to as "Father" and "Son." This suggests the analogy of a family, or, more generally, a society. Thus, the persons of the Trinity might be thought of as one in precisely the way that, say, Abraham, Sarah, and Isaac are one: just as these three human beings are one family, so too the persons are one God. But, since there is no contradiction in thinking of a family as three and one, this analogy removes the contradiction in saying that God is three and one. Those who attempt to understand the Trinity primarily in terms of this analogy are typically called *Social Trinitarians*. This approach has been (controversially) associated with *Greek* or *Eastern* Trinitarianism, a tradition of reflection that traces its roots to the three great Fathers of the Eastern Church – Basil of Caesarea, his brother Gregory of Nyssa, and their friend Gregory of Nazianzus.

Initially, the social analogy might look no better than the egg analogy. No member of a family is itself a family; thus, we seem to be faced again with the suggestion that no member of the Trinity is God. But there is an important difference. The members of a family are also full and complete instances of a single nature, humanity. So, unlike the parts of an egg, there are really *two* ways in which the members of a family "are one." They are *one family*; but they are also "of one nature" or "of one substance." By analogy, then, Father, Son, and Holy Spirit, are one in two senses: (a) they are members of the single Godhead, and (b) they each fully possess the divine nature. Thus, when we say there is exactly *one* God, we can take the word "God" to refer to the Godhead, that is, the society of which the persons are members. But when we say that the Father is God, the Son is God, and the

Holy Spirit is God, we can take the words "is God" to express the property or characteristic of being divine, which is had by each of the persons. So, since each of the persons is both divine and part of the Godhead, we can say truly that each is God, despite the fact that they are distinct.

To some, it might seem that the social analogy still pushes us in the direction of polytheism. We think that there is something to this criticism. But friends of the social analogy rightly respond that defending the criticism requires, among other things, a serious analysis of what exactly it means to be a polytheist – a task that, as it turns out, is far from simple.

Psychological analogies

Many theologians have looked to features of the human mind or "psyche" to find analogies to help illuminate the doctrine of the Trinity. Hence the label "psychological analogies." Historically, the use of such analogies is especially associated with *Latin* or *Western* Trinitarianism, a tradition that traces its roots to Augustine, the great father of the Latin-speaking West. Augustine himself suggested several important analogies. But since each depends for its plausibility on aspects of medieval theology no longer taken for granted (such as the doctrine of divine simplicity), we'll pass over them here and focus instead on two analogies in this tradition that have been developed by contemporary philosophers.

Thomas V. Morris has suggested that we can find an analogy for the Trinity in the psychological condition known as multiple-personality disorder: just as a single human being can have multiple personalities, so too a single God can exist in three persons (though, of course, in the case of God this is a cognitive virtue, not a defect). Others – Trenton Merricks, for example – have suggested that we can conceive of the persons on analogy with the separate spheres of consciousness that result from *commissurotomy*. Commissurotomy is a procedure, sometimes used to treat epilepsy, that involves cutting the bundle of nerves (the *corpus callosum*) by which the two hemispheres of the brain communicate. Those who have undergone this procedure typically function normally in daily life; but, under certain kinds of experimental conditions, they display behavior that suggests there are two distinct spheres of consciousness associated with the two hemispheres of their brains. Thus, according to this analogy, just as a single human can, in that way, have two distinct spheres of consciousness, so too a single divine being can exist in three persons, each of which is a distinct sphere of consciousness.

It might appear that the analogy with multiple-personality disorder is no better than the water analogy, and therefore similarly leads us into modalism. After all, the personalities of those who suffer from the disorder might seem to be nothing more than distinct states of a single (albeit divided) consciousness which, like the states of water, cannot be manifested at the same time. And the commissurotomy analogy might appear on closer inspection not to be interestingly different from the social analogy. For if there really can be several *distinct* centers of consciousness associated with a single being, then the natural thing to say is that the "single being" in question is either an additional sphere of consciousness composed of the others, or else a "society" whose members are the distinct spheres of consciousness. But it is far from clear that these criticisms are decisive. And, at least on the surface, these two analogies seem to have a great deal of heuristic value; for both seem to present real-life cases in which a single rational being is nonetheless "divided" into multiple personalities or spheres of consciousness.

The statue–lump analogy

The third and final solution to the problem of the Trinity that we want to explore invokes what might be called the "relative-sameness" assumption. This is the assumption that things can be the same *relative to* one kind of thing, but distinct *relative to* another. More formally:

(RELATIVE SAMENESS)   It is possible that there are x, y, F, and G such that x is an F, y is an F, x is a G, y is a G, x is the same F as y, but x is not the same G as y.

If this assumption is true, then it is open to us to say that the Father, Son, and Holy Spirit are the *same God* but *distinct persons*. Notice, however, that this is all we need to make sense of the Trinity. If the Father, Son, and Holy Spirit are the same God (and there are no other Gods), then there will be exactly one God; but if they are also distinct persons (and there are only three of them), then there will be three persons.

The main challenge for this solution is to show that the relative-sameness assumption is coherent. This challenge has been undertaken by a number of prominent contemporary philosophers, including Peter Geach and Peter van Inwagen. Despite the efforts of these philosophers, however, the relative-sameness assumption has remained rather unpopular. The reason appears to be that its defenders have not provided any clear account of what it would mean for things to be the same relative to one kind, but distinct relative to another. Recently, however, it has been suggested that reflection on statues and the lumps of matter that constitute them can help us to see how two things can be the *same material object* but otherwise *different entities*. If this is right, then, by analogy, such reflection can also help us to see how Father, Son, and Holy Spirit can be the same God but three different persons.

Consider Rodin's famous bronze statue *The Thinker*. It is a single material object; but it can be truly described both as a statue (which is one kind of thing), and as a lump of bronze (which is another kind of thing). A little reflection, moreover, reveals that the statue is distinct from the lump of bronze. For example, if the statue were melted down, we would no longer have both a lump and a statue: the lump would remain (albeit in a different shape) but Rodin's *Thinker* would no longer exist. This shows that the lump is something distinct from the statue, since one thing can exist apart from another *only* if they're distinct. (Notice that the statue can't exist apart from itself.)

It might seem strange to think that a statue is distinct from the lump that constitutes it. Wouldn't that imply that there are two material objects in the same place at the same time? Surely we don't want to say that! But then what exactly are we to say about this case? Notice that this isn't just a matter of one thing *appearing* in two different ways, or being *labeled* as both a statue and a lump. Earlier we noted that Superman and Clark Kent can appear differently (Clark Kent wears glasses, for example); but the names "Superman" and "Clark Kent" are really just different labels for the same man. But our statue analogy isn't like this. Superman can't exist apart from Clark Kent. Where the one goes, the other goes too (at least in disguise). But the lump of bronze in our example apparently *can* exist apart from *The Thinker*. As we have seen, when melted, the lump survives while *The Thinker* does not. If that's right, then, unlike Superman and Clark Kent, the statue and lump of bronze really are distinct things.

Philosophers have suggested various ways of making sense of this phenomenon. One way of doing so is to say that the statue and the lump are *the same material object* even though they are distinct relative to some other kind. (In ordinary English, we don't have a suitable name for the kind of thing relative to which the statue and the lump are distinct; but we can perhaps borrow some terminology from Aristotle and say that the statue and the lump are distinct *form-matter compounds*.) Now, it is hard to accept the idea that two distinct things can be the same material object without some detailed explanation of what it would mean for this to occur. But suppose we add that *all it means* for one thing and another to be "the same material object" is just for them to share all of their matter in common. Such a claim seems plausible; and if it is right, then our problem is solved. The lump of bronze in our example is clearly distinct from *The Thinker*, since it can exist without *The Thinker*; but it also clearly shares all the same matter in common with *The Thinker*, and hence on this view is the same material object.

By analogy, then, suppose we say that all it means for one person and another to be the same God is for them to do something analogous to sharing all of their matter in common (say, sharing the same divine nature). On this view, the Father, Son, and Holy Spirit are the same God but different persons in just the way a statue and its constitutive lump are the same material object but different form-matter compounds. Of course, God is not material; so this can *only* be an analogy. But still, it helps to provide an illuminating account of inter-Trinitarian relations, which is all that we are presently asking for.

Arguments for belief in the Trinity

Regardless of whether one is inclined actually to endorse any of the analogies offered in the previous section, their availability and coherence cast serious doubt on the claim that the doctrine of the Trinity ought to be rejected as flatly contradictory. But why would someone *accept* it? What is there to recommend it?

For those already committed to the divine inspiration of the whole Christian Bible, there is a persuasive biblical argument to be made. The Bible forbids us to worship any being other than God (e.g. Exodus 20:3–5; Isaiah 42:8). So Jesus is worthy of our worship only if he is God. But the Bible also makes it clear that the Father deserves our worship (e.g. Matthew 5:9–13 and 7:21; John 2:16), and that Jesus is not the Father (e.g. Matthew 24:36; Luke 22:42; John 1:14, 18). So, if we are to go on worshipping both Jesus and the Father, we *have* to say that Jesus is God *and* that the Father is

God. But, again, we cannot say that Jesus *is* the Father, nor can we say that they are *two Gods* (Deuteronomy 6:4). Likewise in the case of the Holy Spirit (e.g. John 14:26; Acts 5: 3–4; Romans 8:26–27). But what if one rejects the biblical case? Is there any purely philosophical argument for thinking that the very nature of God must be Trinitarian rather than Unitarian?

Surprisingly, there is. Richard Swinburne has offered the following *a priori* argument for the doctrine of the Trinity. Start with the premise – which most theists accept – that God is a perfectly loving being and, indeed, cannot exist without being perfectly loving. (In other words, being perfectly loving is essential to God.) Now consider the following apparently obvious truths: first, God was free not to create anything. So there might have been no creatures for God to love. But, second, perfect love requires a beloved. So if God had not created anything, there still would have been *someone* for him to love – someone who would not have been a *creature*. But who could that someone have been, except another divine person? Moreover, Swinburne also thinks it obvious that truly perfect love requires not only one beloved, but also a third object of love – an additional person whom lover and beloved can cooperate together in loving. He argues, for example, that though the love between husband and wife is a beautiful thing, there is something more perfect about marital love that issues in the production of and love for children, or in a cooperative effort to bestow love upon (say) the poor or downtrodden. In other words, love between two people that is *both* inwardly and outwardly focused is better than love that is just inwardly focused. Thus, Swinburne concludes, there must be a third uncreated person. But there is no reason to suppose that there must be more than three. So, respecting the principle that one ought not to believe in more entities than one has reason to believe in, we ought to believe that there are exactly three divine (uncreated) persons. Admittedly, this conclusion is consistent with polytheism as well as Trinitarianism; but Swinburne has additional arguments to rule out polytheism – arguments that we won't explore here.

Should we believe Swinburne's argument? Those who share his intuitions about the requirements for perfect love will have a hard time resisting it. They might insist that, though God *is* perfectly loving, he might not have been – and would not have been in just those worlds in which he created nothing. But being capable of being less loving than one in fact is seems itself to be an imperfection. So those of us who are attracted to the method of perfect-person theology will resist this line of response.

But those who do not share Swinburne's intuitions about the requirements for perfect love will likely be left cold by this argument. Moreover, one might be suspicious in general about drawing conclusions about the very nature of God from intuitions about love. It does not seem to be a straightforward conceptual truth about love (or about goodness) that a love that is both inwardly and outwardly focused is somehow better than a merely inwardly focused love. So one who rejected that view would not be manifesting a failure to grasp the concept of love (in the way that one who rejected the claim that there can be no married bachelors *would* manifest a failure to grasp the concept of bachelorhood).

Incarnation

In the last section, we noted that one of the main forces driving Christians in the direction of a Trinitarian rather than a Unitarian view of God is the following conjunction of views: (a) only God is worthy of worship; (b) Jesus of Nazareth is distinct from the Heavenly Father whom we rightly worship; and (c) Jesus of Nazareth is himself worthy of worship. And, of course, the reason why Christians think that Jesus is worthy of worship is just that they believe him to be God incarnate. But what could possibly lead someone *rationally* to think that a thirty-something-year-old Palestinian man, born to a local carpenter and raised in a town of little import, was none other than the Lord of the Cosmos in human flesh? And what could it possibly even *mean* to say that someone is God incarnate? These are the questions that we shall explore in the present section.

Believing in the Incarnation

Why should anyone believe – as generations of Christians throughout history *have* believed – that Jesus of Nazareth was divine? Various reasons for belief have been cited throughout the history of Christian thought; but in contemporary Christian apologetics, two arguments come to the fore. The first is the so-called Lord–Liar–Lunatic argument, first formulated in the seventeenth century by Blaise Pascal as an argument for the conclusion that the testimony of the Evangelists (Matthew, Mark, Luke, and John) is reliable, and more recently popularized in the 1950s by C. S. Lewis. The second is an appeal to the historical evidence in support of the greatest alleged miracle of Jesus' life – his resurrection. In what follows, we shall focus on the first argument. Those interested in the historical argument can look to the sources in the Further Reading list at the end of this chapter.

The Lord–Liar–Lunatic argument starts with the premise that Jesus claimed, at least implicitly, to be divine.[3] It then notes that this claim must be either true or false and, if it is false, it must be a claim that Jesus either knew to be false or didn't know to be false. If Jesus knowingly falsely claimed to be divine, then he was (by definition) a liar. On the other hand, if he unwittingly falsely claimed to be divine, then he was crazy. Remarkably few people, however, want to say that Jesus was either a liar or a lunatic – and this not just because doing so would be politically incorrect. The influence of Jesus' teachings on Western intellectual history has been enormous. Literally hundreds of millions of people have found peace, sanity, and virtue in orienting their lives around his teachings. Indeed, even those who do not worship him as God incarnate nevertheless often regard him as a sage or a saint. All of these facts together make it seem very likely that Jesus was neither so wicked and egomaniacal as to try deliberately to deceive others into thinking that he was divine, nor so mentally unbalanced as to be fundamentally confused about his own origin, powers, and identity. If Jesus was not a liar or a lunatic, though – so the argument goes – then there is only one alternative left: his claim to divinity was true.

The argument has at least a certain surface plausibility. And, obviously enough, it will be most persuasive to those who are already convinced that Jesus claimed to be divine and that it's implausible to view him as either a liar or a lunatic. On the other hand, it will have little purchase on those who either reject these two claims or are simply not yet persuaded that they are true; for *establishing* that Jesus was neither a liar nor a lunatic is a very tall order indeed. Nevertheless, even if we grant these two crucial premises, there are still other ways of resisting the argument.

The main point of resistance will be the claim that if Jesus unwittingly falsely claimed to be divine, then he was a lunatic. As Daniel Howard-Snyder has recently argued, one apparently overlooked possibility is that Jesus might have been sincerely mistaken. But, we might ask, how could a sane

---

[3] There is controversy over whether the New Testament documents *really* portray Jesus as explicitly claiming to be divine. Those interested in this controversy should see, for starters, the works by Wright and Davis *et al.* in the Further Reading list at the end of the chapter, as well as the references therein.

person sincerely mistake himself for *God*? Here three suggestions are worth pursuing.

First, one might note that plenty of people throughout history have apparently sincerely believed themselves to be divine without being insane. Some of the Roman emperors, for example, were sane; and belief in the divinity of the emperor was widespread throughout the empire, and apparently sincerely and sanely held by some of the emperors themselves. Likewise, rulers in ancient Egypt, in China, and elsewhere have believed themselves to be god or the sons of gods without being obviously crazy. (This is not necessarily to say that these people were *reasonable* in believing themselves to be divine. There is some distance between unreasonability and insanity; and the point here is just that they were not clearly insane.) Why then couldn't Jesus' case have been similar? Why couldn't he have been mistaken in the same way in which we think, say, Julius Caesar or Akhenaton were mistaken?

In response, it is important to note that the concepts of divinity in play in ancient Rome, Egypt, and elsewhere were very different from the Jewish monotheistic conception of deity that Jesus applied to himself. Roman and Egyptian gods, for example, were little more than superhuman beings. They were powerful but not omnipotent; knowledgeable but far from omniscient; sometimes but not nearly always good; and so on. It is not hard to see, therefore, how a sane person raised in a culture that viewed rulers as deities of this sort might come to believe himself to be divine without being refuted outright at every moment of introspection. By way of contrast, Jesus' claim to divinity was nothing short of a claim to being the omnipotent, omniscient, omnibenevolent creator of all things. It is hard to see how an ordinary person could think *that* of himself without insanity. For if Jesus weren't divine, he, like the rest of us, would be confronted with his own limitations at every turn. There would be questions whose answers he did not know, rocks he could not lift, vices he would recognize but be unable to eradicate from his life, and so on. Moreover, he would have no memory of creating the cosmos – quite a lacuna in a person who purportedly knows all things and *did* create the cosmos.

Second, one might argue – as Daniel Howard-Snyder has – that a mere mortal might sanely think that he is God incarnate if he has good reason to think that (a) he has been called by God to do and be the things that the Jewish Messiah was supposed to do and be, (b) that the Messiah would have been God incarnate, and (c) that what it would be like to be God incarnate would (or might) be very much like being an ordinary human being. It seems not terribly implausible to think that a sane person *could* have good reason to endorse (a) to (c). After all, prophets in various religious traditions seem to have sanely taken themselves to have divine callings; there were strands of thought about the Jewish Messiah that could well have suggested to a reasonable first-century Jew that the Messiah might be God incarnate; and many contemporary theologians endorse something like (c) on the basis of arguments that we'll examine in the next section. And so, one might think, if one *did* have good reason to endorse (a) to (c), then one would have good, though clearly fallible, reason to believe that one was God incarnate. But if you have good reason to believe a proposition, it could hardly be considered *insane* for you to believe that proposition (unless your reasons themselves were a product of insanity; but there is no reason to think that would have to be the case here).

The trouble, however, is that this line of argument ignores the fact that sane people will have and respond to *defeaters* for the belief that they are God incarnate. (To have a defeater for a belief is to have other beliefs that some-how undermine whatever justification you might otherwise have for the first belief.) Suppose Jesus was a mere mortal; and suppose he had good reason to endorse (a) to (c). Then he would have some reason to think that he is God incarnate. Nevertheless, even if being God incarnate would be very much *like* being an ordinary human being, the Jewish conception of God rules out the possibility that it could be *exactly* like being an ordinary human being. In particular, being subject to vice and sinful desire is quite plausibly both a universal characteristic in (mere) human beings and one wholly incompati-ble with being divine. A sane person who understood the concept of God would be aware of this fact, and aware of at least some of his own vices and sinful desires; and so he would have a defeater for any evidence supporting the claim that he was divine. The proponent of this line of resistance, then, would have to say that if Jesus believed that he was divine on the basis of his endorsement of (a) to (c), then one of the following claims was true: (i) he had no vices or sinful desires; (ii) he had them, but was wholly unaware of them; or (iii) he didn't understand that being God was incompatible with being vicious or sinful. It is hard to imagine someone who doubts the divinity of Jesus believing that (i) is true of him; and it is hard even to take seriously the idea that (ii) might be true of someone. (And if it were true of

Jesus, wouldn't that be some evidence of a different kind of insanity – an insanely grandiose self-image?) And if (iii) were true of Jesus, then it is doubtful that he was really succeeding in applying the Jewish conception of deity to himself. In other words, if (iii) were true of him, it is doubtful that he *really* thought of himself as the incarnate God of Abraham, Isaac, and Jacob.

These first two suggestions, then, seem untenable. But there is a third to contend with, also due to Howard-Snyder. Suppose Jesus actually *was* God incarnate, and that he truthfully and sanely believed that he was. Surely, then, he had grounds for this belief – some sort of experience or memory or argument, or some combination thereof. But if he had grounds for the belief, those grounds could, in principle, be duplicated in a mere man. (Just imagine the man having exactly the same sort of internal experience or apparent memory or argument available.) *How* exactly these grounds might be duplicated is immaterial; the relevant fact is just that they could be. And if they were, then a mere man who believed himself to be divine on the basis of those grounds would still be sane. For, again, by stipulation *Jesus* believed himself to be divine on the basis of those grounds, and *he* was sane. Thus, it is at least possible for a mere man to believe sanely but mistakenly that he is divine.

There is something persuasive about this line of reasoning, but it too has a weakness. It was presumably on the basis of certain kinds of experiences and bits of evidence that Napoleon (sanely) believed that he was a short man who ruled France in the eighteenth century. If you now were to find yourself with precisely the same grounds for believing that *you* are a short man who is ruling France in the eighteenth century, you would be insane. This not because it is insane to hold the relevant belief on the basis of those grounds. Rather, it is because *having those grounds*, given who, what, and where you are, is a mark of insanity. (Compare: someone who believes that she ought always to wear a football helmet because she also believes that her head is made of glass has reasoned to a sensible conclusion from an insane belief.) Perhaps it is *possible* for you to have those grounds without being insane – if, for example, you were the victim of some elaborate *Matrix*-style hoax. But we would need to hear a lot more about how you came to be in possession of those grounds before granting that they were not the product of insanity. And likewise, it seems, in the case of someone who finds him- or herself with the same grounds that a divine Jesus would have had for sanely believing himself to be divine. We are not entitled simply to assume that being in possession of such grounds is consistent with sanity; for upon initial consideration it seems not to be.

The foregoing objections to the Lord–Liar–Lunatic argument seem, then, to be unsound. This is not to say that the argument is bulletproof. But it does seem to us, at any rate, to be stronger than some contemporary critics have given it credit for being.

The doctrine of the Incarnation and its problems

The orthodox Christian understanding of the doctrine of the Trinity has been laid out most fully in the Chalcedonian Creed (451). The Creed, in its entirety, reads as follows:

> Following, then, the holy fathers, we unite in teaching all men to confess the one and only Son, our Lord Jesus Christ. This selfsame one is perfect both in deity and in humanness; this selfsame one is also actually God and actually man, with a rational soul and a body. He is of the same reality as God as far as his deity is concerned and of the same reality as we ourselves as far as his humanness is concerned; thus like us in all respects, sin only excepted. Before time began he was begotten of the Father, in respect of his deity, and now in these "last days," for us and on behalf of our salvation, this selfsame one was born of Mary the virgin, who is God-bearer in respect of his humanness.
>
> [We also teach] that we apprehend this one and only Christ-Son, Lord, only-begotten, in two natures; [and we do] this without confusing the two natures, without transmuting one nature into the other, without dividing them into two separate categories, without contrasting them according to area or function. The distinctiveness of each nature is not nullified by the union. Instead, the "properties" of each nature are conserved and both natures concur in one "person" and in one reality. They are not divided or cut into two persons, but are together the one and only and only-begotten Word of God, the Lord Jesus Christ. Thus have the prophets of old testified; thus the Lord Jesus Christ himself taught us; thus the Symbol of Fathers has handed down to us.[4]

---

[4] Translation by Robert Outler, in John Leith (ed.), *Creeds of the Churches*, 3rd edn. (Atlanta, GA: John Knox Press, 1982), pp. 34–5; bracketed Greek insertions omitted.

So, in short, according to the doctrine of the Incarnation, Jesus of Nazareth was fully divine and fully human; he has *two* natures (rather than, say, a single divine, single human, or single "God-man" nature); he has a rational (human) soul and body; and he is not to be understood as a sort of composite of two separate persons.

As with the doctrine of the Trinity, there are various errors that must be avoided if one wants to have a fully orthodox understanding of the Incarnation. Below is a bulleted list of the major heresies associated with the doctrine of the Incarnation, together with their distinctive claims:

- Arianism: Jesus was not divine, but was rather the highest of the created beings.
- Ebionism: Jesus was a mere man (not even the highest among created beings).
- Docetism: Jesus was not really human at all, just divine. His apparent humanity and suffering were an illusion.
- Nestorianism: There were two separate persons in the incarnate Christ, one divine and the other human.
- Monophysitism: Jesus had just one nature, a divine nature.
- Appolinarianism: Jesus lacked a human soul.
- Monothelitism: Jesus had just one will, not two.

As should be clear, all but the last of these claims is condemned by the Creed that arose out of the Council at Chalcedon. Monothelitism was condemned at the Second Council of Constantinople in 680 CE. In proscribing each of these different views, the Creed manages to give us a fair bit of insight into what was supposed to have been involved in God's becoming incarnate. A moment's reflection, however, reveals that a great many questions still remain. Indeed, a bit of reflection makes it clear that there is at least superficial cause for concern that the Chalcedonian understanding of the Incarnation is flatly incoherent.

Consider a time prior to the birth of Jesus of Nazareth. At this time, the second person of the Trinity – the Word (as he is called in the Gospel of John), the divine *logos* – existed as a non-incarnate person. On the Chalcedonian understanding, the Word's becoming incarnate involved his taking on a full human nature – a nature which included both a body and a rational soul. So in the incarnate Christ, we have one divine person, the

Word, as well as a human body and a human soul. Moreover, the divine person has one will – the divine will; but there is a second, human will associated with Christ's human nature. But now don't we have *two* persons in the incarnate Christ – the Word, and the human body-soul composite in whom the Word is incarnate? It seems that we ought to say yes. For Jesus of Nazareth apparently had *on his own* – i.e. apart from whatever was contributed by the Word – everything that it takes to be a full-blown human person. In particular, he had a body, a soul, and a will of his own. In fact, the principle "one will per person, and one person per will" seems highly intuitive. So if there are two *wills* in the incarnate Christ, as orthodoxy requires, then it seems that there *must be* two persons in the incarnate Christ. But saying this contradicts the Creed; for the Creed explicitly condemns the view that there are two persons in the incarnate Christ.

The appearance of contradiction here is not the only problem with the doctrine of the Incarnation, however. There is at least one other that demands attention. Nothing counts as fully divine, one might think, unless it has all of the attributes that are definitive of deity – among them, omniscience, omnipotence, and perfect goodness. Yet, the biblical account of the life of Jesus might seem to indicate that he lacked at least one or more of these characteristics.

For example, the Gospel of Luke (2:52) reports that Jesus grew in wisdom. But nothing can grow in wisdom without at some time lacking complete wisdom. An omniscient being cannot lack complete wisdom, however; for an omniscient being would always know what the wisest course of action would be in any circumstance. (That is, he would know every truth of the form "The wisest course of action in this circumstance ... is to behave as follows ... ") Thus, if Jesus grew in wisdom he was not omniscient. Likewise, the Gospel of Matthew has Jesus reporting lack of knowledge of the day and the hour of his own second coming. You might think that he lacks this knowledge just because the day and the hour are not yet decided – the facts about when Jesus will return are somehow indeterminate. But this response is ruled out by Jesus' claim in the same passage that "only the Father knows" when the second coming will occur (which, of course, implies that there *is* a determinate fact of the matter). So again, there is reason to doubt that Jesus is omniscient.

Moreover, the gospels, as well as the Epistle to the Hebrews, report that Jesus was tempted to sin. But one cannot be tempted to do that which one has no desire to do. Thus, for example, it would be literally impossible (apart from outright deception) to tempt a severely claustrophobic person to allow herself to be buried alive. Whatever cajoling you might do to try to persuade the person to submit to such a thing, it couldn't really be called *temptation*. And, though it is not sin simply to *desire* sinful behaviors, it does seem to be a moral defect. A person who desires to torture small children but refrains is surely better than a person who gives in to the desire. But it would be better still not even to have the desire in the first place; and if we found out that one of our friends had such a desire, we would be appalled. Plausibly, then, a morally perfect being cannot desire to sin. But if such a being cannot desire to sin, then such a being cannot be tempted to sin. But Jesus was tempted to sin. Thus, it would appear that he lacked moral perfection.

In light of these considerations, there seems at least initially to be good reason for thinking that the Bible says things that imply that Jesus lacked some important divine attributes. But then it is puzzling, to say the least, how he could have been fully divine.

So believers in the Incarnation have at least two important objections to address. First, there is the objection that the orthodox view seems to be contradictory. Second, there is the objection that the Bible itself seems to provide reason for doubting one of the doctrine's central claims: the claim that Jesus was divine. In answering these objections, it will be helpful to begin by distinguishing two different views about what is involved in "taking on a human nature." Once this is done, we will then be in a better position to see how the two objections can be answered.

It is clear from the Chalcedonian Creed that, from the point of view of the Creed's framers, having a human nature amounts at least to having a human body and a rational (human) soul. But this by itself doesn't answer the question of what exactly is involved in taking on a human nature. There are at least two different ways of answering that question, depending on what you think it means to have a human soul. Suppose you think that a person has a human soul just in case that person *is* a soul (of any sort) that inhabits a human body. On this view, then, a natural story to tell about the Incarnation is one according to which the Word's becoming incarnate was just a matter of the Word's coming to inhabit – and thus *be* the soul of – a human body. For the sake of terminological housekeeping, let us refer to this view as a Two-Part Christology (where the two parts of the Incarnate Christ are just the Word and the human body of Jesus of Nazareth).

The Two-Part Christology goes a long way toward solving our first problem. For, on the Two-Part view, there is no pressure at all to suppose that there are two persons in the incarnate Christ. The reason is that, on the Two-Part view, there is just one soul, not two, associated with the body of Jesus of Nazareth. Precisely this advantage, however, makes it hard to avoid monothelitism – the view that Jesus had only one will. For, again, it is plausible to think that there is one will per soul and one soul per will; so if there is not a human soul in addition to the Word in the Incarnate Christ, then it is hard to see how Jesus could have a human will in addition to his divine will. Moreover, many will resist the Two-Part view simply on the grounds that a "soul" with divine powers (as would be the soul of Jesus on the Two-Part view) can't be a human soul, since it doesn't have the right sorts of limitations.

For these and other reasons, then, many have been attracted to a Three-Part Christology. According to the Three-Part view, the person of Christ consists in the human body and soul of Jesus of Nazareth, plus the Word. It is this view that most naturally gives rise to concerns about Nestorianism (the view that there were two separate persons present in the Incarnate Christ); but proponents try to mitigate those concerns by insisting that the body-soul composite that is Christ's human nature does not, in the context of the Incarnation, have what it takes to be a person in its own right. To be sure, they say, a body-soul composite *typically* has what it takes to be a person. But the difference between Jesus' body-soul composite and a typical body-soul composite is just that the former has been *assumed* by the Word. What exactly "assumption" amounts to in this context is hard to say; and opponents of the Three-Part view typically complain that the reason it is hard to say what assumption amounts to is just that the term, as it is used here, is meaningless. But advocates of the Three-Part view respond (rightly in our estimation) that whatever assumption is, it is something that happens to Christ's human nature, and when it happens to a body-soul composite, that body-soul composite no longer constitutes a person in its own right. So long as this minimal characterization is coherent, it doesn't really matter what assumption is *exactly*, for this minimal bit of information is all that will be needed to show that there is no incoherence in endorsing the Three-Part view while rejecting Nestorianism. And once this has been shown, the first of our two problems is solved.

But what of the second problem? How can we make sense of the idea that Jesus was fully divine in light of the fact that the Bible itself portrays him, apparently, as lacking some of the divine attributes? Of course, one way to solve the problem (already mentioned above) is just to set aside the New Testament testimony as unreliable at least in those places where Jesus is portrayed as lacking divine attributes. We shall ignore this option – not because objectors to the reliability of the New Testament are not to be taken seriously, but just because "saving" Christian doctrine by simply throwing out inconvenient data (and data that most Christians will, in fact, want to respect) seems to provide a rather shallow victory at best. By ignoring this option, we thereby set aside views according to which the New Testament authors misspoke themselves about what Jesus did or did not know, or about his temptations, or whatever. But not only this. We also set aside views according to which Jesus *pretended* to be suffering from certain temptations and to be ignorant of certain facts. For our purposes, then, an acceptable solution to the second problem will take one of two forms: it will explain how a being can count as fully divine despite lacking divine attributes; or it will explain how the New Testament witness, despite appearances, is in fact consistent with the claim that Jesus possessed all of the divine attributes.

The place to start in trying to answer the second objection is with the doctrine of *kenosis*. The term *kenosis* comes from the Greek verb *hekenosen* (ἐκένωσεν) which is translated as "emptied" in the following passage from St. Paul's epistle to the Philippians:

> Have this attitude in yourselves which was also in Christ Jesus, who, although He existed in the form of God, did not regard equality with God a thing to be grasped, but emptied Himself, taking the form of a bond-servant, [and] being made in the likeness of men.[5]

Kenotic theories of the incarnation say that the Word either *abandoned* some of the traditional attributes of divinity when he became incarnate or at least *simulated* their abandonment by imposing certain restraints upon himself.

Saying that the Word abandoned some of the traditional attributes of divinity upon becoming incarnate just raises, rather than answers, the question we are trying to answer – namely, how can he be divine if he lacks some of the traditional attributes of divinity. The answer given by kenoticists, though, is fairly simple: not all of the traditional attributes of

---

[5] Philippians 2:5–7, in *The New American Standard Bible*, Copyright 1995 by the Lockman Foundation.

divinity are *necessary* for divinity. Compare: human beings are sinful. Does the fact that Jesus was (according to Christian doctrine) not sinful count against his humanity? Clearly not; for being sinful isn't a *necessary* condition for being human. Something can count as human without being sinful; it's just that, apart from Jesus (and, according to Roman Catholics, Mary) being sinful is a *universal* (though non-essential) human trait. Likewise, then, it is possible to admit that Jesus was not omniscient or omnipotent while at the same time insisting that he was divine. One need only say that those attributes are not essential to divinity.

Two problems linger, however. First, there is still the concern about perfect goodness. But perhaps that problem can be mitigated in another way – say, by denying that temptation must appeal to desire (rather than some other cognitive state), or by saying that the sense in which Jesus was tempted by the devil is only the rather benign sense in which a vacuum-cleaner salesman might be said to be "tempting" you to purchase his wares with various enticing offers even though you haven't the slightest inclination really to purchase them.

Second, there is the concern that if attributes like omniscience aren't necessary for divinity, then it is hard to know what is. Some have suggested that just the property of *being divine* is what's necessary for being divine. But the trouble is that precisely what we are looking for now is a characterization of what is involved in possessing that property. In other words, what we want to know is what other properties a being must have in order to qualify as a possessor of the property of being divine. A better response, then, would be to cite traditional divine attributes (like aseity or necessary existence) as the properties necessary for or constitutive of divinity. Either that, or simply deny that *any* properties are necessary for divinity. Indeed, the latter move is plausible on independent grounds. It is widely held in the philosophy of biology, for example, that there are no properties possession of which are jointly necessary and sufficient for membership in, say, the kind *humanity*. Moreover, it is very hard to find any interesting properties – apart form properties like "having mass" or "being an organism" – that are even merely necessary for being human. That is, it seems that for any (interesting) property you might think of as partly definitive of humanity, there are or could be humans who lack that property. Thus, many philosophers think that membership in the kind is determined simply by family resemblance to paradigm examples of the kind. Something counts as human, in other words, if, and only if, it shares enough of the properties that are *typical* of humanity. If we were to say the same thing about divinity, there would be no in-principle objection to the idea that Jesus counts as divine despite lacking omniscience or other properties like, perhaps, omnipotence, omnipresence, or even perfect goodness. One might just say that he is knowledgeable, powerful, and good *enough* that, given his other attributes, he bears the right sort of family resemblance to the other members of the Godhead to count as divine.

Still, some Christians will balk at the mere suggestion that Jesus lacked omniscience or other divine attributes. For these believers, option (a) above – explaining how Jesus might count as divine while lacking certain divine attributes – is a non-starter. Option (b) will be the only choice, then; and saying that Jesus merely simulated the abandonment of divine attributes (rather than actually abandoning them) will help to make that option palatable.

The trouble with saying that Jesus merely simulated the abandonment of divine attributes is that it is hard to see how one could simulate (say) loss of knowledge without outright pretense. How, for example, would you simulate not knowing the answer to "What is the sum of two and two?" You could take drugs that would make you forget; but that wouldn't be *simulation*; that would bring about a temporary (or permanent) genuine loss of knowledge. You could *act* like you don't know. For example, you could say "I don't know," shrug your shoulders, look pensive and bewildered, and so on whenever someone asked you the question. But here too you wouldn't be *simulating*; you'd be pretending. To simulate the loss of knowledge you would have to make it seem to yourself as if you didn't know, despite the fact that you really did know. But how exactly would this go?

We can start to get a clue if we couple our understanding of the psychological phenomenon of *denial* or *self-deception* with an adapted version of a view that is commonly taken to be a rival to kenotic Christologies – Thomas Morris's "Two Minds" view of the Incarnation. When someone enters denial or is self-deceived – say, about an addictive problem or about a great trauma or loss – what seems to happen is that that person loses conscious awareness of a fact or range of facts that they know all too well. The addict who comes out of denial is unlikely to say "I never knew I was an addict." Rather, she will say something like "I knew it all along, but just couldn't see it." Plausibly, this is a case where someone seems to herself not to know something that in fact she does know. Denial, one might think, *simulates* a loss or absence of a certain kind of knowledge. You don't actually, genuinely forget or fail to recognize that you are an addict or that you were a victim of the trauma or loss about which you are in denial. Rather, you just make it *seem* to yourself as if you are unaware of these things.

Of course, the suggestion here isn't that Jesus is in denial about being omniscient or omnipotent or perfectly good. But consider what has just been said about denial in light of the following passage describing the Two Minds view of the Incarnation:

> [I]n the case of God Incarnate, we must recognize something like two distinct ranges of consciousness. There is first what we can call the eternal mind of God the Son with its distinctively divine consciousness, whatever that might be like, encompassing the full scope of omniscience. And in addition there is a distinctly earthly consciousness that came into existence and grew and developed as the boy Jesus grew and developed. It drew its visual imagery from what the eyes of Jesus saw, and its concepts from the language he learned. The earthly range of consciousness, and self-consciousness, was thoroughly human, Jewish, and first-century Palestinian in nature. We can view the two ranges of consciousness (and, analogously, the two noetic structures encompassing them) as follows: The divine mind of God the Son contained, but was not contained by, his earthly mind, or range of consciousness. That is to say, there was what can be called an asymmetric accessing relation between the two minds. Think, for example, of two computer programs or informational systems, one containing but not contained by the other. The divine mind had full and direct access to the earthly human experience resulting from the Incarnation, but the earthly consciousness did not have such a full and direct access to the content of the overarching omniscience proper to the Logos, but only such access, on occasion, as the divine mind allowed it to have. There thus was a metaphysical and personal depth to the man Jesus lacking in the case of every individual who is merely human.[6]

As it is presented in the passage just quoted, the Two Minds view really does *appear* to be a rival to kenotic theories of the incarnation. There is no abandonment or simulation of abandonment of attributes like omniscience; for each of Christ's two minds – the divine mind and the human mind – are fully conscious. The way in which the Two Minds view (thus construed) proposes to answer our second problem, then, is just to say that,

[6] *Our Idea of God* (Notre Dame, IN: University of Notre Dame Press, 1991), p. 169.

although it *appeared* that the Incarnate Christ lacked certain kinds of knowledge and power and perhaps suffered from certain kinds of moral defect, the fact is that it was really only *part* of the Incarnate Christ – the human mind – that suffered from these limitations.

The problem, however, is that, if we adopt this view, Nestorianism again rears its ugly head. Why aren't the two minds two persons? We might insist that the human mind has been assumed by the divine mind. But what could that possibly mean if, as would seem to be the case, it is the *human* mind with all of its limitations that (at least sometimes) answers questions that are addressed to Jesus, determines what miracles he can and cannot perform, and renders him subject to temptation? The human mind is, on this view, apparently quite active in its own right – as is the divine mind, which governs the degree of access that the human mind has to the divine mind's contents. It is hard, then, to see how heresy can be avoided.

But the Two Minds view *can* be adapted in such a way as to dodge these and other problems. Suppose we think that the human mind and the divine mind are related in a way similar to the way in which a person's conscious mind is said to relate to her "subconscious" mind. (Never mind questions about whether there is *really* any scientifically respectable distinction to be drawn between the conscious and subconscious mind.) One's first person perspective – her self-awareness and conscious life – are associated with the conscious mind; but (at least in the popular talk about such things) there is quite a lot of further mental content – beliefs, desires, goals, and even acts of will – that allegedly reside in and well up from the subconscious. And it is not uncommon to hear people talk about denial as nothing other than an act of pushing a certain kind of conscious awareness down to the level of the subconscious.

If we suppose that this is how the two minds of Christ are related, the main problems that we have been discussing thus far disappear. We have a clear model for how it might seem to Jesus of Nazareth that he is not omniscient, omnipotent, or even perfectly good when in fact he is. The "subconscious" divine mind can provide or deny access to all of the knowledge, power, and moral fortitude characteristic of divinity; but it can also leave the conscious human mind ignorant of certain facts, unable to tap into certain sources of power, and subject at least to the desire to succumb to certain kinds of temptation. We can also see how to avoid Nestorianism. Just as your conscious and subconscious minds (if there are such things) do not count as two separate persons, neither do the conscious human mind and subconscious divine mind of Christ count as two separate persons. And, finally, we can see how sensibly to avoid monothelitism: just as your subconscious mind might be said to have a "will of its own," so too there might well be a separate will (not consciously available to the conscious human mind of Christ) associated with the divine mind of Christ.

Conclusion

In this chapter, we have considered a variety of problems connected with the distinctively Christian doctrines of the Trinity and Incarnation. As we said at the outset, it is central to Christianity to suppose that God has the attributes of being triune and incarnate. There are, as we have seen, objections that threaten to shipwreck this supposition on the rocks of incoherence; but so far as we can tell, those objections are entirely answerable.

Further reading

Copan, Paul and Ronald Tacelli (eds.), *Jesus' Resurrection: Fact or Figment?* (Downers Grove, IL: InterVarsity Press, 2000).

Crisp, Oliver, *Divinity and Humanity: The Incarnation Reconsidered* (Cambridge: Cambridge University Press, 2007).

Davis, Stephen T. *et al.* (eds.), *The Trinity* (Oxford: Oxford University Press, 1999). *The Incarnation* (Oxford: Oxford University Press, 2002).

Hick, John, *The Metaphor of God Incarnate* (Louisville, KY: Westminster/John Knox Press, 1993).

Howard-Snyder, Daniel, "Was Jesus Mad, Bad, or God? . . . or Merely Mistaken?" *Faith and Philosophy* 21 (2004), pp. 456–79.

McCall, Thomas and Michael Rea (eds.), *These Three Are One: Philosophical and Theological Essays on the Doctrine of the Trinity* (Oxford: Oxford University Press, 2008).

Morris, Thomas, *The Logic of God Incarnate* (Ithaca, NY: Cornell University Press, 1986).

Rea, Michael (ed.), *Oxford Readings in Philosophical Theology* (Oxford: Oxford University Press, 2008).

Swinburne, Richard, *The Resurrection of God Incarnate* (Oxford: Oxford University Press, 2003).

Wright, N. T., *The Resurrection of the Son of God* (Minneapolis, MN: Fortress Press, 2003).

The Challenge of Jesus (Downers Grove, IL: InterVarsity Press, 1999).

Part II

The Rationality of Religious Belief

4　Faith and rationality

Faith, according to the Christian scriptures, is "being sure of what we hope for and certain of what we do not see."[1] So defined, however, doesn't faith look a bit like wishful thinking, or a stubborn refusal to allow one's beliefs to be judged at the tribunal of hard evidence? In short, doesn't this make faith seem like an irrational or, at the very least, non-rational way of acquiring and hanging on to beliefs?

Some people are content with the idea that their religious faith is some-how either contrary to reason or not subject to reason. The ancient church father Tertullian is often quoted as saying, "I believe *because* it is absurd."[2] The quotation is not accurate; but those who misquote him in this way often approve of the idea themselves. One who thinks this way about religious faith – that is, one who thinks that religious faith is irrational or non-rational and, furthermore, that it is still somehow okay or even a good thing to have religious faith – is called a *fideist*.

Fideism has been taken very seriously by a variety of philosophers and theologians. But a moment's reflection reveals that most of us will not be the least bit comfortable with it. Suppose you arrive at the doctor's office to be treated for a cold, and the doctor tells you she thinks it would be a good idea to remove one of your kidneys. Naturally, you would want the doctor to give you some reason for this opinion; and you would be quite unimpressed if she responded simply by saying, "Oh, I don't really have any *reason*. I just have a strong conviction that removing your kidney would be a great thing." When matters of great importance are at stake – health, survival, desires of the heart, and the like – we want hard evidence, not ungrounded

---

[1] Hebrews 11:1, in *The Holy Bible: New International Version*, Copyright 1984 by The International Bible Society.

[2] The phrase is derived from remarks Tertullian makes in his *De Carne Christi*. However, the Latin does not contain this phrase nor even anything equivalent to it.

convictions. We want, in other words, to be sure that the beliefs on which we and others are acting are rational. If we find that others are risking harm to us or to others because of irresponsible, irrational, or non-rational belief-forming practices, we are quite justifiably angry.

So we should not be at all content if it turns out that religious faith is the product of irresponsible, irrational, or non-rational belief-forming practices. For religious beliefs typically are about matters of great importance, and acting (or failing to act) on one's religious beliefs often has significant consequences for the well-being of others. Indeed, according to some, one's very eternal destiny might depend critically on one's own personal religious beliefs; and so (from this point of view) those who either deliberately or unwittingly invent false religious views risk leading others astray and jeopardizing their immortal souls. So to blithely insist that it is okay to embrace religious beliefs in an irrational or non-rational way – or, worse, *because* those very beliefs are absurd – will strike many of us as wrongheaded to say the least.

But can religious faith escape the charge of irrationality? Answering this question will occupy our attention for the bulk of this chapter. We will begin by discussing the nature of faith and some alleged requirements on rationality. We will then turn to a discussion of the grounds of religious belief. We will consider different views about what religious belief would have to be based on in order for it to be justified. We will also examine the question of whether the phenomenon of widespread religious disagreement somehow undermines whatever justification we might have for our religious beliefs. We will close the chapter by considering an argument which tries to turn the tables on those who oppose religious belief, arguing that it is not religious faith but rather atheism that is ultimately irrational.

The nature of faith

Before we get very far along in discussing different conceptions of faith and their philosophical merits, we need to be clear that there are some senses of the word "faith" – perfectly respectable ones – that will not be the focus of our attention here. In what follows we will be considering faith as a *propositional attitude*, that is, a cognitive stance towards a proposition. Take the proposition "The Cubs will win the World Series this year." There are different cognitive stances (or attitudes) one might take towards this proposition. I might *doubt* it, or *believe* it, or *fear* it, or *hope in* it, and so on. Each of the italicized words or phrases represents a different *propositional attitude*. In this chapter, we will be concerned primarily with faith as a propositional attitude. In particular, we shall be thinking of faith as (merely) a species of *belief*. The reason we focus on this sense of the term, to the exclusion of others, is that this is the sense primarily at issue when people raise questions about the *rationality of faith* or about the relationship between *faith and reason*.

There are, of course, other senses of the term "faith." For example, some philosophers point out that, in many religious traditions, faith is a *virtue* (and lack of faith a *vice*) and, as such (it is argued), it cannot be primarily a matter of *belief*. After all, virtues and vices are states for which we are morally responsible. As such, those states must be directly or indirectly under our voluntary control. But it is not clear whether, or to what extent, beliefs are under our voluntary control. (Try as you might, you cannot bring yourself to believe that you don't have a head, or that you are Shakespeare. And many people will say that they have similarly found it impossible to acquire or retain belief in God.) Consequently, some think that the sort of faith that matters for religious purposes is not any sort of belief, but rather something like hope plus a disposition to act on your hopes as if they are really true.[3] This may be a perfectly respectable notion of faith, but it is not the one we will discuss here.

Alternatively, many religious believers use the word "faith" to refer to a type of *personal trust*. Consider, for example, someone who hates God, believes that God is out to make her life miserable, and therefore actively spends her time defying God. Does she have *faith* in God? Here it seems that we want to say that, though she might *take it on faith* that God exists, she does not have *faith in God*. The first occurrence of the word "faith" refers to her attitude toward the proposition that God exists; the second occurrence refers to her lack of any sort of trusting relationship with God. This second use of the term, on which faith involves some sort of personal trust, is a perfectly respectable use; but it is not the one we will be concerned with here.

There are, no doubt, other uses of the term "faith." But from here on, we shall talk about faith as if it is just a kind of belief. But what sort of belief is

---

[3] See Louis P. Pojman, "Faith Without Belief," *Faith and Philosophy* 3:2 (1986), pp. 157–76.

it? Whatever else faith might involve, pretty much everyone agrees that having faith in a proposition involves believing that it is true *while having neither proof nor direct sensory evidence* of its truth. Proof, in this context, is to be understood in the way that it is understood in geometry – i.e. as involving deductive reasoning from premises that are supposed to be self-evident to every sane and competent thinker. (Thus, as we shall be using the term, one does not generally get *proof* from natural science. At best, one gets very strong evidence.) Direct sensory evidence is what we get from specific exercises of our senses: seeing, hearing, touching, and so on. Much of the confusion in discussions of faith arises from a failure to distinguish proof from *evidence*, as well as from a failure to distinguish between different kinds of evidence. Further confusion arises from a failure to pay careful attention to what can and cannot sensibly be taken to be the requirements for knowledge. In this section, we will briefly try to sort out some of the confusions; then we will discuss the ingredients of faith and the conditions under which it occurs.

Faith, evidence, and knowledge

Mark Twain colorfully characterized faith as "believing what you know ain't so."[4] Of course, it can't be that faith is *literally* believing what you know to be false. Nevertheless, Twain's remark is amusing because, for most of us anyway, it has a ring of truth to it. What, then, might be the seemingly correct idea lurking in the neighborhood? Here four related characterizations of faith come to mind:

(i)   Faith is believing something in the absence of proof.
(ii) Faith is believing something in the absence of supporting evidence.
(iii) Faith is believing something in face of overwhelming counter-evidence.
(iv) Faith is believing something that we do not know to be true.

Do any of those look like conceptions of faith we might want to endorse? Let's consider each in turn.

   Is there any good reason to accept the first characterization? Not really. We have already granted that faith *involves* belief in the absence of proof – where, again, having proof amounts to having a deductive argument all of

---

[4] From *Following the Equator*. Available at www.gutenberg.org/dirs/etext02/dwqmt11.txt.

whose premises are self-evident to every sane and competent thinker. But it seems too strong to say that just anything believed in the absence of proof amounts to faith. Scientists believe the theories they believe in the absence of proof. Jurors convict people and sentence them to prison without proof. In both of these cases, the believers in question have lots and lots of evidence (we can assume), but not proof. And in these cases it would seem odd to say that all of these beliefs are held on *faith*.

What about the second characterization? Can we sensibly say, with Richard Dawkins (among others), that faith is "belief that isn't based on evidence"?[5] It doesn't seem so. It takes a lot of faith, for example, for Charlie Brown to believe that *this time* Lucy won't pull the ball away when he tries to kick it. And this will be true even if Charlie Brown has a *great deal of evidence* that Lucy won't pull the ball away. Suppose Lucy tells him that she has no intention whatsoever of pulling the ball away, and suppose that this claim is supported by her passing a lie detector test. Suppose further that, for the past year, she has participated in a rehabilitation program geared toward curing her of her sadistic football-yanking tendencies. Recently, she has come to Charlie Brown with an apparently sincere, heartfelt apology for all of the times she has pulled the football away in the past; and she has soberly declared her intention to reform. Here we have a lot of genuine evidence that, today anyway, Lucy will not pull the ball away. Still, won't it take faith for Charlie Brown actually to believe that she will not pull it away? Surely it will. So it is a mistake to suggest that faith always involves belief in the absence of evidence.

Likewise, our third characterization is mistaken in suggesting that faith involves belief in the face of overwhelming counter-evidence. No doubt we sometimes use the word "faith" in this way. This is an especially common way for coaches and athletes, for example, to use the word. When a lousy sports team has to play the best team in the league, coaches and players on the lousy team will often report that they have faith that their team will win; that is, they (claim to) believe that their team will win, even in the face of overwhelming evidence to the contrary.

Yet while we sometimes use the word that way, we are equally comfortable using it to describe our attitude towards claims for which we have

---

[5] "Science versus Religion," in Louis Pojman and Michael Rea (eds.), *Philosophy of Religion: An Anthology*, 5th edn. (Belmont, CA: Wadsworth, 2007), p. 426.

quite a lot of evidence. Consider again our two teams. We can imagine a player on the league-leading team (let's call him Aaron) being interviewed before the game and being asked: "Aaron, even though you are playing the worst team in the league, do you have any worries about this game?" And we can imagine Aaron responding, "None at all; I have complete faith that we will be victorious." This seems a fair use of the word, despite the fact that Aaron does not hold the belief "in the face of compelling counter-evidence." As a result, this characterization of faith is not adequate either.

There seems, then, to be nothing in the concept of faith that would preclude us from having evidence – even a lot of evidence – for the things that we take on faith. Still, maybe, as our fourth characterization has it, believing by faith just means believing in cases where the beliefs fall short of full-fledged knowledge.

Can we know the truth of something that we take on faith? Many will say no. The main reason is that those who accept this fourth characterization are inclined to think that to know something is to believe it on the basis of some sort of firm and unshakeable evidence. Faith on the other hand does not rest on such evidence. There is some truth to this. But to see exactly how much, we will have to think a bit about evidence, and how evidence figures into knowledge (and other sorts of believing, including faith).

Often when people think of evidence, they have primarily in mind something like *forensic* evidence – physical traces, testimony, and the like. And it is certainly true that faith usually involves believing in a way that goes beyond our forensic evidence. But notice that knowing also sometimes involves believing in a way that goes beyond our forensic evidence. For example, unless you live in the neighborhood of the South Pole (or an ill-attended zoo) you almost certainly know that there aren't any penguins in your house. But your grounds for this belief will not be any sort of forensic evidence. (Indeed, you probably haven't even checked for penguins lately.) Rather, your belief will be based solely on a variety of background beliefs, together with the fact that you have no reason seriously to entertain the hypothesis that your house contains penguins. And the background beliefs will be beliefs about the typical habitat for penguins, the migratory habits of penguins, the location of your house and the ability of penguin owners to easily access the inside of your house, and so on. They won't be, say, memories of the presence of penguin exterminators. Thus, your belief that there are no penguins in your house goes beyond what could be justified by forensic evidence. Nevertheless, you know it all the same. So, believing in the absence of forensic evidence doesn't provide the distinction between knowledge and faith that we were looking for.

When philosophers talk about evidence, however, often they are not thinking only (or primarily) of forensic evidence. Rather, they are thinking more generally of what is typically called *propositional* evidence. Perhaps the easiest way to understand the notion of propositional evidence is just to say that propositional evidence is evidence that can be believed. So, for example, if you are sitting on a jury and you come to believe that the defendant is guilty, you will almost certainly do so because you acquire beliefs that support the claim that she is guilty. So, for example, you might come to believe that:

a) security cameras place the defendant at the scene of the crime at the time the crime was committed,
b) her fingerprints are on the door and on the murder weapon, and
c) she has no alibi.

Here, then, your evidence for your belief that the defendant is guilty is a set of propositions – in this case, propositions about the forensic evidence. A great many of our beliefs are based on evidence of this sort. But not all of them. Perceptual beliefs – or, at the very least, beliefs about our perceptual experiences, such as *I seem to see a tree* – are based on perceptual experiences. But experiences aren't propositions; they aren't things that we believe; they can't be assessed for truth or falsity. Nevertheless, they often serve as the grounds for belief, and it seems undeniable that we know a great many things on the basis of perceptual experience.

Moreover, some of what we know – for example, that we are not victims of the *Matrix*, or that certain elementary logical axioms are true – seems not to be based on *any evidence whatsoever*. Just think of how you might try to offer evidence for the claim that you are not a victim of the *Matrix*, or the claim that contradictions cannot be true. Any evidence you might put forward would already presuppose the truth of the claim in question. In order to prove that contradictions cannot be true, you would have to assume that they cannot be true; in order to show that you are not a victim of the *Matrix*, you would have to assume that your perceptual faculties are reliable (which they wouldn't be if you were a *Matrix*-victim). To borrow an analogy from Thomas Reid, it would be like referring to a man's own word as evidence that he is not a liar. But, of course, to do that is to give no real evidence at all.

If all that we have just said is correct, then there are things that we know that are not known on the basis of any of the types of evidence we have identified: forensic, propositional, or experiential. Above we saw that we cannot distinguish faith and knowledge by saying that the latter are based on forensic evidence while the former are not. But now we have learned something more. We cannot even distinguish faith from knowledge by saying that the latter are based on some sort of evidence while the former are not, since there are indeed cases of knowledge in the absence of evidence. The result of all of this is that the four characterizations of faith that we tried out above all fail.

Toward a positive conception of faith

Above we saw that faith involves belief in the absence of proof or direct sensory evidence. This at least provides the beginnings of a negative characterization of faith. Thus, for example, St. Thomas Aquinas argued that claims believed on the basis of proof or direct sensory evidence are claims believed *by reason*. Claims believed on faith, then, are based on something else. But what else? We saw in the last section that faith need not be groundless – that, in fact, we can have a great deal of evidence for things that we take on faith. But what sort of evidence might we have for our religious faith? And why is it hard to shake the conviction that there is *something* true in the suggestion that faith somehow implies a deficiency in our evidence? In the present section, we shall try to take some steps toward a positive characterization of faith; and in so doing, we shall try to answer these remaining questions.

Let us begin with the question of what sources of evidence might ground our religious faith. Here we have a variety of options. St. Thomas took it that faith is belief based on authority, or testimony. But this is not the only possibility. Other candidate sources include religious experience, philosophical arguments, inference to the best (empirical) explanation, and so on. This is not to say that all of these forms of evidence are on a par. One might think, for example, that a scientific argument for some particular religious claim is much better, evidentially speaking, than an appeal to authority. But the point is that all of these are candidate sources of evidence, and there is no reason to decide at the outset that religious faith cannot be grounded in evidence from one or more of these sources.

But now what of the suggestion that faith somehow implies a deficiency in our evidence? Our own positive characterization of faith is designed to address this question; but in order to present that characterization, we need to introduce a new term. When (as is pretty much always the case) evidence doesn't *guarantee* that just one among a set of competing theories is true – when, in other words, there are (in principle or in practice) multiple theories that are compatible with the evidence – philosophers say that the theory is *underdetermined by the evidence*. Where there is underdetermination, it is often natural to speak of faith. Often, but not always; for underdetermination comes in degrees, and when there is overwhelming evidence in support of some hypothesis, and no rivals worth taking seriously on the horizon, faith-talk starts to seem out of place. Thus, for example, it is perhaps quite natural to think that it requires a leap of faith to believe (say) the Bohmian interpretation of quantum mechanics over the rival Copenhagen interpretation – these two interpretations being the main competing stories about what the equations of quantum theory really mean, with virtually nothing by way of hard empirical evidence to support one over the other. But it is hardly natural at all to suggest that it requires faith to believe (say) that the earth revolves around the sun, rather than vice versa.

What we want, then, is an account of faith that respects both the idea that faith is present where there is some reasonably high degree of underdetermination, as well as the idea that faith is not so ubiquitous as to be present just anywhere that we find underdetermination. We therefore tentatively propose the following as our positive account of faith: to say that a person S has faith in a proposition p is to say that S believes p despite the fact that (a) there are alternatives to p that are compatible with whatever evidence supports S's belief that p, and (b) there is genuine and somewhat weighty evidence in favor of one or more of those alternatives. Of course, the phrase "genuine and somewhat weighty evidence" is hopelessly imprecise; but in our view, the imprecision does not diminish the value of this account as at least a viable first pass at a positive account of faith.

One advantage of this understanding of faith is that it allows us to respect the common-sense intuition that faith comes in degrees. The degree of faith one has in a proposition depends on the degree to which it is underdetermined by the evidence, as well as upon the strength of available counter-evidence. Again, it takes little or no faith to believe that the earth revolves around the sun, because, though that view is indeed underdetermined by the evidence, there is an overwhelming lack of evidence pointing to any serious alternative. Likewise, though it is sometimes pointed out in discussions of faith that, for example, we routinely "take it on faith" that the chairs we sit on will continue to support our weight, the fact is that the amount of faith involved in believing that an ordinary chair will support your weight is vanishingly small – again, precisely because there is virtually no evidence in favor of the alternative (that the chair will collapse). On the other hand, believing religious claims often requires a substantial amount of faith, precisely because one typically has at least somewhat weighty evidence pointing toward a variety of alternatives, each of which is compatible with the data.

Another advantage of the account that we have offered is that it allows us to say that faith will sometimes be rational and sometimes not, depending on the degree of underdetermination and the strength of the counter-evidence. One who has faith in the flat earth hypothesis is deluded. On the other hand, it is probably quite rational to have whatever faith it takes to believe (as opposed to merely *use*) our best theories in physics – though, in fact, there is controversy about this among philosophers of science. In any case, there won't be a single categorical answer to the question whether faith is rational: it will depend, rather, on the circumstances under which it is held.

The presence of these advantages does not by any means clinch the case for our understanding of faith being superior to its rivals. But it is surely a virtue that it can respect these facets of our common-sense talk about faith.

Does our conception of faith have any disadvantages? There are at least two. First, as we have noted, our account of faith commits us to thinking that faith is present (albeit to a small degree) even in cases where our belief is strongly backed by the available evidence. But it might seem rather jarring to suggest that even when our evidence very strongly supports one proposition over its competitors, believing in accord with the evidence is a matter of faith. This seems jarring because we are often inclined to speak as if *believing on evidence* is incompatible with *believing on faith*. In light of the foregoing, however, it seems that the right response to this is that (a) it is, strictly speaking, a mistake to think that these two modes of believing are incompatible, but (b) it is somewhat natural to think this way in light of the fact that the paradigm examples of believing on faith are precisely those cases where the available evidence doesn't point so strongly toward any of the alternatives.

Second, some might think that it is a disadvantage of our view that "believing by faith" does not turn out to be wholly distinct from "believing by reason." After all, very many of the beliefs that we would normally say are "believings by reason" are beliefs that are both underdetermined by the evidence and perhaps also contradicted by "somewhat weighty" counter-evidence. For example, scientific beliefs are sometimes like this; so too, sometimes, are the beliefs that jurors form when they try to determine guilt or innocence. To our minds, it is appropriate to say that faith is involved in such cases. Still, we acknowledge that this consequence might lead one to doubt that our account is the best way to divide the territory between believing by faith and believing by reason.

In the next section, we leave aside the question of what faith is and turn to discuss the rationality of faith. In light of the way we are here thinking of faith, it should come as no surprise that we take the question of whether religious *faith* is rational to be equivalent to the question of whether religious *belief* is rational. Those who hold a different conception of faith will, accordingly, see those two questions as different; but even so, they will doubtless recognize the latter question as of genuine interest in its own right.

Faith and rationality

In the preceding section we argued that nothing in the concept of faith excludes the idea that one might have evidence for faith, or that one might know some of the things that one takes on faith. Given that one can only know what one rationally believes, it follows from this that faith can, in principle anyway, be rational. And, in fact, this should not be the least bit surprising. After all, if the conception of faith that we have defended is correct, faith is present in science as well as in religion. But, of course, scientific beliefs are widely regarded as paradigms of rational belief.

But is distinctively *religious* faith rational in this way? If so, then the objection raised above – that our version of faith looks too much like ordinary reason – will be no objection at all. Still, the question is a hard one, and the answer depends partly on just what we think it would take for our religious beliefs to be rationally held.

According to some philosophers, a belief is rational only if it can be *seen* to be supported by the balance of one's evidence. If this view is right, then the rationality of religious belief (like any other sort of belief) depends ultimately on the strength of the arguments we can produce on its behalf. If we can demonstrate (to ourselves, at least, if not to anyone else) that certain experiences of ours, or certain facts about the world, evidentially support our religious beliefs and, furthermore, that whatever counter-evidence we have doesn't outweigh our positive evidence, then our religious beliefs are rational. Otherwise, they are not. Call this position *evidentialism*.

Others, however, deny that the rationality of religious belief depends on our ability to produce supporting arguments. A belief, they say, is rationally held (roughly) just so long as the following two conditions are satisfied: (a) it is produced by reliable, properly functioning cognitive faculties; and (b) the person holding the belief does not think or have overriding reason to think that the belief is irrational. Call this position *reliabilism*. To be sure, forming beliefs in the absence of argument is sometimes either unreliable or a sign of cognitive malfunction. Normal human jurors, for example, need arguments and evidence in order to form reliable beliefs about guilt in homicide cases, and properly functioning human beings can see this. So a person who tends to form such beliefs in the absence of argument is, at best, unreliable and, at worst, insane. But there is no obvious reason to think that forming beliefs in the absence of argument is *always* unreliable or a sign of cognitive malfunction. Thus, the reliabilist (unlike the evidentialist) is in a position to resist the claim that religious beliefs are rational only if they are supported by arguments.

Who has the better of this dispute? The evidentialist or the reliabilist? In our view, the reliabilist is on surer footing. In the remainder of this section we explain why.

Let us begin by considering what might motivate someone toward evidentialism. Suppose you have some belief – any belief that isn't *self-evident* in the way that logical truths are – for which you can't see any supporting evidence. In that case, you have no story to tell – none whatsoever – about why it might be sensible for you to hold that belief. But if that's right, then how is this belief of yours any different, say, from the (absolutely unsupportable and irrefutable) belief that, exactly one hundred light years from here, there is a small planet entirely populated by leprechauns? The latter sort of belief is clearly ridiculous. But isn't this other belief of yours in exactly the same boat? At any rate, not being acquainted with anything at all that supports it, you have no story to tell that would differentiate the two beliefs. If that's right, however, then from your point of view, the two beliefs should be on a par with respect to their justification: the one should be justified only if the other is. But clearly you wouldn't be justified in believing in the leprechaun planet; so your other belief is unjustified too.

We have already indicated that some beliefs – the belief that your cognitive faculties are reliable, for example – might be rationally held in the absence of any evidence whatsoever (they are not even self-evident). So evidentialists will have to include something in their view about how beliefs get justified that either respects this fact or else explains to us why it seems to be true even though it is mistaken. But whatever evidentialists say about bedrock-level beliefs like the belief that your cognitive faculties are reliable won't apply in the case of religious belief; for nobody really thinks that religious belief is like that. That is, nobody thinks that religious belief is rationally held in the absence of any evidence whatsoever (not even experiential evidence).

So nobody really thinks that we'll be left with *no story* to tell about why it might be sensible for us to hold our religious beliefs. But, according to evidentialists, unless we have arguments to back up our religious beliefs, whatever stories we can tell to explain why our religious beliefs are sensible just won't be good enough. The reason is simple: to say that we have no arguments in support of our religious beliefs is just to say that we have no *propositional evidence* for those beliefs. So either we have no evidence at all for them (which even the reliabilist will resist saying) or else we have nothing more than experiential evidence for them. But what sort of experiential evidence might we have? There is perceptual evidence; but probably nobody nowadays has anything like direct perceptual evidence in support of his or her religious beliefs. Alternatively, there are mystical experiences – visions or other sorts of overwhelming experiences that present themselves as experiences of God. There are also more common and mundane sorts of religious experiences – a sense of divine forgiveness, a subtle awareness of the presence of God, an internal impression that this or that sacred book is divinely inspired. But it is very hard to make a case for the conclusion that we can *see* that such experiences evidentially support our religious beliefs; and if we can't see that they evidentially support our religious beliefs, it is hard to see how we can justifiably take them as a basis for our religious beliefs.

By way of illustration, let us borrow one of the stock examples from the literature on faith and rationality. Linus has a quasi-religious belief in a being called the Great Pumpkin. The Great Pumpkin is a lot like Santa Claus: he has super powers, distributes presents to deserving people, and appears in public only one day during the year. The Great Pumpkin's day of choice is Halloween; the "deserving people" are those who manage to find a "sincere" pumpkin patch and wait in it all night. Needless to say, most of us will want to say that belief in the Great Pumpkin is not anywhere close to being justified. And the reason seems just to be that there is nothing even approaching a decent argument that can be given for belief in the Great Pumpkin.

But now suppose that Linus has had certain experiences that point him toward belief in the Great Pumpkin. Perhaps, for example, he feels that the Great Pumpkin has spoken to his heart of hearts and so revealed himself specially to Linus. Or perhaps he just finds himself with the unshakeable conviction that, arguments or no arguments, the Great Pumpkin exists and the basic story of Great-Pumpkinism is true. Would this help? Most of us will want to say no. In fact, most of us will think that the additional story makes matters worse. Linus gives up his Halloween every year to sit, miserable and cold, in a pumpkin patch waiting for the Great Pumpkin to show up – and now we find that it is all because he has a manifestly unsupported, unshake-able conviction that the Great Pumpkin's existence and intentions have been specially revealed to him? How sad! How crazy! Perhaps such behavior can be overlooked in children; but an adult who behaved this way should, at the very least, be admonished to pay more attention to the cold hard evidence.

But note that the craziness of Linus's belief consists not in the mere fact that it is held on the basis of experience. After all, perceptual beliefs are held on the basis of experience, and justifiably so. What then is the problem? It is tempting to think that the problem is just that nobody (Linus included) can *see* any connection between his experience and the truth of his belief. There is simply no reason to think that the experience indicates that the belief is likely to be true; and so there is no reason to think that the experience confers justification on the belief.

Reasoning along these lines seems to be the primary motivation for evidentialism. And to the extent that we find it persuasive, we might think that we see here a reason for preferring evidentialism to reliabilism. For the reliabilist is committed to thinking that Linus's belief can be justified *even if there is no reason for thinking that his quasi-religious experience indicates that the belief is likely to be true*. What is crucial for justification is just that the belief be formed by reliable, properly functioning cognitive faculties. It doesn't matter whether Linus has any reason to think that his faculties are reliable or properly functioning. But if we grant this, then can't we claim justification for any crazy belief that we might have? Do you want to believe that your real parents are Spiderman and Wonder Woman? No problem; just get yourself to firmly hold the conviction that this is true, and then declare the belief to have been formed by a properly functioning, reliable cognitive faculty. But that is silly; so if reliabilism is committed to saying that justification can come in this way, then so much the worse for reliabilism.

But it would be a mistake to suppose that reliabilists are committed to thinking much differently from the rest of us about Linus's Great-Pumpkinism (or the belief that your parents are Spiderman and Wonder Woman, or other, similarly silly beliefs). To be sure, the reliabilist will not be bothered by the fact that neither Linus nor anyone else can see a connection between his quasi-religious experiences and the truth of his beliefs about the Great Pumpkin. But the reliabilist can nevertheless acknowledge that, just as propositional evidence comes in varying degrees and can be defeated by other evidence, so too experiential evidence comes in varying degrees and can be defeated by other evidence. And in the case of Great-Pumpkinism, whatever evidence Linus might have in support of his belief in the Great Pumpkin seems overwhelmingly to be defeated by attention to the details of the Great Pumpkin story together with the fact that probably nobody else on the planet has had the sorts of internal experiences that Linus might claim in support of his belief in the Great Pumpkin. A sentient pumpkin? Who flies? Who judges pumpkin patches on the basis of sincerity? Who manages to stay hidden from the world all year, and yet somehow can reveal himself telepathically to small children? Great-Pumpkinism is ridiculous, and it is not widely held. There is, in short, good reason to *doubt* that belief in the Great Pumpkin is produced by *reliable, properly functioning cognitive faculties*. Thus, we rightly judge that Linus's belief in the Great Pumpkin is unjustified.

The case of religious belief, however, is different; and, according to the reliabilist, the difference matters. A great many people throughout history have had experiences that they have taken (rightly or wrongly) to involve some sort of direct awareness of God, or of God's communicating something to them. In his book *Perceiving God*, William Alston notes that such experiences are analogous to perceptual experience. Religious experiences, like perceptual experiences, force themselves upon the subject and seem to the subject to be about some external reality. In the case of perception, there is a "community" of perceivers, and we can consult other members of this community – other people with eyes and ears and so on – to find out whether our experiences are veridical. We can also check our experiences against what we know from science and other theory-building disciplines. (Could that cat really have been flying under its own power as it seemed to be? No, the biology textbook tells me. Someone must have thrown it across the room.) Likewise, there are communities of people who have had similar sorts of religious experiences; and those who have religious experiences in their community, or in their religious tradition, who have had similar experiences in order to find out whether their experiences are veridical. They can also check their experiences against what they know from theology and related theory-building disciplines. (Could God really have been communicating to me that it's a good thing to worship Baal? No, the [Jewish and Christian] theology textbooks tell me. That thought must have come from another source.) To be sure, there is no *independent* way of checking the validity of religious experience – that is, no way independent of religious experience and the theological traditions built upon it. But likewise there is no way of checking the validity of perceptual experience that is independent of perceptual experience and the theories built upon it. Very little of this, however, is true of Linus's Great Pumpkin experiences. Reliabilists will say that this helps to explain why the evidential value of Linus's Great Pumpkin experiences is *obviously* defeated whereas the evidential value of religious experience is not.

One way of expressing this view that religious beliefs can, like perceptual beliefs, be justified on the basis of experience is just to say that religious beliefs (or certain kinds of religious beliefs) are *properly basic*.[6] A *basic* belief is any belief that is held not on the basis of other beliefs. So, for example, if you believe on the basis of your own perceptual experience that there is an elephant in the room, your belief that there is an elephant in the room will

---

[6] For the seminal defense of the view that belief in God might be properly basic, see Alvin Plantinga's "Reason and Belief in God," pp. 17–93 in Alvin Plantinga and Nicholas Wolterstorff (eds.), *Faith and Rationality* (Notre Dame, IN: University of Notre Dame Press, 1983).

be held in the basic way. *Properly* basic beliefs are just beliefs that can be *justifiably* or *rationally* held in the basic way. Most of us think, for example, that perceptual beliefs and memory beliefs are properly basic. On the other hand, most of us think that beliefs about guilt or innocence in court are not. If you believe that the defendant, whom you have never seen before today, is guilty, and if you don't have a shred of propositional evidence for her guilt, then your belief is unjustified. The belief that she is guilty is not at all properly basic. Thus, to say that certain kinds of religious beliefs are properly basic is to say nothing more than that they can be experientially justified. Alston's analogy with sense perception thus constitutes a defense of the claim that belief in God is properly basic.

Note too that, in saying that religious experience might justify religious belief, we do not thereby commit ourselves to saying that religious belief is always (or ever) justified. Nor do we commit ourselves to saying that nothing can defeat the evidential value of religious experience. The point is just that there is at least *prima facie* reason for thinking that religious experience can justify religious belief in just the same way perceptual experience justifies perceptual belief. In the case of perception, the reliabilist will say that beliefs formed on the basis of perceptual experience are justified if, and only if, (a) forming beliefs in that way is reliable and consistent with proper cognitive function – as we think it is in the case of normal human beings; and (b) we do not ourselves think or have reason to think that forming beliefs in that way is irrational – as we don't in the case of normal human beings. And she will say the same about religious experience. To *show*, then, that religious experience *can't* justify religious belief, the objector will have to show either that forming religious beliefs on the basis of religious experience is unreliable or a sign of cognitive malfunction, or that there is some other reason for thinking that forming beliefs in that way is irrational.

But this will be a hard row to hoe, and this for two reasons. First, as William Alston has argued, it is very hard to find reasons for thinking that religious experience ought not to be trusted that do not also indict perceptual experience.[7] Second, as Alvin Plantinga has argued (in *Warranted Christian Belief*), the Christian story, at any rate, is such that, if it is true, then there is very good reason for thinking that religious experience is both reliable and consistent

---

[7] Though Alston does recognize that religious diversity poses a problem for the evidential value of religious experience that doesn't have a parallel in the case of perceptual experience. The problem of religious diversity will be taken up in the next section.

with (indeed, may be a sign of) cognitive proper function. Thus, among other things, in order to show that religious experience can't possibly justify religious belief, the objector will have to show that Christianity is false.

A further point in favor of reliabilism is the fact that evidentialism itself is problematic. Note what happens if we take very seriously the idea, central to evidentialism, that a non-self-evident belief can be justified only if we can see that it is supported by evidence. Consider some belief of yours for which you have supporting evidence. Call that belief B. Now ask yourself: what is involved in seeing that B is supported by evidence? Obviously enough, if we say that "seeing that B is supported by evidence" involves *justifiably believing* that B is supported by evidence, then we face an infinite regress. The regress would go like this:

- B is justified only if B1 is justified, where B1 = the belief that *B is supported by evidence*; but
- B1 is justified only if B2 is justified, where B2 = the belief that *B1 is supported by evidence*; but
- B2 is justified only if B3 is justified, where B3 = the belief that *B2 is supported by evidence*; and so on.

But it is hard to believe that we have all of these higher-level beliefs, in no small part because it is hard to believe that we could even grasp many of the relevant propositions. (What, exactly, would the belief that *B948,125 is supported by evidence* come to?) So it seems that "seeing that B is supported by evidence" must involve something other than the justified belief that B is supported by evidence. If that is right, however, then there is no reason to think that one who "sees that B is supported by evidence" will have any justifiable *story* to tell about the evidential support enjoyed by B. And if so, then she will not be able to differentiate B from belief in the leprechaun planet.[8]

The upshot of the objection we have just raised is that evidentialism demands too much from us. If we really think that we can justifiably believe something only if we can *see* that the balance of evidence supports it, then we will have very few, if any, justified beliefs. For, again, we will either face

---

[8] This objection to evidentialism is highly simplified version of an objection marshaled in much fuller and more careful detail by Michael Bergmann against a closely related position called *internalism*. See his *Justification and Awareness* (Oxford: Oxford University Press, 2005).

an impossible infinite regress or else we will be forced to admit that all of our non-self-evident beliefs depend ultimately for their justification on some belief (probably something like B2 or B3 above) which we can't recognize as supported by evidence and which is therefore itself unjustified (at least by the lights of an evidentialist). But surely a great many of our beliefs are justified. Thus, evidentialism must be false.

In sum, then, it is doubtful that we need arguments in support of religious belief in order for religious belief to be justified. Something in the neighborhood of reliabilism seems to be correct. Even if this is right, however, it hardly follows that religious belief *is* justified for anyone. For it might turn out both that there are no good arguments in support of religious belief *and* that whatever experiential evidence we have in support of our religious beliefs is defeated by other things we know. Above, we argued that theistic belief isn't nearly as bad off as Great-Pumpkinism. But that doesn't mean that there is *nothing* to defeat the evidential force of religious experience. And, in fact, there is one candidate defeater that we have so far been ignoring: the fact of widespread religious disagreement. We take up this problem in the next section.

Religious disagreement and religious pluralism

In the previous section, we drew analogies between sensory experience and religious experience. But there is one important point of disanalogy. To see the disanalogy it will be helpful to draw a comparison between science and religion. We might reasonably think of our total body of scientific theory as a collection of attempts to build theories that explain various features of human *sensory experience*. Similarly, we might also reasonably think of our total body of religious theory as a collection of attempts to build theories that explain various features of human *religious experience*. But now there is something further to note: there is a great deal of harmony among our scientific theories (even if the harmony is not perfect), and about which scientific theories are on the right track and which ones aren't; but the field of religion is a morass of disharmony and widespread disagreement. Contradictions abound among various religious theories, whereas they are not nearly so widespread among scientific theories.

What shall we infer from this fact? Many conclude that religious experience differs from sensory experience at precisely this point: sensory experience and the theories that are built on it are reliable sources of information about the world outside our own heads; but the same is *not* true for religious experience. Those who reach this conclusion about religious experience, and who also think (as many do) that the *arguments* for particular religious doctrines are inconclusive, then face a question: what ought we to think of religious belief, religious discourse, and religious practice? Some think we should abandon religion altogether. Our faculties for producing religious theories are not successfully aimed at truth (as evidenced by the widespread intractable disagreement between religions); thus, we ought simply to give up whatever religious beliefs we hold and, consequently, we ought to give up the practices that are inspired by or otherwise grounded in those beliefs. This is *religious skepticism*.

Others agree with the skeptics that religious diversity shows that religious theorizing is not truth-aimed; but, on their view, we should not conclude from this that religion or religious belief should be abandoned. Rather, what we should conclude is just that religious theorizing is aimed at a goal other than true belief. (We'll identify several candidate goals momentarily.) On this view, no one religion is *correct*; though some might be better at achieving the goals of religion than others. It might turn out that various religions do manage to say things that hit on some truths about the world – for example, that there is some transcendent reality, that love is important, and so on. But, according to this picture, it won't be the case that some very detailed religious theory gets the story right, or even mostly right, to the exclusion of all others. Rather, multiple religious traditions (though not necessarily *every* religious tradition) will constitute *equally valid* attempts to achieve the goals of religion, and equally valid responses to the diverse "religious phenomena" (religious experience, and so on) that give rise to religious belief. And the sense in which they are equally valid is roughly just this: there is no *reason*, all things considered, to think that one of these religions has managed to discover more of the truth about religious matters than the others, or that God or the gods prefer one set of rituals over the others, or that one is significantly morally superior to the others. This position is called *religious pluralism*.

Within the pluralist camp, there are various views about what the goal of religious theorizing might be. Here we shall mention just two:

(i) Some think that the goal is to provide a way of expressing and reinforcing a variety of human goals, values, and preferences. On this view, religious claims have no truth value at all (or, if they do have a truth value, they do so only because they express, in an oblique way, truths about what we value and disvalue).

(ii) Others think that the goal is to provide a framework for understanding certain aspects of the world (primarily those involving religious experience), but one that is not at all meant to be taken with literal seriousness. Though there might well be objective facts about what spiritual reality (the nature of God, and so on) is like, those facts are so far beyond our ken that we cannot at all reasonably aspire to anything like substantive knowledge of them. Rather, religious doctrine functions primarily as a sort of crutch for organizing our thoughts and feelings. On this view, anything but the most general of religious beliefs will count as unjustified; but it might have a kind of instrumental or practical value nonetheless. Thus, for example, believing that Jesus is God Incarnate might be *epistemically* irrational (that is, irrational from the point of view of trying to reach the truth about things); but it will not necessarily follow that it is *wholly* irrational – it might, for example, be one among many practically useful (and therefore practically rational) ways of responding to one's religious experience.

Note that one can endorse either of these two views about the goal of religion *without* being a pluralist. So, for example, one might think that religious claims merely express or reinforce our values and preferences but nonetheless think that there is one mode of expressing such attitudes – the Muslim mode, for example – that is so much better (morally, or otherwise) than all the others that it alone counts as a legitimate attempt to achieve the goals of religion. This is a rather unnatural view. Those who construe the goals of religion along the lines laid out in the preceding paragraph much more naturally fall into the view that at least the most prominent human religions – the theistic religions, Buddhism, Hinduism, and the like – are on a par. But for the sake of conceptual clarity it is important to bear in mind that what is natural in this regard is by no means inevitable.

But must we be forced into either skepticism or pluralism by the phenomenon of (widespread) religious disagreement? Are we committed to thinking that even if some very general religious beliefs (such as, perhaps, those that are held in common by the theistic religions, Buddhism, and Hinduism) are epistemically justified, our justification for any more detailed or specific sort of religious belief would be defeated by the facts of religious diversity? Not obviously; and this brings us to a third position, to which both religious skepticism and religious pluralism are opposed: namely, what is typically called *religious exclusivism*.

The view bears that label because religious exclusivists, in contrast with pluralists, deny that diverse religious doctrines and practices might all count as equally valid attempts to achieve the goals of religion. But there is more to the view than just the denial of pluralism. (For this reason, the label 'exclusivism' is rather unfortunate; but we shall stick with it because it is fairly well entrenched in the literature on these matters.) The denial of pluralism is the negative aspect of religious exclusivism. The positive aspect is the claim that there is one objectively true story about religious matters, and that this story is knowable (and, most exclusivists would add, *known*) in some substantial detail. Exclusivists thus agree with the skeptics that the aim of religious theorizing is to tell us the objective truth about spiritual matters, but they disagree with skeptics in that they see no reason yet to think that the goal is unattainable.

Many religions make exclusivistic claims. Christianity and Islam, for example, each claim (in their orthodox versions, anyway) to be the one and only correct story about the nature of God and about how human beings ought to relate to God. Note, however, that many exclusivists would agree that there is much about the nature of God, and about how human beings ought to relate to God, and so on that we do not yet know and might never know. Moreover, many would agree that multiple *strands* of a particular religious tradition – the various denominations within Christendom, for example – are more or less "equally valid" responses to spiritual reality. Thus, exclusivism should not be identified with the view that there is exactly one religious system that tells us everything that can be known about spiritual matters. What is central to exclusivism is, again, just the idea that we can know the truth about spiritual matters in some substantial detail, and that, in light of what we know, we can see that many human religions fall far short of expressing the truth or of telling us how we ought to relate to God (or the gods, or the cosmos) and one another.

Our question for the remainder of this section, then, is whether and to what extent the phenomenon of (widespread) religious disagreement speaks against religious exclusivism. To answer this question, it will be helpful to break it down into two smaller questions.

QUESTION 1   Does widespread religious disagreement show that multiple religious traditions are equally valid responses to religious phenomena?

QUESTION 2   Does widespread religious disagreement make it somehow unreasonable to believe the doctrines of a particular religion?

If, as we shall argue in the remainder of this section, the answer to each of these questions is "no," then it is hard to see how the phenomenon of religious disagreement would count against exclusivism.

Let us begin with QUESTION 1. Many people, especially people who are not professional philosophers, are inclined to see a connection between widespread religious disagreement and religious pluralism. But it is rather hard to say what precisely the connection is supposed to be. For starters, we might try something like the following line of reasoning:

> There is a great deal of disagreement on matters religious. Moreover, disagreement persists even among people who are very smart and very well-informed (and equally well-informed as well). But when many of your well-informed peers disagree with you, it is arrogant (to say the least) to think that *you're* the one who has gotten things right and that they have all somehow been misled. It is therefore better – more tolerant, more humble, more likely to foster peace, and so on – simply to acknowledge that there are many paths to God, all equally valid. It is better, in other words, to accept religious pluralism.

If this line of reasoning is correct, then religious disagreement does indeed provide a kind of *pragmatic* support for religious pluralism. In noticing the disagreement, we can see that it will be in our best interests in various ways to accept pluralism. But, of course, this argument goes no distance toward showing that religious disagreement *implies* that there is no single correct religious theory. Becoming a pluralist might well be the tolerant, humble, peacemaking thing to do; it might foster happy, loving relationships with our neighbors. But, for all that, the central thesis of religious pluralism might nevertheless be false.

Another way to try to draw a connection between religious disagreement and religious pluralism is to argue that the phenomenon of widespread disagreement somehow forces us to reconstrue the *goal* of religious theorizing or religious discourse along one of the lines described above. Consider the case of moral discourse, for example. You hold one view; your equally informed peers hold another, incompatible view. Furthermore, protracted (competent) argument and investigation fail to resolve the matter. Should we infer that there is no single correct moral view? Many people do. To be sure, there isn't general agreement that we should make this inference; but, at any rate, the suggestion isn't nearly as implausible as it was in the previous example. And the reason is that it is, at least initially, not terribly implausible to suppose that the goal of moral theorizing and moral discourse is something other than telling the truth about the world. The goal might, for example, simply be the expression of values, preferences, or attitudes.

But isn't it plainly silly to try to infer the goals of (say) moral theorizing and moral discourse from the mere fact of moral disagreement. Wouldn't a better way of discovering the goals of moral theorizing and moral discourse simply be to ask the participants in those activities what their goals are? Of course, it might be that the goal of moral theorizing is to discover moral facts when, sadly, there are no such facts to be discovered. But the phenomenon of moral disagreement won't by itself be what tells us that there are no moral facts to be discovered; nor will it be what tells us the goals of moral discourse. Likewise, then, for the case of religious theorizing and religious discourse.

What would not be silly, however, would be an attempt to draw conclusions about the goals of religious theorizing via a somewhat more complicated argument, such as this one:

4.1. The phenomenon of widespread religious disagreement shows that it is unreasonable, or unjustifiable, to believe anything but the most general and commonly held religious claims.

4.2. If premise 4.1 is true, then either religious belief is wholly irrational and religious practice is pointless, or else the goal of religious theorizing and religious discourse is something other than truth.

4.3. Religious belief is not wholly irrational, and religious practice is not pointless.

4.4. Therefore: the goal of religious theorizing and religious discourse is something other than truth.

Taking the first premise for granted, there is something quite plausible about this argument. The religious skeptic, of course, will reject premise

4.2; but those who are committed to the idea that religion is valuable (even when it involves a lot of false belief) will likely find premise 4.2 rather attractive. We shall not try to resolve that issue here. Rather, we want to draw attention to the fact that premise 4.1 is true if, and only if, the answer to QUESTION 2 is affirmative.

Is there any reason to give an affirmative answer to QUESTION 2? At first blush, it seems not. Suppose – to adapt an example from Alvin Plantinga – that you are accused of a crime, that the forensic evidence against you is overwhelming and widely known, but that you distinctly remember being out for a walk in the woods at the time the crime was committed. You might have nothing apart from your own memory (an internal experience, notably) to support your view; and it might be that virtually all of your peers (who are just as smart and just as well-informed as you) disagree with you. But, for all that, the disagreement won't count one bit against the reasonability of your belief that you were out walking in the woods at the time the crime was committed. Thus, there is at least some superficial reason for thinking that, in general, disagreement doesn't render belief unreasonable.

But this is a superficial reason only, however. For the fact is, sometimes we think that widespread disagreement *does* make a difference with respect to whether we are justified or reasonable in persisting in our beliefs. Suppose you are in a heated argument with someone. In the course of the argument, it comes out that the person is offended by the fact that, earlier in the discussion, you declared that her position was "foolish." You have no recollection of saying that, and, moreover, you insist that you never said that. However, some twenty people who have been bystanders to the conversation and listening intently all agree that yes, you said the very words that your interlocutor claims that you said. Isn't it now unreasonable, unjustified, to persist in the belief that you never said what you are being accused of saying? Or suppose you are the plate umpire for a baseball game. The runner slides; you declare him safe. Many bystanders, however – all of whom you regard as equally competent judges of such matters – insist that he was tagged out. Indeed, even members of the runner's own team insist that he was tagged out. Isn't it now wholly unreasonable for you to persist in your belief that he was safe?

What's going on in these examples? The answer seems to be that, at least in the two cases just mentioned, the phenomenon of disagreement casts doubt on your reliability as a judge about the relevant subject matter. Notably too, it seems that the reason we don't think that disagreement counts as reason to abandon belief in your whereabouts at the time of the crime is just that we don't think that the disagreement counts as evidence that you are an unreliable judge of your whereabouts. If that story were fleshed out in more detail – so that, for example, it turns out that you are prone to grossly misremember your whereabouts about as often as, say, people generally are prone to forget some of what they have said during a heated argument or about as often as umpires are prone to misjudge goings on at home plate, then we probably would think that disagreement counts as reason not to persist in your belief about your whereabouts.

The crucial question for our purposes, then, would seem to be whether widespread disagreement on religious matters counts as evidence that we are unreliable judges about such matters. If it does, then this casts significant doubt upon the whole enterprise of religious theory-building. Just as we wouldn't trust the scientific theories of people who are known to be unreliable judges about empirical matters, so too we shouldn't trust theologies constructed by people who are known to be unreliable judges about religious matters. Thus, to the extent that religious disagreement counts as evidence that we are, in general, unreliable judges about religious matters, widespread disagreement then also gives us reason to reject exclusivism.

In fact, however, it seems that widespread religious disagreement does *not* count as evidence that we are unreliable when it comes to making judgments about religious matters. Note that even in the cases described above, it is not disagreement *alone* that leads us to think that you are unreliable. We have background beliefs about a typical person's ability to remember walks in the woods, to remember what she has said in a heated argument, and to judge close calls at home plate. This background information helps to determine the evidential force of the disagreement. In the case of religion, however, *we* don't have much at all by way of background beliefs about a typical person's ability to judge religious matters. A Christian's background beliefs on that topic might differ wildly from a Jew's or a Buddhist's or even another Christian's. Some Christians, for example, believe that apart from divine revelation and special grace, it is literally impossible for someone to acquire true beliefs about God, and that such revelation and grace has not been distributed universally, or even, necessarily, widely. For such a person, widespread disagreement is precisely what we ought to expect. Far from being evidence of unreliability, her particular circumstances are precisely what she should expect if she were among the more reliable judges of religious matters (i.e. a beneficiary of the right sort of revelation and grace).

To illustrate, consider the following modified version of our umpire example. Suppose now that, instead of having the typical background beliefs about the abilities of umpires to make close calls at the plate, you have these background beliefs: you have been given superpowers, among which is the uncanny ability to be a perfect judge of close calls at the plate. Moreover, everyone around you has taken a drug that makes them generally unreliable about such matters. You now find widespread disagreement with your judgment. Well, your background beliefs are surely insane; but *given* those beliefs, it is not the least bit unreasonable for you to persist in your belief that the runner is safe and that your peers are wrong. For, really, the people who take themselves to be your peers are not, in your view, genuine peers at all.

So, in sum, whether disagreement casts doubt upon human faculties for religious judgment depends quite a lot on our background beliefs, many of which might well come from our religious theories themselves. And if this is right, then whether religious disagreement renders exclusivism unreasonable will also depend a lot on our background beliefs. Thus, strictly speaking, it looks as if the answer to QUESTION 2 is "no": it takes a lot more than mere widespread disagreement to show that it is unreasonable to believe the doctrines of a particular religion.

What we have said in this section does not constitute an all-out defense of exclusivism. And so it does not refute religious pluralism. It does, however, address the concern that widespread religious disagreement might, by itself, somehow count against exclusivism; and, in so doing, it addresses what we highlighted as the main concern for reliabilist stories about the rationality of religious belief – namely, the concern that widespread disagreement by itself might count as a defeater for whatever experiential justification we might have for our religious beliefs.

Is atheism irrational?

Thus far in the chapter we have primarily been concerned to address questions about the rationality of religious belief. The presumption has been that religious *non-belief* is the rational default mode, and that the primary question to be addressed is whether one can sensibly, rationally be moved from that position. In closing this section, we would like to consider briefly a recent argument by Alvin Plantinga (discussed at length in James Beiby's collection, *Naturalism Defeated?*) for the conclusion that, in fact, matters are in some ways worse for religious non-believers. On Plantinga's view, given the current scientific story about the origin of species (and hence about the origin of humanity), atheism is positively irrational, and agnosticism leaves us in the position of not being able rationally to believe anything.

Let us begin with an analogy. Suppose you believe that there is a particular substance that, when ingested, induces massive cognitive unreliability in the person who ingested it. Following Plantinga, let's call it XX (but let's not confuse it with the popular beer that bears the same label and that has somewhat similar effects when ingested in large quantities). You believe, for example, that if you had recently ingested XX, it might seem for all the world to you that you are sitting here reading a book when in fact you are elsewhere doing something entirely different. Suppose furthermore that you have come to think that the probability that you have recently ingested XX is high or, at the very least, inscrutable. (Perhaps a prankster friend of yours whom you believe to possess large quantities of XX has called and said that, as a joke, he put some XX in the milk in your fridge; and not ten minutes ago you just drained the last of the milk from the carton.) Now, what should you – let's call you S for the sake of our example – believe about the following proposition, R:

(R) S's cognitive faculties are reliable.

Normally, of course, you accept R. But haven't you just acquired a defeater for the justification for your belief in R? Isn't it now unreasonable for you to accept R? It is, after all, a *live hypothesis* for you that your cognitive faculties are massively unreliable. And, of course, you never had any (non-circular) evidence for R in the first place. (How could you? All such evidence would depend for its evidential force upon the presupposition that R is true.) But if you now have reason to think that R is false, and you can't marshal any non-circular evidence in support of R, isn't the rational thing to do just to withhold belief in R? But if you withhold belief in R, then you ought to withhold belief in everything: you can have no rational beliefs whatsoever. You are, in other words, plunged into a kind of global skepticism.

According to Plantinga, this is precisely the position of the person who embraces atheism. According to the standard evolutionary story, the primary function of our cognitive faculties is to enable us to survive and reproduce. Those are the sorts of functions for which natural selection selects; and there is no particular reason to suppose that our cognitive faculties would have any function or purpose apart from serving those very general goals. But, Plantinga argues, the ability to arrive at the *truth* about the world is largely irrelevant to the function of enabling us to survive and reproduce. A male hominid, for example, who desires death and who believes that the best way to secure death is to run away from things like tigers and bears and to copulate frequently with many different females of his species will do as good a job at surviving and reproducing as a male with more normal desires and beliefs. Moreover, there are more ways for our beliefs to turn out false-but-still-useful than for them to turn out true. Thus, Plantinga concludes, in light of evolutionary theory and the supposition that there is no God or any other supernatural being who has somehow ensured that reliable, truth-aimed cognitive faculties would evolve in humans, the probability that our faculties are reliable is low, or inscrutable. But if so, then the atheist who accepts evolutionary theory (as atheists ought to, given the current state of science) is in a position very analogous to the position of someone who now finds the probability that she has ingested XX to be low or inscrutable. And if that is right, then the atheist has a defeater for R (specified to herself), and so for all of her beliefs – including her atheism.

Moreover, even if you *don't* believe that we could, in the end, survive and reproduce if we had mostly false beliefs, it surely seems true that we could survive and reproduce if we had mostly false theoretical beliefs, of which *philosophical and religious beliefs* constitute two sorts. Any theory that makes the same empirical predictions as quantum theory will enable us to do all of the fantastic things that quantum theory enables us to do; any theory that makes the same empirical predictions as contemporary biological and physiological theories do will enable us to make the sorts of medical advances that we have made; and so on. And, again, there seem to be many more ways for our scientific theories to turn out false-but-useful than for them to turn out true. So, it would seem, given evolutionary theory and atheism, the probability that our *theoretical* faculties are reliable is low or inscrutable. Thus, if the XX analogy holds, this too will suffice to provide the atheist with a defeater for the belief that her theoretical faculties are reliable, in which case, again, she will have a defeater for both atheism and evolutionary theory.

Is an agnostic in any better position? Apparently not. For agnostics too ought, given the current state of science, to accept evolutionary theory (at least initially). But reflection upon the above reasoning will provide the agnostic, as much as the atheist, with a defeater for R (or, at the very least, with a defeater for the belief that her theoretical faculties are reliable). Agnosticism, of course, won't turn out to be self-defeating – after all, agnosticism is just *withholding* belief about the existence of God. But the agnostic will have as much trouble as the atheist in maintaining her other beliefs; for, again, once it is a live option that one's theoretical or other faculties are unreliable, it is hard to see how one can sensibly hang on to beliefs that arise out of exercises of those faculties.

The challenge to atheism posed by this argument is provocative and difficult to assess. The argument has been criticized by theists and atheists alike; and there is no consensus among the critics as to what is wrong with it. Some insist that it is a mistake to take seriously the idea that evolution might not select for reliable cognitive faculties; others say that even despite our inability to assess that probability, atheists, agnostics, and theists alike are perfectly rational in accepting R specified to themselves; and still others point to various ways in which the XX analogy breaks down and that other analogies actually seem to undermine Plantinga's argument. Space will not permit us to explore these criticisms in detail, but interested readers can find objections in abundance in some of the sources listed in our Further Reading section.

Further reading

Alston, William, *Perceiving God* (Ithaca, NY: Cornell University Press, 1991).

Beilby, James (ed.), *Naturalism Defeated?* (Ithaca, NY: Cornell University Press, 2002).

Bergmann, Michael, *Knowledge and Awareness* (Oxford: Oxford University Press, 2006).

Kvanvig, Jon, *Warrant in Contemporary Epistemology* (Lanham, MD: Rowman & Littlefield, 1996).

Plantinga, Alvin, *Warranted Christian Belief* (New York: Oxford University Press, 2000).

Plantinga, Alvin and Nicholas Wolterstorff (eds.), *Faith and Rationality* (Notre Dame, IN: University of Notre Dame Press, 1983).

Swinburne, Richard, *Epistemic Justification* (Oxford: Clarendon Press, 2001).

Faith and Reason, 2nd edn. (Oxford: Clarendon Press, 2005).

5 Theistic arguments

The famous twentieth-century British philosopher and atheist Bertrand Russell was once asked what he would say to explain his atheism if he were to confront God after his death. Russell's famous reply was: "Not enough evidence, God! Not enough evidence."

Russell's response has an implicit and an explicit side. Implicitly his remark indicates that a certain amount of evidence – presumably propositional evidence – is required for reasonable belief in God. Explicitly, he is claiming that there isn't any such evidence. In the last chapter we saw some powerful reasons for thinking that Russell is wrong when it comes to the implicit claim. Belief in God might be justified even in the absence of propositional evidence. It might, for example, be grounded in and justified on the basis of some sort of religious experience.

Still, there are many people who would say that they have had no religious experiences and who furthermore find themselves with no other sort of non-propositional evidence for theism, not even an initial inclination toward belief in God. Others might at least have the initial inclination toward belief in God, but they might think that whatever evidential force that initial inclination carries, as well as the evidential force of whatever religious experiences they might have had, is defeated by other things that they know about the world – for example, that the world contains vast amounts of evil and suffering. For these individuals, the availability of arguments marshaling propositional evidence in support of theism might be an important, if not indispensable, precondition of their acquiring justified belief in the existence of God. And that leads us to consider Russell's explicit claim – the claim that there really is no good evidence. The question of whether or not there is good evidence for the existence of God, and what that evidence might be, is the subject of the present chapter.

Ontological Arguments

It is traditional to divide arguments for the existence of God into two broad categories. *A posteriori* arguments rely on premises that we come to know through our experience of the world around us. Arguments that appeal to the fact that our universe had an origin or that it appears to be designed fall into this category. *A priori* arguments, on the other hand, rely on premises that one can know to be true simply by thinking about them. The first sort of argument we will consider, Ontological Arguments, falls into that second category.

As the title of this section makes clear there is not one single Ontological Argument but rather a class of arguments that philosophers have referred to as Ontological Arguments. (Though it is sometimes convenient to talk as if there is just one argument, but many versions of it.) What these *a priori* arguments have in common is that they aim to demonstrate the existence of God from the mere concept of God or from the mere fact that we can think about God. As one might guess, it is for this reason that people commonly regard Ontological Arguments as wild or outrageous.

Ontological Arguments trace their roots to the writings of the eleventh-century Christian theologian Anselm of Canterbury. The initial formulation of the Ontological Argument appears in Anselm's famous work *Proslogion*, a work in which, Anselm reports, he sought to develop an argument that God exists and has the nature or character that orthodox Christian theism claims God to have.[1] As we have seen earlier, Anselm is a perfect-being theologian and thus takes as his starting point the idea that, as he put it, God is the being than which none greater can be conceived. Once we latch onto this concept of God, Anselm thinks that something truly remarkable follows, namely, that *the non-existence of God is downright impossible*. Anselm's argument seems to go as follows:

5.1. God is the greatest conceivable being.
5.2. God exists in the understanding.
5.3. To exist in reality is better than merely to exist in the understanding.
5.4. Thus, if God exists merely in the understanding, then we can conceive of something greater than God, namely a being just like God, but who also exists in reality.

---

[1] Anselm of Canterbury, *Monologion and Proslogion With Replies by Gaunilo and Anselm*, trans. Thomas Williams (Indianapolis: Hackett, 1996).

5.5. But it is impossible to conceive of a being that is greater than greatest conceivable being.

5.6. Thus it is impossible that God exists merely in the understanding.

5.7. Thus God exists in reality as well as in the understanding.

5.8. Thus God exists.

Put just this way, however, the argument contains some confusing claims. For example, what does it mean to say, in premise 5.2, that "God exists in the understanding"? It does not, of course, mean that there is an omnipotent, omniscient, all-good being residing inside our brains or minds somewhere. It can only mean that the "idea of God" exists in our minds. Once we make this clear, the argument begins to unravel quite quickly. The reason for this is that we are now compelled to re-write other parts of the argument. We will have to start out, for example, as follows:

5.1. God is the greatest conceivable being.

5.2.* An idea of God exists in the understanding.

5.3. To exist in reality is better than merely to exist in the understanding.

We are now left to wonder how to proceed from there. Perhaps we might add:

5.4.* Thus, if an idea of God exists merely in my understanding, then there might have been something greater than God.

But 5.4* is puzzling at best. It is odd to talk about ideas existing "merely" in a mind. Where else would ideas exist? Further, how could the status of the *idea* of God have any connection to or implications for the greatness of *God himself*? The argument thus seems to grind to a halt.

One problem here is that we might be trying to extract the argument from Anselm's text in a way that is much too literal. Perhaps we should step back and see what the main point is supposed to be, and then see if we might be able to reconstruct the argument in a more coherent form. The seventeenth-century philosopher René Descartes offers a related version of the argument in his work *Meditations on First Philosophy*. While commentators typically regard Descartes' version as even more vexing than Anselm's, Descartes offers some hints as to how a better version of the argument might be constructed. Rather than defining God as the being than which none greater can be thought, Descartes defines God as a being *containing all perfections*. With this definition let's consider the following variation of the Ontological Argument as a reconstruction of the argument Anselm might have had in mind:

5.1.* God is the greatest possible being.
5.9. The greatest possible being possesses every perfection that would make a being great.
5.10. Existence is a perfection that would make a being great.
5.11. God possess existence.
5.12. Anything that possesses existence exists.
5.13. Thus God exists.

Anselm thought that since the Ontological Argument was evident and elegant, and since it followed from mere consideration of the idea of God, no one could fail to accept the existence of God once they considered it. In fact, Anselm took this argument to provide an explanation of the remark in the Hebrew Bible that "The Fool says in his heart, 'there is no God'."[2] Only someone who is a fool could fail to grasp that God exists, Anselm thought, since it follows from the concept of God alone.

Objections: Gaunilo

Shortly after the publication of the *Proslogion* a contemporary of Anselm, Gaunilo of Marmoutier, penned a response to Anselm's argument wittly entitled "In Defense of the Fool." In this work, Gaunilo argues that Anselm's argument fails since the same logic would force us to conclude that many things exist which obviously do not. Gaunilo uses the example of a "Lost Island" which has every perfection an island could contain. If we define the Lost Island in this way, it seems that an argument for the existence of the Lost Island follows straightaway.

5.14. The Lost Island is the greatest possible island.
5.15. The greatest possible island is an island which possesses every perfection that would make an island great.
5.16. Existence is a perfection that would make an island better.
5.17. The Lost Island possesses existence.

---

[2] Psalm 14:1, in *The Holy Bible: New International Version*, Copyright 1984 by The International Bible Society.

5.18. Anything that possesses existence exists.

5.19. The Lost Island exists.

Interestingly, although Anselm wrote a reply to Gaunilo's objection, many commentators agree that he did not manage to address the worry raised by the Lost Island objection.

Does the objection sink the Ontological Argument? Defenders have argued that it does not. Gaunilo is in one sense correct that anything that we can describe as *the greatest possible of its kind* will have existence among its perfections. And this leads to the worry that we can substitute any old thing described as the "greatest" of its kind into the first premise and thus conclude that it exists. But there are limits to what can be coherently described as the greatest possible of its kind, and this means that there will be limits to what sorts of things we can substitute in for that first premise. We can see this in the case of the Lost Island when we start to fill out the list of "perfections that would make an island great." What sorts of perfections are those? We might say things like: never rains, cool, breezy nights, lots of palm trees, miles of beaches. But wait: how many miles of beaches? 100 miles? 1,000 miles? More? It looks as if no matter how many miles we specify, we can imagine a greater island: one that has at least one more mile of beach. And so on to infinity.

The fact that there is no such thing as "the greatest number of miles of beaches" shows us is that there really is no such thing as the "greatest possible island" any more than there is such a thing as "the highest number." The problem here is that the perfections that would make for a perfect island do not have an *intrinsic maximal value*, and as a result no object can in fact have what it takes to count as the "greatest possible island."

Among other things, this gives us at least one test that something would have to pass before we could plug it in to the argument in the way that we plugged Lost Island into premise 5.14. In short, it would have to be the kind of thing whose great-making properties admit of an intrinsic maximum. Given this constraint, could we argue for the existence of Frosty, the greatest possible snowman? Probably not, since it seems that size would be a great-making quality for snowmen, and there is no maximum possible size. The same will end up being true for lots of potential substitutes into the argument. One might suppose in fact that the only thing that can be coherently plugged into the argument is "God, the greatest conceivable being."

Of course, the critic could reply by offering other examples in which the great-making qualities of a thing admits of intrinsic maxima and yet we know that the thing does not exist. The defender of the argument might also have reason to worry that some of the great-making qualities of *God* do not admit of intrinsic maxima either. For example, what would it mean to say that being *perfectly* loving admits of an intrinsic maximum?

Objections: Kant

The eighteenth century German philosopher Immanuel Kant offered a different criticism of Anselm's argument. Kant's objection is aimed at premises 5.10 and 5.16 in our arguments above. There are two ways to object to these premises. First, one might object to the idea that existence is a *great-making* property of beings or islands. Second, one might object to the idea that existence is a great-making *property* of beings or islands. The first objection is easy to understand, though it seems misplaced. The second objection is much harder to understand, and it is the objection Kant presents.

We have a general idea of what it is for something to be a property or feature of a thing. Being six feet tall, being located twenty miles from Chicago, being less than five minutes old – all of these are properties of things. On Kant's view, when we *attribute* or *ascribe* properties to a thing, we presuppose the existence of that thing. If you ask a friend to describe her cat, she might say things like: he is five years old, male, mostly black, and so on. But she would not say something like this: "Oh, and I forgot to mention – he exists." The reason she would not do that, Kant thinks, is that when a person starts ascribing properties to something, she *presupposes* that the thing exists. So existence is not itself a property; rather, it is a precondition for having properties – something that is implicitly assumed when we start ascribing properties. Thus, the ontological argument assumes something that is false.

For many years a number of philosophers took Kant's objection to be a fatal one. However, there are various reasons to think that the objection actually misses the mark. One reason is that, in thinking about properties, many philosophers have found it quite natural to suppose that there is a property corresponding to every predicate (except where paradox forces us to say otherwise). Since "it exists" is something that can be said of a thing, and since no known paradox seems to force us to think that existence can't be a property, this way of thinking about properties pushes us in the direction of saying, against Kant, that existence *is* a property. A second reason is that the objection takes it for granted that *preconditions for ascribing properties* cannot themselves *be* properties. But why should we believe this? Consider the properties of "taking up space" and "being red." Something can't be red unless it occupies a region of space. Taking up space is thus a precondition for having the property of being red. Does this mean that "taking up space" cannot be a property? Of course not. Kant might reply that existence is different from "taking up space" because existence is a precondition for ascribing not just *some* other properties but *any property at all*. But even if this were true, why should it disqualify "existence" from being a property? It is hard to imagine any good answer to this question.

Objections: question-begging

There is, however, a third objection to this argument that appears to be much more potent. Critics of the Ontological Argument often assert that it begs the question. That is, the argument seems, in some way, to smuggle the notion that God exists into the premises, and then (unsurprisingly) draws the conclusion that God exists. Does the argument beg the question in this way? To see why one might think it does, consider the first premise:

5.1.* God is the greatest possible being.

All along we have been treating this premise as a definition for the term "God." So, in the interests of being more clear and perspicuous, we should probably restate the premise as follows:

5.1.** For anything to count as God, that thing would have to be the greatest conceivable being.

Once we restate the premise this way, other adjustments will have to be made to the argument. Once that is done, the argument will read as follows:

5.9. The greatest possible being possesses every perfection that would make a being great.

5.10. Existence is a perfection that would make a being greater.

5.11.* For anything to count as God, that thing would have to possess existence.

5.12.* Anything that possesses existence exists.

5.13.* Thus anything that counts as God would have to exist.

But 5.13* is a rather underwhelming conclusion. How might we get the sort of conclusion we are looking for? Rather than reading premise 5.1* as we did in 5.1**, we could read it as:

5.1.*** There is a God who is the greatest possible being.

Of course it is easy to derive the claim that God exists from *this* premise; but, obviously, to do so would be cheating. The premise simply asserts what we were trying to conclude. As a result, many think that the argument fails either because it does not show that God exists, or it begs the question.

The modal version

Over the centuries these three criticisms have been regarded as the most potent criticisms of Anselm's and Descartes' versions of the argument. However, recent discoveries in the area of philosophy known as modal logic have provided some new resources that some think support a novel version of the argument. Modal logic is the logic of possibility and necessity – possibility and necessity being two "modes" of truth and falsity, two ways in which a proposition might be true or false. Logic in general tells us what sorts of inferences are good ones and what sorts of inferences are bad ones. Modal logic tells us about good and bad inferences specifically in the domain of claims about what is possible and what is necessary. This new version of the ontological argument, known as the Modal Ontological Argument, requires that one grasp a few key concepts related to our understanding of the logic of possibility and necessity. So before we discuss the Modal Version, we will have to take a brief detour to acquaint ourselves with these concepts.

The first key concept is that of a "possible world." A possible world might be thought of as a comprehensive description of the way the universe might be.[3] One such description is the description of how the universe actually *is*.

---

[3] This isn't the only way of thinking of possible worlds, nor even the most popular way. Most philosophers would deny that worlds are "descriptions," preferring instead a view according to which worlds are propositions or states of affairs or some such thing. We don't intend to take a stand on these issues here. Our characterization of worlds as comprehensive descriptions is adopted simply for ease of presentation.

That description would include an account of everything that has happened, is now happening, or ever will happen here on earth, and indeed on every other planet (and *off* of every other planet for that matter) now and forever. This description is *maximally comprehensive*.

The maximally comprehensive description of our universe is called the *actual world*. But note, things might have unfolded differently than they did in the actual world. For example, it could have happened that rather than choosing to pick up this book and read it today, you called your friends and went on a hike in the mountains. That didn't happen, of course. But it could have. The description of the world in which you did so represents another *possible but non-actual* world. As you can see, there are many possible worlds – infinitely many in fact.

In different worlds, different truths hold. "Iron atoms exist" is true in the actual world, but it is false in worlds in which the universe expanded too quickly for star formation (since iron atoms form in the core of stars which explode at the end of their "life"). So when we consider any proposition, we must assess its truth or falsity relative to a world. Note that we might, in addition to talking about *propositions being true in a world*, talk about various *things* existing (or not) *at* or *in* a world. When speaking this way, we can say that iron atoms exist in some worlds, and not in others.

While it is true that some individuals (iron atoms for example) exist in some worlds and not in others, it equally also true that some individuals can exist in *more than* one possible world. Arnold Schwarzenegger exists in at least one world (the actual world) in which he is an actor and a governor. But he also exists in worlds in which he is a plumber. But he doesn't exist in every world – the fast-expansion universe, for example. If something *were* to exist in every possible world, it would exist no matter how things went or how they turned out; such a being would be a *necessary being*. We encountered the notion of a necessary being back in chapter 1 where we saw that, on the classical conception of God, God is taken to be a necessary being. Beings that exist in some worlds but not in every world are *contingent beings*.

One final concept that needs to be discussed before presenting the modal argument is the concept of *possessing properties necessarily* and *contingently*. Whether a being is necessary or contingent, there are some properties that a being will have in every world in which it exists. Arnold Schwarzengger is a person, and he is just over six feet tall. The first property, being a person, is one that he has in every world in which it exists. It is reasonable to think this because we seem to lapse into incoherence whenever we try to imagine how things would be if he were a ping-pong ball or a cube of Jello. We can't imagine such things because they are impossible.

On the other hand, the property of being just over six feet tall is a property that Schwarzenegger has in some worlds but not in others. In worlds in which he grew up eating only Cocoa Puffs and Mountain Dew, he likely would not have received adequate nutrition to grow to the size (or shape) that he is now. He would perhaps be only four or five feet tall in those worlds. Thus, the property of being just over six feet tall is one that Schwarzenegger has only contingently.

Using these concepts we can now formulate the Modal Ontological Argument:

5.20.   God is the greatest possible being.
5.21.   The greatest possible being is one that possesses all perfections necessarily.
5.22.   Necessary existence is a perfection.
5.23.   It is possible that the greatest possible being exists.
5.24.   If it is possible that the greatest possible being exists, then that being exists necessarily.
5.25.   God exists necessarily.
5.26.   God exists.

Is this argument any good? We can begin by noting that if the premises are indeed true then the conclusion must be true. The real issue here is whether or not the premises are true. Premises 5.20, 5.21 and 5.22 are merely definitional. The first just restates the claim that God is the greatest possible being. 5.21 is the claim that the greatest possible being has every perfection, and that it would have those perfections no matter what. It is not a contingent matter that the greatest possible being is perfect. Finally, premise 5.22 holds, perhaps controversially, that necessary existence follows from the notion of perfection. We won't say much in defense of this premise here since we considered the arguments for it in chapter 1.

Notice that premises 5.25 and 5.26 are just conclusions that follow from what comes before them. So the real substantive work in the argument is being done in premises 5.23 and 5.24. Let's consider them, starting with the seemingly more controversial premise 5.24. What would entitle us to assert, as this premise does, that something exists necessarily simply because it is *possible* that it exist? The answer is straightforward even if it is not simple.

Premise 5.24 is a conditional or an "if . . . then" statement. As a result, we will be in a better position to think about it and assess its truth if we break it down into its component parts. Let's consider the "if" part first: "it is possible that a greatest possible being exists." What does this mean? Simply put, it means that in some possible world there exists a greatest possible being, that is, a being which has all perfections – including necessary existence – necessarily. This premise does not tell us *which* possible world the greatest being exists in. So, let's imagine that there are only five possible worlds, World 1, World 2, World 3, World 4, and World 5. Let's stipulate that the actual world is World 1, and that the greatest being exists (at least) "over there" in World 3. Now let's think about this greatest being "over there" in World 3. What do we know about it? One thing we know is that it has the property of *necessary existence*. That is, as we think about it "over there" in World 3, we realize that since it has the property of necessary existence, it must indeed exist *in every world*. The reason for this is really quite simple: there is just no way to have the property of necessary existence in any world (our world or World 3) without existing in *every possible world*.

So, now, rather than supposing that our greatest possible being exists *merely* in World 3, we are forced to admit that this being – because it has the property of necessary existence in World 3 – exists in every other world as well! And of course, that is just what the "then" part of our conditional says: "that being exists necessarily." Hence 5.24 is true.

That brings us, finally, to Premise 5.23. Premise 5.23 seems innocent enough. After all, it merely asserts that this greatest being exists in *some possible world or other*. It does not ask us to affirm that this greatest being exists in the actual world – just that it is possible. In order to assess this premise we need to ask how we decide or determine that a being is possible in the first place. The easiest way to make this determination is by constructing a test that will tell us whether or not that being is *impossible*. If the test shows a thing to be impossible, then we can conclude that it is *not possible*. If the test shows that the thing is not impossible then we can conclude that it is *possible*.

One test for determining whether or not something is impossible is this: if we can deduce some impossible claim from the concept of the thing, then the thing is impossible. Take for example the concept of "round square." Is a round square possible? Of course not. Anything that is a square has corners, while anything that is a circle lacks corners. But a round square would both have and lack corners, and that is impossible. As long as nothing impossible follows from the concept of a thing, then that thing is indeed possible.

What about a greatest possible being? Can we deduce any impossibilities from its concept? As we saw in chapters 1 and 2, some people think that we can. They argue, for example, that a greatest possible being would be both omnipotent and impeccable and yet that nothing can have these two properties. An impeccable being *cannot* sin while an omnipotent being can *do anything*. Thus a perfect being is impossible. In chapter 1 we saw that there are good reasons to think that this argument fails. Whether it does or not, it seems open to the critic of the argument to claim that other attributes or collections of attributes in the concept of the perfect being entail other impossibilities. And so, the critic might argue, until we are sure there are not other latent impossibilities in the concept of the greatest being, we cannot be confident that premise 5.23 is true. As a result, we cannot be confident that the conclusion is true either.

The defender of the Modal Ontological Argument might seem to have an easy reply to this objection. It is this:

> You think that we cannot endorse premise 5.23 until we are sure that the concept of the greatest being does not entail any impossibilities, but in fact this is no worry at all. The reason for this is that premise 5.23 affirms only that it is possible that the greatest *possible* being exists. So let's imagine that you are right and that some attribute or set of attributes that we think belong in the concept of the greatest being, for instance impeccability and omnipotence, are impossible. No problem. We will just have to agree that the being we have described is *not* the greatest *possible* being after all. We have mistakenly described an *impossible* being. Thus perhaps the concept of the greatest possible being includes only *as much power as an impeccable being can have* or something like that. Premise 5.23 only affirms that the greatest possible being is possible, and that, as you can now see, is true by definition!

While this is a powerful way of deflecting many objections to premise 5.23, one final objection must be considered. Our imaginary defender of the argument has argued that any attempt to undermine premise 5.23 will fail because we can simply readjust the concept of a perfect being in order to weed out any impossibilities it contains. If omnipotence is not really possible, we just backtrack and hold that the greatest being has as much power as it is possible to have, and so on. There is, however, *one* way of objecting to premise 5.23 that cannot be circumvented in this way.

What if someone were to object that the notion of a thing having *necessary existence* is impossible? That is, what if we could derive some impossibility from the concept of a being because it included the property of necessary existence? This would be a problem. The defender of the argument can't backtrack on this property and adjust the concept of the greatest being to purge the impossibility. That is, they cannot say something like: the greatest being exists in as many worlds as it is possible for it to exist in, but not in all of them. They cannot say that because doing so would undermine premise 5.21. Thus if the concept of something having necessary existence is impossible, the argument would unravel.

Is necessary existence impossible? No one has offered a convincing argument that it is. Thus, apart from a prior commitment to atheism, we have no clear reason to reject premise 5.23. On the other hand, the most that can be said in its favor at this point is that philosophers tend to presume that things are possible unless they can be shown to be impossible. But that will hardly be a persuasive consideration for someone who is looking for hard evidence in support of the existence of God. Thus, as things now stand, it appears that theists and their opponents will be at a stand-off with respect to the truth of 5.23.

Cosmological arguments

The first *a posteriori* argument that we will consider is the Cosmological Argument. Like the Ontological Argument, there are in fact many Cosmological Arguments, each of which has as its starting point the claim that there are contingent things or contingent truths. Such contingencies provide starting points for the argument because of the impression we have that contingencies require *explanations*. You pull some poison ivy out of your flower beds and, a few days later, you wake up to find small, red, itchy bumps on your arm. What explains the bumps? Probably the poison ivy. Still, it could be that you ate shellfish and are allergic to it. Or it could be that you were stung by mosquitoes while sleeping. We may not know which answer is right, but we know that *something* has to explain the bumps. Such things don't happen *for no reason*.

The same sort of reasoning that we apply to red bumps on our arms seems equally applicable to other things: a dent in the car, water in the basement, a crater on the moon, and so on. It also seems to apply to things like the existence of the earth, our solar system, the Milky Way galaxy, and even the universe taken as a whole. Once we extend our reasoning to the universe as a whole, the totality of all the natural things that exist, we are led to look for something extra-natural as an explanation for the existence of the universe, and we are well on our way to formulating a Cosmological Argument.

There are different ways in which philosophers have tried to formalize and refine this argument over the centuries, and two different versions have received a good deal of attention in recent philosophy of religion. It is those two arguments that we will consider here.

Dependence version 1

The first version of the argument goes as follows:

5.27. Every being is either dependent or self-explaining.

5.28. Not every being can be dependent.

5.29. Therefore: at least one self-explaining being exists (a being which in turn explains the existence of the dependent beings).

A dependent being is one that depends for existence on something else – a being, in other words, whose existence stands in need of some explanation. A self-explaining being, on the other hand, is one that does not depend for its existence on something else – a being which somehow explains its own existence and whose existence therefore does not require any (further) explanation. Most of the dependent beings we are aware of depend for their existence on other dependent beings. You, for example, are dependent on, among other things, your parents. They in turn are dependent on their parents. And so on.[4] As we travel back through these chains of dependent beings, the chains either come to an end or they do not. According to this version of the Cosmological Argument, as we will see, a self-explaining being will be required in either case. Of course, it takes further argument to move from the bare claim that there is a self-explaining being to the claim that there is a God. But if the argument is successful, it shows that a being

---

[4] Bear in mind, too, that both objects and events count as "beings." To simplify our discussion, we will usually talk as if it is just *objects* – trees, horses, particles, and so on – that depend on one another and explain one another's existence. But typically, of course, the dependence relations will involve both objects and events.

exists which has one of the properties that many have taken to be distinctively characteristic of God.[5]

What should we think of this argument? Both premises are controversial
and in need of defense. Let's start with premise 5.28. Above we said that
whether the chain of self-explaining beings terminates or not, an argument
can be made that a self-explaining being is required. Let's consider each case.

First, imagine that the chain *terminates*. What sort of being would be at
the terminus? It would have to be a self-explaining being (since the only
other option is a dependent being and, being dependent, it couldn't be the
terminus). Second, imagine that the chain *does not terminate*. That is, imagine
that the chain of dependent beings, each one explained by another which
precedes it, goes on infinitely into the past. In that case, each dependent
being would depend on something else for its existence, and that something
else would always be another dependent being. If that is how things are
then, contrary to what premise 5.28 claims, it *is* possible for every being to
be dependent.

The possibility of an infinite chain of dependent things, each explained
by the one preceding it, is called the *infinite regress objection* to premise 5.28 of
the argument. The defender of the argument thus needs to explain why the
infinite regress objection is mistaken. One way to respond to the infinite
regress objection is to point out that it seems to fit poorly with an important
fact we know about our universe, namely, that it is not infinitely old.
Normally when we think of cases of one dependent being that is explained
by another, the explaining being exists before the one that is explained. If
this is right, then an infinite regress of dependent beings would require an
infinitely old universe. We don't have one. So there is no infinite regress.

However, throughout history, philosophers and scientists have flip-
flopped on the question of whether or not the universe is infinitely old.
Perhaps we don't want a reply to the infinite regress objection to rest on
such scientifically tenuous facts. Are there other replies to the objection
that do not rest on such facts? Some have argued that the problem with an
infinite regress of this sort is that it violates a fundamental principle of
human reasoning about explanation, namely, the Principle of Sufficient
Reason:

---

[5] As we will see, however, some might be tempted to argue that the self-explaining being
shown to exist is nothing other than the universe itself. Below we will examine this
suggestion and argue that it is wanting.

PSR There must be a sufficient cause, reason, or explanation for the existence of every thing and for every positive fact.

PSR holds that there must be a sufficient explanation for every thing *and* every positive fact. The infinite regress of dependent things contains an explanation for every *thing*, but it does not give us an explanation for a couple of important *positive facts*:

FACT 1: There is something rather than nothing at all, and
FACT 2: There exists a certain infinite collection of things, namely, an infinitely long chain of dependent beings, each one depending on prior ones in the chain.

No appeal to individual dependent things is going to be able to explain either of these facts. Thus there must be some thing, over and above the set of dependent things, which provides the sufficient explanation for these two facts.

That might seem to close the case against the infinite regress objection, at least if the Principle of Sufficient Reason is true. But defenders of the infinite regress objection have replied that FACT 1 and FACT 2 *are* explained by the infinite regress after all. The reason for this, they argue, is that once we have explained *each member* of a set of dependent things, we have explained *the entire set* (FACT 2) and its *existence* (FACT 1). We can see the mistake, they claim, by considering a rather mundane example. Imagine the following conversation:

A: How much money do you have?
B: Fifteen dollars.
A: Oh. Why do you have fifteen dollars?
B: Well, I have ten dollars in this pocket that I got from the ATM, and I have five dollars in this pocket that someone gave me in repayment of a loan.
A: I see why you have the ten dollars and why you have the five dollars. Now tell me, why do you have *fifteen* dollars?
B: (confused) As I said I got the ten from the ATM, and five from someone earlier today, got it?
A: No, no. I understand the explanation for your having the five and the ten, but you have not explained two further Facts: Fact 1: that you have some money rather than none at all, and Fact 2: that there exists this

certain collection of two things: the five dollar bill and the ten dollar bill. How do you explain those two facts?

B: (annoyed) You must be a philosopher. Goodbye.

Obviously A is confused (or deliberately provoking her interlocutor). Once B has explained where the five and the ten came from, there is nothing left to explain. Explaining each part explains the whole. And, says the defender of the infinite regress objection, that is why we don't need any *further* explanation for Fact 1 and Fact 2 over and above the explanation that we have for each individual dependent thing. That is, the defender of the infinite regress objection thinks that the following principle is true:

> EXPLAINING EACH EXPLAINS ALL PRINCIPLE:
> A set of dependent beings is explained "with no explanatory remainder" when each member of the set has an explanation.

If that principle is right, Facts 1 and 2 are not unexplained after all.

Unfortunately, this ingenious defense of the infinite regress objection fails. To see why, consider another example. A and B are standing at the edge of the train tracks, looking at a train that is not moving and which stretches off into the distance as far as the eye can see. Suddenly they hear a bang and a creak and the cars of the train start to move off to the right. Now imagine that B points to the car just in front of them and asks "Why did that car move?" The event of the car accelerating is, of course, a dependent thing in the sense that something has to cause it to accelerate in this way. A replies:

A: Well of course, it moved because the car right in front of it moved, and the two are hooked together.

B: Alright, but what caused *that other* car to move.

A: The one in front of it, of course!

B: Yes, but what caused *that* one to move?

A: The one in front of *it*?

B: (seeing where this is going, and becoming annoyed) Why do I talk to you? Look, what I want to know is, what is the ultimate cause of the train moving?!

There is more than one reasonable response that A could give. But one thing that A could not reasonably say is this: "There is no ultimate cause for the movement of the train; there is just a string of train cars that goes on and on to infinity, and each car is moved by the one in front of it." Such an explanation would be unsatisfying because we have postponed the explanation for the movement of the car by appealing to the next one, and the next one, and the next one. But in doing so we never, in fact, get an explanation at all.

What does all of this show us? The Fifteen Dollar example seems to argue in favor of the Explaining Each Explains All Principle while the Train Car example seems to argue against it. So which is it? Actually, if we think carefully about the two cases we will see that in fact they teach us the very same lesson. The difference between the two cases is that in the Fifteen Dollar case our explanation of each dependent thing (the five and the ten) was a thing *outside the set* of the things to be explained (the repaying friend and the ATM). In the case of the Train Car, the explanations of each dependent thing came from *within the set* of things to be explained. That should lead us to think that a principle like the following is true:

External Explanations Principle:
A set of dependent beings is explained "with no explanatory remainder" when each member of the set has an explanation *and at least one member of the set is explained by appeal to something outside the set of dependent beings to be explained*.

This shows why the Fifteen Dollar example provided us with a complete explanation and the Train Car example did not. The former explained each item by appeal to something outside the set while the latter did not explain *any* by such an appeal.

So much for premise 5.28. How about premise 5.27? That first premise claims that we can divide all of the things that exist into one of two categories: dependent or self-explaining. While examples of self-explaining beings might be hard to think up, examples of dependent things are easy. Look around the room in which you are now sitting. Every one of the things you can see is a dependent thing: the walls, the lights, the carpet on the floor, and so on. All of these things exist because certain parts were put together by someone or something and transported to the location where you now are. In this sense they are all dependent.

Still there is at least one category that we can imagine over and above the two recognized by premise 5.27: things that are *explained by nothing at all*. Why does premise 5.27 exclude the possibility of such things? It does so for reasons similar to those outlined above. When we encounter things that could have failed to exist (red bumps on our arms, the planet Earth), we think that they must somehow be explained. Defenders of the Cosmological Argument argue that this exclusion is grounded in the Principle of Sufficient Reason. If PSR is true, then the set of all dependent beings will in fact need some explanation, and that explanation will have to involve appealing to some self-explaining being, exactly as the conclusion claims.

Is PSR true? Some have argued that the principle is self-evident. Others have argued that it is a fundamental principle of human reason. However, PSR faces three serious objections.

The first objection to PSR arises out of the fact that our best theories in physics claim that there are events that occur in nature which simply do not have sufficient causes or reasons. Radioactive decay provides a good example. According to the most widely accepted theory about such things, it would be impossible to predict when a radioactive atom will decay because decay events are indeterministic; there are no conditions that are *sufficient* for their occurrence. Thus, PSR is false.

The second objection concerns free choice. According to one widely accepted notion of free choice, when I choose between two or more things that I desire, the action is free only if at the moment of decision I could have chosen either thing. If my desire for one thing was sufficient for my choice (that is, such that given the desire, the choice was inevitable), then the choice was not free. As a result, if my choice between alternatives is genuinely free, that choice must lack sufficient conditions. There would, then, be no sufficient reasons for free choices. As a result, if there are such choices, PSR is false.

We could revise PSR, trying to amend it with various exceptions to steer clear of these objections. But PSR faces an even more serious third objection. The objection was first given careful expression by the philosopher who coined the Principle of Sufficient Reason, Gottfried Leibniz, and has been defended recently by others. According to PSR, every positive fact requires an explanation. But, of course, one positive fact about the world is just the grand totality of all of the other positive facts – the fact that would be expressed by, say, a (very large) book that tells the *complete* story about how things are, have been, and will be in the cosmos. Call that fact the SUPERFACT. If PSR is true, then the SUPERFACT needs an explanation. Let's call that explanation, whatever it might be, simply "THE REASON." What could THE REASON possibly be? For our purposes it doesn't really matter.

What does matter is that THE REASON would have to be either a necessary truth or a contingent truth; and, unfortunately, there are serious problems for either alternative.

Consider what would follow if THE REASON were a necessary truth. In that case, THE REASON would be true in all possible worlds: the actual world (the world that is the SUPERFACT), and all other possible worlds (Possible World 1, Possible World 2, Possible World 3, and so on). Recall, however, that the THE REASON for the SUPERFACT is supposed to be a *sufficient reason* for it. This means that in every world where THE REASON is true, the SUPERFACT will obtain. But this means that the SUPERFACT obtains in *every world*, which is just another way of saying that the SUPERFACT obtains *necessarily*. The result is that the actual world would be *necessarily* actual. And that is a problem because we are committed to the idea that other worlds might have been actual (since things might have gone some ways that they did not go).

What if THE REASON is not necessary? The first thing we have to note is that if it is not necessary, it is true in only *one* world, namely, the world described by the SUPERFACT. The problem in this case is that only very special propositions are true in just one world. This should be obvious once we think about such propositions. Consider first propositions that are true in many worlds. Propositions like "Ernest Hemingway exists (or existed)" are true in the actual world, but it will be true in many other worlds as well. Unlike these truths, truths that are true in only one world are hard to think of. It turns out that the only propositions that are true in a single world, say the actual world, are propositions that are logically equivalent to this proposition: "The world described in the SUPERFACT exists." Unfortunately, such propositions just state that the SUPERFACT is actual. Thus, they can't *explain it*.

What this shows us is that unacceptable consequences follow if we assume that there is a sufficient reason for the actuality of our world. And so we should reject that there is such an explanation. And once we do that, we have to reject PSR and its applicability to the question of why our world is actual.

Dependence version 2

Is there a way of salvaging the Dependence Cosmological Argument? The only way would be to defend premise 5.27 using some principle other than PSR. As we think about what principles might play a substitute role, it is important to remember the exact role that PSR played. That role was to exclude the possibility of things that are explained by nothing. But if that is all we need, then a much weaker principle than PSR will do the trick. For example:

NICT: There can be no independent contingent thing.

With NICT we can now reformulate our Dependence Argument as follows:

5.30. Every being is either dependent or necessary.
5.28. Not every being can be dependent.
5.29. Therefore: at least one necessary being exists (a being on which dependent beings at least partially depend for their existence).

How should we assess this argument? If NICT is true, premise 5.30 is true. Defending premise 5.28 will require once again ruling out the possibility of an infinite regress. Does NICT rule out such a possibility? Not exactly. Note that if the universe consists of an infinite sequence of contingent things, each one dependent on another, then there are no independent contingent things. As a result, it appears that every being can be dependent after all.

There are only two ways to circumvent this objection. The first is to defend the claim that the universe as a whole is itself a contingent thing, and then argue, via NICT, that *it* cannot be an independent contingent thing. Unfortunately, this is no easy task since defending this claim would require articulating a view on when a collection of entities constitutes or adds up to a single thing. The second is to note that this sort of infinite regress seems no more satisfying than the infinite regress that was defended in the Train Car case earlier.

The kalam version

Another version of the Cosmological Argument, which finds its roots in medieval Islamic philosophy, has been defended recently by William Lane Craig. Rather than arguing from the existence of contingent or dependent things to a cause, this argument contends that everything that begins to exist, including the universe, must be caused to exist. The argument can be formulated most simply as follows:

5.31. Whatever begins to exist has a cause of its coming to exist.
5.32. The universe began to exist.
5.33. Therefore: the universe has a cause of its coming to exist.

Many defenders of the Kalam Argument find the first premise to be simply obvious. They would be surprised to learn, then, that some cosmologists have recently argued that particles and indeed the universe as a whole can come into existence entirely out of nothing. Pre-existing our material universe is a pre-space or quantum vacuum from which, on this model, our universe emerged. Does this spontaneous creation of matter out of "nothing" contradict premise 5.31?

It is not at all clear that it does. When physicists or cosmologists speak of the universe coming into existence out of "nothing" or out of the "quantum vacuum" we must interpret their words carefully. Perhaps there is a sense in which these prior or simultaneous conditions are nothing. But there is another sense in which they are surely *something*. After all, these conditions (the quantum vacuum included) seem to be governed by the laws of nature, "they" can be *described* (as fluctuating, for example), "they" can be said to "produce" particles, and so on. Nothing sure seems to be capable of a lot! All of these things should instill serious doubt about whether such claims add up to a counter-example to premise 5.31 after all.

The second premise of the argument has been defended in two different ways. The first way is simply to make appeal to the claims of current cosmology. Our very best current science supports the claim that the universe came into existence roughly 14.5 billion years ago. As a result, science supports premise 5.32. However, since the medieval period, some philosophers have argued that we can know premise 5.32 to be true in ways that have nothing to do with science. According to this second argument, it is *impossible* for the universe to have had no beginning. The reason for this is that such a beginningless universe must contain an actually infinite series of past moments and such actual infinities are impossible.

To see the force of this argument imagine that you are told to start counting by ones from the number one. One, two, three ... "When should I stop?" you ask. "When you get to infinity," comes the reply. Very funny. You know, for a variety of reasons, that the answer can't be serious. One reason is that you *can't* count to infinity – not because there isn't enough time, but rather because, no matter how long you keep counting, reaching infinity is just *impossible*. Likewise, if you were to say that you have just finished the very arduous task of counting to infinity, we would think you were joking (or crazy). You simply can't do it. The very idea makes no sense.

These illustrations are relevant, defenders of the argument say, because if the universe contains an actually infinite series of past moments then the universe will have, as it were, succeeded in counting to infinity! But what is impossible for you is just as impossible for the universe.

Assessing the success of this particular argument is difficult because infinity itself is a vexing topic. But assessing the success of this argument is somewhat less relevant at the moment because we have good independent scientific support for premise 5.32, as we have seen.

One interesting feature of the Kalam Cosmological Argument is that it proposes that the universe had a beginning in time. This means that there was a first moment in the universe and thus that if there is a cause of the coming-to-be of the universe, this cause cannot have preceded the existence of the universe in time. How could this be? That is, how could the universe be caused-to-come to be if the cause did not exist *before* it?

Craig has argued that we must understand this causal relationship to be one where the cause exists not *prior to* the effect, but *simultaneously with* the effect. Causal relationships like this exist in many places throughout nature. For example, when we place a cup on a table, the table holds the cup in place and keeps it from falling. And as long as there is no earthquake or other disruption, the table continues to keep the cup from falling. This might seem like an arrangement in which one thing (putting the cup on the table) causes another thing (the cup being sustained in its position in space). But in fact, if the cup had been sitting on the table forever, the table would be simultaneously causing the cup to maintain its position forever. It would not be the case that one event was causing a succeeding event. In the same way, Craig argues that God's causing the universe to come to be could be simultaneous with its coming to be.

Craig also thinks that we can draw conclusions about specific attributes of the cause of the universe. For example, he argues that since the existence of the universe depends on its cause, and since there is no space or time without the existence of the universe, we can infer that that cause of the universe is a non-temporal being – a being which does not reside in the spatio-temporal continuum. While the argument does not entail that the cause of the universe is omnipotent or omniscient, Craig argues that it does entail that the cause of the universe is capable of something like free choice. If the cause of the universe is a non-temporal entity which exists eternally, then any of its effects would presumably exist for eternity unless this being had within itself the power to bring about effects "at will."

As we have noted, the success of the Kalam Argument depends on two claims: that the universe had a beginning and that whatever has a beginning requires a cause. While some critics have focused on the first claim, and especially on the argument concerning the impossibility of actual infinities, most recent criticism has been focused on the second claim. How could we know that everything that begins to exist has a cause? Hume and others argued that we cannot know this on the basis of reason alone. If it were true, it is something that we would know through experience. That is, we would know it to be true because we would be aware of many things which come into existence and we would see that those things all have causes. We might then infer that what holds true in these cases holds true in all cases. However, (inductive) inferences of this sort are only good when we have experience of a number of cases, and when the unobserved cases are relevantly similar to the case in question.

Are we aware of enough cases to conclude that premise 5.32 is true? It is hard to be confident that we do. Further, are the sorts of things that we are acquainted with similar enough to universes-as-a-whole that we can apply the lessons learned in one case to the other case? That question seems even harder to answer. However, some have argued that the answer is easy; it is "no." The objects that we are acquainted with that begin to exist are objects that are *in time*, with causes that are *in time*. With the Kalam Argument we are applying our experience to a case in which a non-temporal entity causes the existence of the totality of space, time, and matter. The two cases seem highly dissimilar.

Finally, some critics have raised objections to the coherence of the idea of a non-temporal being causing a temporal universe or of a non-temporal person making "choices" or exercising "act of will" since both of these things seem to require sequences of events.

Design arguments

Cosmological arguments take as their starting point the existence of dependent, contingent, or non-timeless things and argue that there must be a supernatural being with sufficient power or stature to explain such things. Design or *teleological* arguments take as their starting point the existence of natural objects displaying patterns that are best explained or only explained by the activity of rational, designing beings.

Arguments which try to show the existence of a designer from the evidence of apparent design have been defended by philosophers since at least the time of Plato. Here we consider two classical versions of the argument and one more recent version.

The analogy argument

There has been much discussion about exactly how to frame the argument from design. And the framing makes a great deal of difference since some ways of stating it leave it open to obvious and fatal objections. For example, we might begin with an argument like this:

5.34.   The universe is like a machine.

5.35.   Machines are typically caused by designers.

5.36.   Therefore: the universe is likely caused by a designer.

It is not uncommon for those who believe in the existence of God to offer design arguments like this. But put this way, the argument is very unclear. First, what does it mean to say that the universe is *like* a machine? Second, even if the universe is like a machine, perhaps it is even more like something else: an experiment by a sadistic mad scientist, or a largely cold, dark, lifeless rock, or ... Which of these analogies is the most relevant, and who decides?

We can begin to make the argument more clear and rigorous by trying to find some specific feature that both the universe (or some of its natural parts) and things known to be designed share in common, where the shared feature is a sure sign of design in the case of things known to be designed. If, for example, we were to direct our telescopes to a region of the sky and find a large collection of stars spelling out the words "This universe was designed by God" we would conclude that this part of the natural world was designed because (a) it shares something in common (grammatical English sentences) with things we know to be designed (books, magazines, and so on) and (b) designed things have that very feature *because* they are designed.

Revised in this light, the argument would look something like this:

5.37.   There is some property P such that (a) some natural object N (or perhaps the cosmos as a whole) has P, (b) many artifacts (watches,

for example) have P, and (c) artifacts that have P do so because they
are the products of design.

5.38. Things that are alike generally have causes or explanations that are
alike as well.

5.39. Therefore: it reasonable to conclude that N has P because it is likewise the product of design.

For this argument to work we are going to have to identify some property P
that natural objects and artifacts have and that reliably signals design
among artifacts. It isn't hard to imagine at least a few candidates for P:
being machine-like, being composed of machines nested within other
machines, having parts which are accurately adjusted to one another so
that they accomplish certain ends.

What shall we think of the premises of this argument? Consider premise
5.37. It claims something like this: some natural objects and human artifacts are alike in that they are machine-like, and artifacts are machine-like
because they are designed. Unfortunately, none of this is even close to being
straightforward or obvious. Is the universe machine-like? That depends on
what it means for something to be a machine. If we mean by "machine" a
collection of interacting parts which are designed to perform a function of
some sort, then calling the universe machine-like will simply beg the question. We cannot use such a claim as a premise in an argument aimed at
showing that the universe is designed.

Perhaps a machine is a collection of parts that interact in a regular and
orderly way. But why should we think, as premise 5.38 requires, that things
that are machine-like have similar causes for their being that way? As Hume
pointed out, and as we saw earlier, some things might be machine like
because they are products of design, but others are machine-like because
they are living organisms. So, is the universe machine-like because it was
designed, or because it is a giant organism?

Design as an inference to the best explanation

All of this makes it clear that design arguments based on analogy are quite
difficult to defend. Because of this, most design arguments discussed in
contemporary philosophy of religion are constructed as "inferences to the
best explanation." Earlier we considered an example in which you wake up

one day with red, itchy bumps on your arm after pulling poison ivy a day or two before. We all agree that something other than the poison ivy *could* explain the bumps. Still we will all also agree that the most reasonable thing to believe, in this case, is that the poison ivy is the culprit. In drawing this conclusion you make an inference to the best among a number of possible available explanations.

Arguments of this sort work only when there are no good competing explanations. If in addition to pulling poison ivy yesterday, you wrestled someone a week ago who was covered with chicken pox, your confidence in the poison ivy explanation should drop dramatically. Thus when considering design arguments we first need to know: what other explanations might there be for the apparent design in the world?

The most commonly offered alternative explanations are chance, on the one hand, and evolution on the other. Explaining the existence of something by appeal to chance is really not much different from offering no explanation for its existence at all. Things that occur by chance are things that "just happen" – their occurrence is neither intended by rational agents nor guaranteed by the laws of nature.

Explanations in terms of evolution work quite differently. These explanations hypothesize that apparent design, at least in the biological realm, is to be explained by the workings of an algorithmic natural process, namely, variation and natural selection. Variations appear in the offspring of certain organisms, and when those variations are adaptive (and heritable), they will tend to increase in frequency over succeeding generations. Thus we should expect that organisms will be increasingly well suited to their environments and will display increasingly impressive qualities (perhaps like conscious and morally significant life). Those impressive qualities give the appearance of design; but, on this account, that appearance is misleading.

This alternative explanation is historically quite important since, in their heyday in the early nineteenth century, the vast majority of design arguments focused on the biological realm. However, since the publication of Darwin's *Origin of Species*, the alternative evolutionary explanation has come to seem an even more probable explanation. More recent design arguments focus on a very different type of order, one that seems resistant to explanations in terms of chance or evolution. We turn to arguments of this sort next.

"Fine-tuning" design arguments

In the nineteenth century scientists and philosophers were particularly impressed with the apparent design of nature in the realm of biology. The intricate, integrated internal structures of organisms, the extraordinary well-suitedness of organisms to their environment, and the fact that numerous plants and animals were useful for human purposes were all seen as the work of a divine designer. Darwinism took the wind out of the sails of these arguments since it provided a mindless mechanism for this apparent design.

Since the second half of the twentieth century, scientists and philosophers have focused increasing attention on another area where we find powerful evidence of apparent design: cosmology. Recent cosmologists have been struck by the fact that the conditions, laws, and constants which govern both the origin of the universe and the activity of the matter it contains seem to be "fine-tuned" in such a way as to allow life to occur. This tenuous balance of numerous conditions has been acknowledged by theists and atheists alike, and led the famous twentieth-century cosmologist and atheist Fred Hoyle to remark: "A common-sense interpretation of the facts suggests that a superintellect has monkeyed with physics as well as with chemistry and biology, and that there are no blind forces worth speaking about in nature. The number one calculates from the facts seem to me so overwhelming as to put this conclusion almost beyond question."[6]

This apparent cosmic fine-tuning leads some to favor the following argument:

5.40. The universe exhibits fine-tuning of a sort that makes it suitable for life.
5.41. The existence of fine-tuning is probable under theism.
5.42. The existence of fine-tuning is highly improbable under atheism.
5.43. Therefore: fine-tuning provides strong evidence in favor of theism over atheism.

What sort of evidence do cosmologists offer for the first premise? There is in fact quite a lengthy list of examples of such fine-tuning. Here are just three:

---

[6] Fred Hoyle, "The Universe: Past and Present Reflections," *Engineering and Science* (November 1981), p. 12.

(A) According to the most widely accepted cosmological model, the universe came into existence roughly 14.5 billion years ago at the Big Bang. Very shortly after the Big Bang, the universe underwent a cosmic "inflation" during which it expanded extremely rapidly for a mere fraction of a second. Had the rate of inflation during this period differed by as little as one part in 10^{60} the universe either would have stopped expanding and collapsed back in on itself due to internal gravitational forces, or it would have expanded so rapidly that elementary particles could not have clustered or coalesced in a way that would allow any matter to form.

(B) Atoms are made up of a nucleus and one or more electrons which orbit the nucleus. Aside from hydrogen, the nucleus of every atom contains two or more protons which are held together by something scientists call the "strong force." As with the rate of inflation, the strength of the strong nuclear force must be finely balanced for life to be possible. If for example the strong force were only 10 percent weaker than it is, protons could never begin to "clump" together in ways that allow for the formation of atoms other than hydrogen. In such a universe there would be no possibility of forming any complex molecules at all. And such complexity is required for life. If the strong force were as little as 4 percent weaker, something quite different would happen: nuclei could be formed from either pairs of neutrons or pairs of protons. In that case, the reactions that take place inside stars would happen very rapidly, rather than over the billions of years it now takes, and this would mean that the universe would lack the sources of heat and light which, as best we can tell, are instrumental to the origin and continuation of life.

(C) Not only must the strong force be of a certain strength, it also needs to be proportional to another fundamental force of nature, the electromagnetic force, within a very narrow range. The reason for this is not hard to see. The electromagnetic force is the force that causes protons to seek to fly apart. This force needs to be balanced by the strong force keeping them together. For example, if the strong force were only one-twenty-fifth as strong as it is, half the elements necessary for complex life forms would be unable to exist because the repulsive forces would blow the nucleus of higher elements apart.

These are just a handful of numerous examples of so-called cosmic "fine-tuning."

The second premise seems plausible enough. If theism is true, it is reasonable to assume that the creator would create a universe with conditions that are conducive to the formation of life and, indeed, intelligent life. Such life would be capable of the distinctly personal goods that seem to be of overriding value: love, friendship, morally significant action, and so on.

What about premise 5.42? The claim that fine-tuning is implausible on atheism initially seems right. After all, if these finely-tuned constants and forces could have had other values than the ones they do have, how likely is it that they would be tuned in the way necessary to allow for life for no apparent reason?

Some have argued that this question, and the reasoning in defense of premise 5.42, assumes something false, and this false assumption tricks us into thinking that premise 5.42 is true when it is not. The assumption is that it is highly improbable that the constants and forces would be fine-tuned for life as opposed to being set in some other way. This, they argue, is wrong. To see why let's imagine (for the sake of simplicity) that there are ten fine-tuned constants and forces, and that each of these constants and forces could take ten different values. Think of them as ten dials, each with numbers from zero through nine. For life to be possible, let's say, the value of each dial would have to be set at the number 5. What are the odds of that? One in 10 billion. Those are pretty low odds. But now imagine that the dials are set with the non-life-permitting values of 2,4,6,7,1,3,8,9,1,0. What are the odds of *that*? Actually, the same: one in 10 billion. Thus, our life-permitting settings are no more improbable than any other set of settings that the dials might take. The life-permitting settings are not uniquely improbable; they are in fact as improbable as any set. Since the constants and forces had to have *some value or other* we should not be surprised that they have *these values*, since every set of values is just as unlikely.

Unfortunately this objection misses the mark. We can see this by considering the following example: four friends get together to play poker one night and one of the players, John, draws royal flushes for ten straight hands. On showing the tenth straight royal flush, John's friends accuse him of cheating and threaten to take the money back and throw him out. But John replies as follows: "I know it is improbable that I would get a straight flush of hearts on any given hand. In fact, the probability is just a little more than one in a million. But what is the probability that I get a hand with two spades (a 3 and a 6) and three hearts (a 9, a Jack, and an ace)? That hand is garbage. But the probability of getting it is the same: a little worse than one in a million. Likewise, though the particular sequence of hands that I got is vastly improbable, it is no more or less probable than any other particular sequence of hands. I had to get some series of hands or other, so why do you find one improbable series more surprising or in need of explanation than another? There is, of course, no good reason."

Unless John's friends are very gullible, John should expect to lose his winnings and be pitched out the door. Why? Because what needs an explanation in this case is not that he drew an "improbable series of hands" but that he drew, against incredible odds, a series of unbeatable hands. There are numerous garbage hands and only a handful of hands that beat all others. We want to know why he drew an improbable *and special* series of hands. The same holds true in the case of the fine-tuning arguments. It is no doubt true that any set of settings would be improbable. But this set is improbable and special, and thus in need of an explanation.

Others have argued that premise 5.42 might be mistaken because there are underlying reasons, unknown to us, that would explain why these constants must have the very values that they have. For example, we would at one time have believed that the strength of the force of magnetism and the force of electricity could vary quite independently. But we now know that these forces are not independent of one another after all. Perhaps something similar is true with respect to the fine-tuned forces and constants that seem to be set at random to just the right values. Perhaps for a physical universe to exist at all, the forces and constants must have the very settings they have in the actual world. While this objection may turn out to be right, the view of current physicists and cosmologists is that the laws and constants are not connected in this way. Thus until further notice we have to regard this objection as a failure.

Some have instead objected to premise 5.42 by arguing that while *life as we know it* would be unlikely if the constants and forces of nature were slightly different, perhaps *other forms of life* would be possible. Maybe carbon can only form under highly constrained conditions. But who says that all life must be carbon based? Perhaps forms of life that are now unimaginable to us would be possible were the forces and constants radically different from what they are in our universe.

It is true that we might be unable to predict or imagine the various forms that life might take in universes that differ from our own in fundamental ways. But what we *can* predict is that life would be impossible if the universe did not exist at all, or if it contained no matter, or if it contained only hydrogen. And the fine-tuning argument seems to make a powerful case that if the forces or constants had values that were much different from their actual values, there would be no universe, or no matter, or nothing more complex than hydrogen.

The most formidable objection to premise 5.42 is the so-called "multiverse objection." According to this objection, the existence of a finely tuned universe is unlikely on atheism *if there is only one universe*. But if there are many, many universes, each of which differs with respect to its laws and forces, then it is not so unlikely that one of those universes will be life permitting.

While the existence of multiple universes could lead us to reject premise 5.42, this objection faces three difficulties. First, since we have no actual evidence for the existence of such universes it seems more reasonable to reject than to accept their existence. The reason for this is the more general principle that scientists accept in their theorizing which might be formulated as follows: everything else being equal, we should prefer hypotheses for which we have independent evidence or that are natural extrapolations from what we already know. Since belief in the existence of multiple universes would violate this principle, the principle would lead us to reject this belief.

Second, the reality of multiple universes would only undermine premise 5.42 if those universes were likely to have different forces and constants. However, current models which postulate the existence of multiple universes do not clearly specify that those universes differ from one another in these ways. This is still a very contentious area of scientific theorizing and so it may be that a resolution of this concern is forthcoming. But at the moment, these models do not evidently support such a possibility.

Finally, some physicists have argued that even if there were a mechanism for generating multiple universes, this mechanism would itself have to be fine-tuned in order to be capable of generating viable universes. A "universe generator" would have to have characteristics which make it capable of producing these numerous viable universes with different forces and constants. Yet like any machine-making machine, this universe generator would also have to be fine-tuned for this purpose. Such specificity would likely require higher-level fine-tuning.

One might wonder the following at this point: if the universe generator exhibits complexity that requires an explanation, then wouldn't this also imply that a designer would require an explanation? If so, then a designer provides us with no more of a complete explanation than a universe generator would. But, for reasons we have seen in discussing the Cosmological Argument, it may be that a divine designer would not in fact require some further explanation, since the designer might well be self-explaining or necessary.

Conclusion

In this chapter we have examined a variety of arguments that aim to show that something exists which has many or all of the distinctive characteristics of God. Some of the arguments are less ambitious, attempting to show only that a necessary or non-dependent creator exists (the dependence argument), while others offer more ambitious conclusions (that the greatest possible being exists). Do these arguments succeed? We have seen in each case that there are good reasons for accepting the premises of these arguments. But we have also seen that critics offer some good reasons against accepting them. Your job is to consider each of these controversies and decide which view you find most plausible.

Of course, the outcome of that exercise will not entirely settle the question. Even if these arguments for theism all fail, theism might still be true. Perhaps there are other arguments or evidence for theism we have not yet considered or thought of. In addition, even if the arguments look successful, we might *also* have good reasons for thinking that God doesn't exist. In that case we will have to balance the strength of the evidence on both sides as we draw our ultimate conclusions. Are there any good reasons for thinking that God does not exist? We turn to this question in our next chapter.

Further reading

Barr, Stephen, *Modern Physics and Ancient Faith* (Notre Dame, IN: University of Notre Dame Press, 2006).

Collins, Robin, "The Many Worlds Hypothesis as an Explanation of Cosmic Fine-Tuning: An Alternative to Design?" *Faith and Philosophy* 22:5 (2005), pp. 654–66.

Craig, William Lane, *The Cosmological Argument from Plato to Leibniz* (New York: Barnes & Noble, 1980).

The Kalam Cosmological Argument (London: Macmillan, 1979).

Craig, William Lane and Quentin Smith, *Theism, Atheism, and Big Bang Cosmology* (New York: Oxford University Press, 1993).

Gale, Richard, *On the Existence and Nature of God* (Cambridge: Cambridge University Press, 1991).

Leslie, John, *Universes* (London: Routledge, 1989).

Oppy, Graham, *Ontological Arguments and Belief in the Existence of God* (Cambridge: Cambridge University Press, 1995).

Rowe, William, *The Philosophy of Religion* (Belmont, CA: Wadsworth, 1978).

The Cosmological Argument (Princeton, NJ: Princeton University Press, 1975).

Swinburne, Richard, *The Existence of God*, 2nd edn. (Oxford: Clarendon Press, 2004).

Tegmark, Max, "Parallel Universes," *Scientific American* 288 (May 2003), pp. 41–51.

6 Anti-theistic arguments

Having looked at arguments for the existence of God, we now turn to look at arguments against God's existence. Novices in the philosophy of religion often initially think that there is something wrong-headed about the project of coming up with arguments for the non-existence of God. "How," it is often asked, "can one prove the *non-existence* of something?"

This is a good question. How *can we* prove, or at least provide good reasons to believe in, the non-existence of anything, God included? There are at least three ways. One way we can show the non-existence of something is by showing that the thing described is *impossible*. If someone tells you that she has a round square in her pocket, you would know that she is wrong. You know there is no round square in her pocket (or anywhere else), because you know there *cannot be* round squares. Round things necessarily *lack* corners while squares necessarily *have* corners. One thing can't both have and lack corners. So there can be no such thing as a round square.

Impossibility arguments for the non-existence of God are not uncommon. In fact, in chapters 1 and 2 we looked at a number of arguments that aim to show that the attributes of God are internally incoherent or inconsistent with other attributes. These might be seen as attempts to show that God does not exist because God is like a round square.

A second way we can show the non-existence of something is to show that certain telltale signs are absent which would be present if the thing in question actually did exist (or that certain telltale signs are present which would be absent if the thing in question actually did exist). If there had been a thunderstorm last night, your driveway would be wet this morning. If it is dry, you can safely conclude that there was no thunderstorm last night. The dry driveway provides you with evidence for the non-existence of the storm. Arguments with a similar structure can be and have been used to argue against the existence of God. Below we will examine the two most common such arguments: the argument from evil and the argument from hiddenness.

The argument from evil is familiar enough. If there were a God, the universe would have a telltale sign: it would be a pleasure-filled, evil-free place. But it isn't. And so, there is no God. The argument from hiddenness holds rather that if there were an all-loving God, such a God would, among other things, want us to know of his existence so that we could enter into loving communion with him. This goal seems so important in fact that we would expect God to provide evidence for his existence that is clear and powerful enough that we could only miss it if we were deliberately trying to do so. But, the argument continues, the evidence for the existence of God is not clear and unmistakable. Thus there is no God.

A third way we can argue for the non-existence of something is through an appeal to the lack of evidence for the existence of the thing. There is a famous slogan in philosophy and in law: absence of evidence is not evidence of absence. That is, there is no reason to deny the existence of something simply because we lack evidence for its existence. Strictly speaking that is correct. But it is also true that in some cases if we lack any evidence for the existence of something, the *reasonable thing to believe* is that that thing does not exist.

In this chapter we will bypass impossibility arguments against the existence of God since they were taken up in our discussions of the divine attributes earlier. We will also set aside arguments which claim that the absence of evidence makes belief in atheism more reasonable or obligatory since that issue was addressed in chapter 4. Here we will focus our attention on the two most important "telltale sign" arguments.

The argument from evil

During a recent visit to Germany Pope Benedict XVI visited the death camp at Auschwitz. While surveying the memorial to the nearly 1.5 million Nazi victims he found himself at a loss for words of explanation or consolation: "In this place, words fail. In the end, there can only be dread silence – a silence which is itself a heartfelt cry to God ... How could you tolerate all this?" *Washington Post* columnist Richard Cohen commenting on the Pope's remarks wrote the following:

Religious people can wrestle with the Pope's remarks. What does it mean that God was silent? That he approved? That he liked what he saw? That he didn't give a damn? You tell me. And what does it mean that he could "tolerate all this"? That the Nazis were OK by him? That even the murder of Catholic clergy was no cause of intercession? I am at a loss to explain this. I cannot believe in such a God.[1]

Theists and atheists alike seem convinced that evil does indeed count against the existence of God in some sense. While some evils might seem to make sense in light of a comprehensive divine plan for the universe, how can we accommodate senseless torture, degrading sexual abuse, catastrophic tsunamis, and so on? And what is more, how can theists explain the fact that virtue and happiness do not seem proportional in this life? In the words of the Hebrew prophet Jeremiah:

> You are always righteous, O LORD, when I bring a case before you. Yet I would speak with you about your justice: Why does the way of the wicked prosper? Why do all the faithless live at ease?[2]

Needless to say, the pattern of evil we find in the world does not exactly fit our initial expectations of what a world would look like if theism were true. Does this fact count as a good reason to accept atheism? Does the existence of evil of this sort add up to a telltale sign that atheism is true?

Those who think so offer one of two different types of arguments. According to the first type of argument, the existence of evil is flatly incompatible with the existence of God. According to the second, the existence of God and evil are not incompatible, but the reality of evil makes it unlikely that God exists, and this makes belief in the existence of God unreasonable. Philosophers call the first sort of argument *the logical argument* from evil and the second sort *the evidential argument* from evil.

The logical argument

The logical argument is not difficult to construct. In fact, it is an argument that, for many of us, immediately springs to mind when we think about God and evil. The simplest version would be this:

[1] *Lancaster Intelligencer Journal*, June 6, 2006, A10.
[2] Jeremiah 12:3, in *The Holy Bible: New International Version* (North American Edition), Copyright 1984, International Bible Society.

6.1. If there were a God, there would be no evil.

6.2. There is evil.

6.3. Thus there is no God.

What should we think of this most simple version? The answer hinges on our assessment of premise 6.1. If we are inclined to accept it, it is probably because we think that if there were a God, that God would be all-good, all-powerful, and all-knowing. Any being that is all-good would, by definition, want to prevent evil. And of course, any being that is all-powerful and all-knowing would be aware of all evil and would be capable of preventing it. In light of all this, it seems reasonable to think that if there were a God, there would be no evil.

These considerations lead us to an enhanced version of the Logical Argument:

6.4. If there were a God, He would be omniscient, omnipotent, and wholly good.

6.5. (a) A wholly good being would prevent the occurrence of every evil it is in his or her power to prevent, (b) an omniscient being would be aware of all possible and actual evils, and (c) an omnipotent being would be able to prevent all evils.

6.6. Thus, if there were a God, there would be no evil.

6.7. There is evil.

6.8. Thus, there is no God.

If this argument is a good one, it shows us why the existence of evil and the existence of God are logically incompatible.

Since premises 6.6 and 6.8 merely draw conclusions from other premises, the theist can object to the argument only by rejecting one of premises 6.4, 6.5, or 6.7. Although some religious traditions deny premise 6.7 – that is, they deny the reality of evil – this does not seem to be a very promising response.

Some philosophers have instead rejected premise 6.4. After all, why not simply deny that God is all-powerful or all-knowing? Perhaps God is very, very powerful, but still not capable of preventing *all* evil. Or perhaps God is very, very knowledgeable, but still falls short of knowing every truth that could be known. One could accept these things and thus deny premise 6.4. But to deny 6.4 is just to deny theism, since theism holds that God is all-powerful and all-knowing. So denying 6.4 really just concedes the conclusion.

The theist's last remaining option, then, is to reject premise 6.5. And indeed, this premise has been the primary focus of attention. What should we think of it? The most serious problem for premise 6.5 is part (a). The problem is that it is false. As a moment's reflection makes clear, it is surely false to say that a good being always prevents every evil it can. Doctors (even good ones) will sometimes cause you to feel pain (an evil) because doing so is required to get at some greater good (your cure, for example). Thus, a wholly good being is not one which prevents every evil it can, but rather one that prevents evil unless there is a morally sufficient reason for not doing so.

What would count as a morally sufficient reason for allowing evil? For a wholly or perfectly good being to have a morally sufficient reason for permitting an evil, three conditions must be satisfied:

(A) The Necessity Condition: it must be the case that the good brought about by permitting the evil, E, would not have been brought about without permitting either E or some other evils morally equivalent to or worse than E.[3]
(B) The Outweighing Condition: it must be the case that the good secured by the permission of the evil is sufficiently outweighing.
(C) The Rights Condition: it must be the case that it is within the rights of the one permitting the evil to permit it at all.

If these conditions *are* satisfied for some particular evil, then even an all-powerful and perfectly good being will be justified in permitting it.

What all of this shows us is that it is not the *reality of evil* that is incompatible with the existence of God; rather, it is the *reality of pointless* or *gratuitous* evils. In light of this, we can revise our Logical Argument one more time as follows:

6.9. If there were a God, there would be no gratuitous evils (GEs).
6.10. There is at least one GE.
6.11. Therefore: there is no God.

---

[3] We use the word "would" rather than "could" in this condition intentionally. It might the case that there are certain goods that *could* be secured without allowing some particular instance of evil. But it might also be the case that those goods would not in fact be secured without permitting the evil. Take, for example, the figure of St. Paul in the Christian Scriptures. Christians might contend that it is possible that Paul have repented of his evil ways without being stricken by God with blindness but that, as a matter of fact, he would stubbornly refuse until so stricken.

If there is a problem with this argument, it is with premise 6.10.[4] To defend premise 6.10 the atheist needs to demonstrate that there is at least one GE. Showing this means showing that there is an evil that is either (a) *not necessary* for bringing about an *outweighing* good or (b) *not within the rights* of God to permit. Do some evils fall into one of these two categories? Let's consider them in turn.

One strategy would be to argue, with respect to particular evils – say, a small child's being cruelly beaten – either that such an evil could not possibly be outweighed by a greater good or that it could not possibly be necessary for some outweighing good. The trouble, however, is that it is hard to see how such arguments might go in particular cases. Why not think that there might be goods of which we are unaware – goods, perhaps, that might come to the sufferer herself – that would outweigh the suffering? And why not think that some of those goods might be absolutely unattainable apart from God's willingness to allow such instances of suffering to take place? The only arguments that would seem to have any purchase here would be very general arguments – arguments, in other words, for the general conclusion that *no* evil could be necessary for an outweighing good.

Thus, we have a second way of trying to defend 6.10: namely, to produce an argument showing that no evil could be necessary for a greater good (in which case all evils would be gratuitous). Some atheists have offered such arguments. They claim that if God exists, then, in fact, *all* evils would be gratuitous since an omnipotent being would never have to rely on allowing evil in order to bring about some greater good. To say otherwise would be to say that God is sometimes at the mercy of having to allow certain evils to occur in order to get some outcome that he wants. But how could an omnipotent being be at the *mercy* of anything? We can, they say, imagine such a thing in the case of surgeons. Surgeons sometimes must inflict or allow pain and suffering in their patients in order to cure them. But God? Surely not. An omnipotent being would never be subject to such limitations. If God wanted to bring about a certain good, God would just do it.

Unfortunately, for all we know, this is false. We can see this by way of the following example. Theists and atheists alike largely agree that it is a good thing that God creates a universe, and that it is a good thing if the universe

---

[4] Though a few theists have recently argued that we should reject 6.9. See, for example, the works by William Hasker and Peter van Inwagen in the Further Reading list at the end of this chapter.

God creates contains creatures with freedom. Free creatures can enjoy the very great good of making free and autonomous choices. Furthermore, suitably intelligent and reflective free creatures are capable of producing moral good in the world, engaging in relationships of love and friendship, displaying genuine charity and courage, and so on. Yet free creatures of that sort necessarily have the ability to choose to do evil. And if those creatures are genuinely free in making their choices, they cannot be determined to choose only the good.

Now let's imagine that God is faced with the prospect of creating a universe. Wanting to maximize the varieties of good in the creation, and wanting to fill the creation with the greatest types of good, God decides to create a world containing a number of creatures with free choice. Can God create a world with such freely choosing creatures who never choose to do wrong? Not exactly. On the one hand, it is surely possible that God create a world with free creatures and that those creatures never choose to do wrong. But if the creatures are genuinely free (and if, as many think, freedom is incompatible with any kind of determinism – divine or natural), then it is really up to them and not God whether their world is one in which nobody ever chooses to do wrong. And it might be the case that, no matter what God did, things *would not* have turned out so that everybody always does what is right (even if they *could* have turned out that way). If that is right, then (we might say) though it is possible that everybody always freely does what is right, worlds in which that occurs might not be *feasible* for God. In short: because God cannot leave a creature free and at the same time guarantee that she will do what God wants, it is (on this view) simply not within God's power to ensure that the world he creates contains only free creatures who always do what is right.[5] Thus, for all we know, a universe with evil might be an unavoidable consequence of God's creating a universe that includes the very great good of creaturely freedom.

---

[5] Does this count against God's omnipotence? No; because, given the view of freedom (as incompatible with determinism) that is presupposed by this response to the argument from evil, it is *logically impossible* for God to guarantee that a *free* agent conform to God's will. So long as the agent is free, there are no guarantees about what she will do; and if God does anything to guarantee her conformity to his will, he – by definition – undermines her freedom. And, as we saw in chapter 1, the standard story about omnipotence is that omnipotence does not include the power to do what is logically impossible.

This argument, known as the Free Will Defense, was first developed in detail by Alvin Plantinga. The argument is meant to show that there are, for all we know, some goods (like the good of free choice) which even God cannot bring about without also allowing certain evils (specifically, morally evil choices) to occur. If this is right, then the second way of defending 6.10 also fails: some evils, for all we know, might have to be permitted in order to secure greater goods.

Let us now turn to a third way of defending 6.10. One might try to argue that there are some evils that God has no right to permit – even if permitting them *is* necessary to secure some greater good. Can the atheist argue that there are some evils like that? One might argue, for example, that some evils are so horrendous that no one, God included, could be justified in allowing them even if they were necessary conditions for bringing about some out-weighing good. Perhaps, for example, it would never be permissible to allow a child to die a slow, painful, and lingering death due to cancer, even if it is a necessary means to some great good and even if that good somehow man-aged to outweigh such suffering. Unfortunately, arguments of this sort will all be grounded in moral principles that are highly contentious – principles, moreover, that many theists will be likely to reject. As a result, it is hard to imagine that arguments of this sort will be of much value to the atheist in getting people to accept premise 6.10.

For reasons of this sort, the Logical Argument is not much defended these days. Instead, most discussion of the argument from evil focuses on the second version: the Evidential Argument.

The Evidential Argument part 1: the "Direct Argument"

The first version of the Evidential Argument follows the same general pattern found in the Logical Argument. The difference is that the argument claims only that the premises are likely or probable:

6.12. If there were a God, there would be no gratuitous evils (GEs).
6.13. It is probable that at least one of the evils in our world is a GE.
6.14. Therefore: probably, there is no God.

In discussing the Logical Argument we saw that the atheist is going to have a difficult time defending premise 6.10 (the claim that there are gratuitous evils). The problem is that for all we know, God has good reasons for allowing the evil we see around us to occur. What the defender of this Evidential Argument insists on is that even though there *might* be such reasons, it is not *very likely* that there are.

This way of putting the argument actually resonates with our ordinary way of thinking of the connection between the existence of God and the existence of evil. Though, as we acknowledged earlier, it will be hard to show that any particular evil, or that evil in general, is *definitely* pointless, it is hard to shake the thought that at least some of the evils around us are *probably* pointless. For many such evils, we simply cannot imagine a point; and many are inclined to think that our inability to imagine a point just goes to show that, quite probably, such evils have no point. Thus, 6.13 has a kind of intuitive attractiveness; and so the argument as a whole has, at least initially, some persuasive force.

The G.E. Moore shift

There are three ways for the theist to respond to the argument cast this way. The first is by what William Rowe calls the "G.E. Moore shift." This response is named after the famous twentieth-century philosopher G.E. Moore, who argued that we should reject many of the historic arguments for skepticism because of the implausibility of the conclusions. (To be a skeptic about a domain of inquiry is, roughly, to think that knowledge in that domain is impossible. To embrace *global* skepticism is to think that knowledge in (almost) every domain of inquiry is impossible.)

Moore asks us to consider arguments of two sorts (both placed in the mouth of a person holding one hand in front of his or her face):

The skeptical argument:

(a) If the skeptic is correct, then I do not know that there is a hand in front of me.
(b) The skeptic is correct.
(c) Therefore: I do not know that there is a hand in front of me.

The anti-skeptical argument:

(a) If the skeptic is correct, then I do not know that there is a hand in front of me.
(d) I know there is a hand in front of me.
(e) Therefore: the skeptic is not correct.

The arguments share premise (a). They differ in that one adopts premise (b) and moves to the highly unbelievable (c). The other adopts (d) and concludes the highly plausible (e).

When confronted with arguments like this we must ask ourselves which of the two arguments seems more believable. Since both arguments share premise (a), the only way to decide is to ask ourselves whether premise (b) or (d) seems more reasonable to us. Moore concludes that (d) is more reasonable, and that this gives us reason to reject the arguments offered by skeptics.

How does this apply to our assessment of the Direct Argument? Like someone confronting the skeptical argument, the theist confronted with the Direct Argument must compare that argument to the following one:

6.12. If there were a God, there would be no gratuitous evils (GEs).

6.15. It is probable that there is a God.

6.16. Probably, there are no GEs.

Since the Direct Argument and the above argument share premise 6.12, the only question is whether it seems more reasonable to accept 6.13 (that it is probable that there are GEs) or 6.15 (that it is probable that God exists). The theist confronted with the problem of evil might well conclude that 6.15 is more reasonable and thus that the Direct Argument should be rejected.

What might convince the theist that it is more reasonable to accept 6.15 than 6.13? If one has had religious experiences of certain sorts, or if one finds, say, the Cosmological Argument or the Fine-Tuning Argument rationally persuasive, then one will have good reasons to accept 6.15. And if the strength of those reasons outweighs whatever reasons one has for accepting 6.13, the theist should accept 6.15 and reject 6.13.[6]

Of course, someone who has not had religious experiences of any sort, or who does not find any of the arguments for theism persuasive, might think it more reasonable to accept 6.13 over 6.15. If, upon weighing the considerations for and against these two claims, you find 6.13 more plausible than 6.15, you might reasonably conclude that atheism is correct. William Rowe,

---

[6] It is worth noting, however, that the theist who accepts 6.15 over 6.13 might be rational in doing so even without any religious experiences or acquaintance with theistic arguments. If defenders of Reformed Epistemology are correct, the theist can hold her belief in theism as a properly basic belief. In that case, the mere fact that the theist finds herself believing 6.15 is enough reason to accept it and reject 6.13.

the most formidable defender of the Direct Argument, thus claims: "in the absence of good reasons for believing that the theistic God exists . . . we are rationally justified in believing that probably God does not exist."[7]

But notice this: in order to find 6.13 more plausible than 6.15, you must have *some* reason for thinking 6.13 true. So does (or could) the atheist have some good reasons for accepting "that there probably are some gratuitous evils"? Some theists have argued that the answer is no. And this takes us to the second way that one might respond to the Direct Argument.

Noseeum arguments

What good reason could the atheist have for thinking that there are some evils that happen for no good reason? In the most widely discussed defense of the Direct Argument, William Rowe claims that simple reflection on some of the more heinous forms of evil in our world ought to convince us of this. In the many forest fires that occur each year it is certain that many animals die. And it is equally certain that at least some of these animals die slow and horribly painful deaths. So let's focus our attention on an imaginary deer – one that represents what have surely been many thousands of deer – which dies a slow, agonizing death in the middle of a forest fire. Is this painful death (or some equally bad evil) a necessary condition for some outweighing good? Can we really believe that, were God to miraculously prevent this instance of evil, the world would be an overall worse place? How could we think such a thing? It seems simply obvious when we consider cases like this that there is no greater good to which we might appeal that could justify it. And in light of this, the reasonable thing to conclude is that this is, after all, a genuinely gratuitous evil.

Stephen Wykstra has called labeled arguments of this sort "noseeum arguments."[8] The atheist is arguing that she has looked long and hard for some possible greater good that might come from this evil, and that the long search has come up empty handed. She sees no reason that could

[7] "The Problem of Evil and Some Varieties of Atheism," in William Rowe and William Wainwright (eds.), *Philosophy of Religion: Selected Readings*, 3rd edn. (Oxford: Oxford University Press, 1998), pp. 246–7.

[8] "The Human Obstacle to Evidential Arguments from Suffering: On Avoiding the Evils of 'Appearance'." *International Journal for Philosophy of Religion* 16 (1984), pp. 73–94.

possibly justify God in permitting such suffering; and so she concludes from the fact that she can't see 'em that they just aren't there.

Are noseeum arguments good arguments? Sometimes they are. If your roommate asks you to get the milk from the refrigerator and you open the door, look carefully, and don't see any milk there, it is reasonable for you to conclude that there is no milk in the refrigerator because you don't see it. That is a good noseeum argument. But not all noseeum arguments are good. Imagine that you go to the doctor to get your immunizations. The doctor removes the protective sleeve from the needle and is about to inject you with it when he accidentally drops it on the floor. He picks it up and appears about to continue when you object: "Doctor, I think that needle might be dirty; there might be germs on it!" The doctor holds the needle up to the light, closes one eye, and stares intently at the needle. After a few seconds he says, "I have looked very closely and I don't see any germs on it; there's nothing to worry about." This doctor has made a noseeum inference – and it is a *bad one*.

What separates good noseeum inferences from bad ones? For a noseeum inference to be good two conditions must be met. First, it must be the case that you are looking for the thing in question in the right place. If your roommate asks you if there is any milk and you look in the oven, you are looking in the wrong place. Your failing to see it *there* would not be good evidence that you don't have any milk. Second, it must be the case that you would see the thing in question if it really were there. If your roommate asks if there are ants in the lawn and you look out the window and say, "Nope. I don't see any," you have made a bad noseeum inference. You are looking in the right place, but ants are too small to be seen by you from that distance even if they are there.

With this we can return to the question of whether or not the atheist is in a good position to make a noseeum inference to the claim that there are gratuitous evils. Are defenders of the Direct Argument more like someone who concludes, after looking in the refrigerator, that there is no milk? Or are they instead more like the doctor who proclaims the needle to be clean?

Some philosophers, adopting a position now known as "skeptical theism," argue that atheists affirming 6.13 are more like the doctor. According to skeptical theists there are two good reasons to think that we are not well-positioned when it comes to figuring out the reasons God might have for permitting evil. First, given the immensity of divine goodness and the finitude of our human cognitive and moral faculties, it seems likely that there are some, perhaps many, types of good with which we are not acquainted. If we cannot even grasp the full range of goods that evils *might* be aimed at securing, then our attempts to make judgments about whether or not evils are gratuitous will be futile.

Second, even if we believed ourselves to be acquainted with the relevant goods, there is good reason to doubt that we would have any idea what role particular evils might play in bringing about those goods. How could we possibly know what sorts of ultimate good ends might be accomplished by the permission of this or that evil? It is hard enough to figure out what the good or evil consequences might be of a decision to exercise three times per week. (Will it lower your blood pressure so that you can live longer, or will you get run over by a car while riding your bicycle down the street?) Some evils might be necessary conditions for events hundreds or thousands of years down the road. Without omniscience, we can have very little idea of what events are necessary for what other events distant in time and space. Skeptical theists argue that these considerations should provide us with a healthy dose of uncertainty about our ability to make judgments concerning whether any evil is gratuitous or not. If the skeptical theist is right, the Direct Argument is in trouble because the claims of skeptical theists would undermine any confidence we have that 6.13 is after all true.

William Rowe has offered two responses to skeptical theists. First, he claims that if skeptical theists were right, we would be forced to admit that no matter how much evil there might be in the world, and no matter how terrible it is, we would never have reason to accept 6.13 and thereby doubt the existence of God. Surely, Rowe argues, this is incorrect. Second, he argues that it is not simply that we cannot *see* reasons that might justify God in permitting evils like the deer's agonizing death. Rather, it is that we cannot even *conceive* of them. Rowe thinks this puts the justification for 6.13 on firmer ground. It is one thing to say that we cannot see how the reasons that we are aware of might explain the presence of apparently pointless evils. It is quite another thing, Rowe claims, when *any imaginable reasons* that might justify such evils fail to provide us with explanations. As an example, Rowe asks us to imagine the case of a young girl who is brutally raped and murdered. Might there be some greater good towards which this horrendous evil contributes? It is not simply that we cannot think of one. Rather it is that when we start to consider greater goods that might be candidates, we see that the very idea of greater goods justifying such an evil seems outrageous.

Theodicies

The third way that the theist might respond to the Direct Argument is to offer what might seem to be good reasons for God to allow the evils that there are. To offer such reasons is to offer a theodicy. The difference between a "defense" (mentioned earlier) and a "theodicy" is roughly this: a theodicy aims to set out a believable and reasonably comprehensive theory about why God might have permitted evil of the amount and variety we find in our world, whereas a defense aims merely to provide a *possible* reason – without concern for its believability – why God might permit evil. A defense, in other words, aims just at demonstrating the *possibility* of God's coexisting with evil, whereas theodicy aims at something like a full justification for God's permission of evil. If theists can set out some reasons for some types of evil, this will make us far less confident that other evils which we cannot explain really don't have any explanation. Theodicies can only play such a role, however, if they are genuinely credible, since they are supposed to represent explanations that we can imagine ourselves believing to be true. As a result, good theodicies are ones that we either know to be true or which we can reasonably believe to be true in light of other things that we believe.

The punishment theodicy

Christians, Jews, Muslims, theistic Hindus, and numerous other theistic religions hold that some evil is a result of divine punishment for human wrongdoing. Since successful theodicies must show that the evils they supposedly explain are connected to outweighing goods, we must then ask: is it reasonable to think that divine punishment secures any outweighing goods? Answering that question depends on what punishment is suppose to be good for. Defenders of the punishment theodicy have argued that punishment can be good for one or more of four things: *rehabilitation*, *deterrence*, *societal protection*, and *retribution*. We will consider the first three supposed benefits of punishment first and consider retribution separately.

The first three purported goods of punishment involve good consequences for the wrongdoer or other human agents. In the case of rehabilitation, the result is that the wrongdoer herself learns the wrongness of her action and no longer performs the bad action. In this way, the wrongdoer benefits. The goods of *deterrence* or *societal protection* instead benefit those around the wrongdoer. In the case of deterrence, the punishment inflicted on the wrongdoer leads others to reform their behavior. Protection of society can be secured if the punishment renders the wrongdoer unable to carry out further wrong acts by, for example, incarceration or even death.

If these are the goods that punishment is meant to bring about, it is not clear that they are sufficient. It seems that there are other ways in which God might be able to bring about these goods without inflicting punishment. For example, God could deter wrongdoers simply by making the world in such a way that wrong actions have severe natural consequences.

The fourth and most controversial purported good of punishment is the good of retribution. Many theistic traditions defend the notion that when someone commits a wrong they merit a punishment which exacts a cost that goes above and beyond mere recompense. If you steal money from a bank and are caught, you will be expected to repay what you stole. But merely having to give back the money is not enough. Something more is required: that you pay a fine or spend time in jail. According to retributivists, this additional cost is required simply because you have done something wrong and thus have earned a penalty. Exacting the additional penalty is retribution, and such a penalty is a necessary condition for maintaining justice in the universe. If this is right, then inflicting punishment will be necessary for the greater good of having a globally just universe.

Natural consequence theodicy

Some evil might be the result of divine punishment for moral wrongdoing by creatures. But this is not the only way in which free choosing can lead to bad consequences. Sometimes, bad moral choices lead to bad consequences directly. If you choose to spend your life indulging your every desire, seeking out sensual pleasure at every turn, and having no concern for the wellbeing of others, you may end up fat, lazy, and alone. Those consequences would be bad, but they are not divine punishments. Instead, they are just natural consequences of immoral choosing.

It is reasonable to think that a world designed by God would be one in which choosing badly would also turn out to be bad for us. God might be able to use the bad consequences that arise from bad choosing as a tool for helping us to learn how to live lives of moral uprightness in loving communion with God and others. Recognizing the poverty of a life lived in immorality and out of communion with God and others might be the only way of moving us to change our ways freely. In this way, allowing wrong-doing to have bad natural consequences brings about an outweighing good.

Punishment and natural consequence theodicies can only go so far, how-ever. First, it seems clear that many evils – most notably, evils experienced by infants or non-human animals – cannot be regarded either as divine punishment or as natural consequences for moral wrongdoing. Second, the punishment theodicy explains evils only if there are *prior* evil choices that merit punishment. But then the question arises as to why God per-mitted those earlier evil choices. The punishment theodicy cannot tell us; thus, it will have to be supplemented.

The free will theodicy

Philosophers addressing the topic of theodicy typically divide the types of evil that our world contains into two broad categories: moral evil and natural evil. Moral evil is evil that results from free creatures using their freedom in morally blameworthy ways. Natural evil is evil that does not directly involve blameworthy creaturely action. The most common theo-dicy for moral evil is the free will theodicy. Earlier we looked at the Free Will *Defense*, a response to the Logical Argument from evil that provides us with an argument that if God wants to bring about the good of creatures with the capacity for free choice, it is, for all we know, impossible to avoid the permission of at least some moral evil.

That argument might be good enough to show that the existence of God and the existence of moral evil are logically compatible – something the Logical Argument denies. But there are further questions that arise when considering the connections between free will and moral evil that were not addressed by that argument and which need to be settled for appeals to free will to yield a *theodicy*. The reason for this is that it seems reasonable to believe that, even if *some* evil was unavoidable by God, surely a *lot* of the evil attributed to free choice could have been prevented. This threatens to undermine the use of the free will theodicy as a general explanation for the reality of moral evil.

There are two sorts of evils that can spring from free choice. First, there are the evil moral choices themselves. Second, there are the evil *consequences* that can and sometimes do result from evil choices. It might be reasonable to hold that the reality of free choice makes it inevitable that there will be some bad moral *choices*. But couldn't God allow free choices – both good and bad – without allowing the bad choices to have further bad *consequences*? It might be good for you to have the ability to make a free choice to run out of the restaurant before you pay your bill. But couldn't God safeguard the restaurant owner from harm by miraculously making money appear on the table in an amount equal to the cost of your meal (with a generous tip to boot)? It might be good for you to be able to choose to run over your neighbor's mailbox in anger. But couldn't God make the mailbox post perfectly elastic the moment you strike it so that as you drive away – content that you caused your neighbor harm – the mailbox springs back upright without a scratch?

Some philosophers have argued that, although it is a good thing to allow creatures to have free choice, it is a bad thing to allow those free choices to cause harm or injury to others. Instead, they argue, God should put us all in a *virtual playpen* in which choices can be made without any real harm to others being caused. Good choices could be made, and the good consequences that follow from them allowed. But bad choices, while not prevented altogether, would be prevented from causing additional damage. Couldn't God simply block such negative outcomes?

There are two good reasons to think not. First, if the world were structured this way, we would never be able to learn to do evil in the first place. If nothing we ever did allowed us to jump over large buildings (and, sadly, it doesn't), the idea of trying to do so would never enter our minds (and – at least after a certain age and amount of effort – it generally doesn't). The same would hold true for choosing evil in the playpen. Of course, this might first seem to be an advantage of the playpen. But notice that it comes at the price of keeping us from being able to make genuinely morally significant choices between good and evil alternatives.

Second, reflection on what it would take to set up a virtual playpen casts serious doubt on the idea that there would be much good in setting up such a thing. A person in the playpen will think that she has made choices with evil consequences, but the consequences will have been prevented by God. So what will happen when, say, a person tries to apologize for punching you in the nose, or to return money that she has stolen from you, or to visit the grave of a murder victim? God will have blocked these consequences; and so the apology will make no sense, the returned money will seem like an unexpected boon, and there will be no grave. Moreover, any attempt to discuss the blocked consequences will quickly reveal that all is not as it appears. To prevent everyone from discovering that no negative consequences in fact arise out of attempts to do evil, God would have to cause us to go mute, or to be misheard, every time we intended, in conversation, to refer back to earlier sinful deeds. Different newspapers would have to be delivered to different people: criminals would need an edition that reports (falsely) the negative effects of their crimes; "victims" would need editions that omit all mention of them. Television dramas portraying evil and suffering would leave everyone feeling as if bad things *always* happen to someone else. In short, it seems that, in order for God genuinely to keep us in the playpen, our experience would have to contain increasingly more elaborate illusions, until we would finally (and probably rather quickly) reach a point where we each live in worlds that are largely experientially isolated from each other. It is easy to doubt that there would be much good in creating a world like that.

The free will theodicy thus seems to provide at least a possible explanation for the fact that God allows a world in which creatures can make evil moral choices and in which those choices can sometimes issue in bad consequences. But like punishment theodicies, free will theodicies are not comprehensive. Even if these considerations suffice to explain moral evil, it is hard to see how they could offer any very plausible explanation for natural evil.

The natural law theodicy

Free will theodicies focus on explaining evil as a consequence or result of creatures' free choices. Yet this is not the only way that we might try to connect freedom with the permission of evil. Another way is to argue that evils arise out of certain preconditions that must be in place for creatures to exercise their freedom.

There are many such conditions. For example, if the world proves wholly unresponsive to certain choices you make (to jump over tall buildings, for example), you might lose the ability – and hence the freedom – to choose such things. (Most of us tried to do this as kids but do so no longer because the world "didn't cooperate.") What is required for the world to "cooperate" so that we can start making and continue to make free choices? At least one thing that is required is that the environment around us *be governed by regular, orderly laws of nature*. The reason for this is that in most cases, we act by moving our bodies in certain ways, and those ways cause things to happen in the world around us. When you want to split firewood, you move your body to swing the axe, which in turn causes the wood to splinter. If the environment around you were not regular and law-like, you couldn't do such things, since you wouldn't know that swinging axes could cause wood to split (since they wouldn't regularly do so). And so you would not know how to intend to split wood at all. In a chaotic world, you may desperately want to split some wood, but you wouldn't have any idea how to go about doing it. *Perhaps* swinging an axe would do the job; but for all you could tell, perhaps throwing marshmallows at it, or running about in circles in your neighbor's yard, would achieve the desired result. Thus, it seems that, although we might have desires to do all manner of different things, we would never *actually choose* to do those things because we would have no idea how.

Any world in which there are going to be free creatures capable of carrying out free actions with consequences beyond their own skin must then be a world that operates according to regular, orderly laws of nature. And this can lead to problems. The very same laws of momentum that allow me to drive a nail with a hammer, can cause that hammer to smash my thumb. The very same laws that allow me to tell stories by causing air vibrations with my vocal cords, allow tornadoes to knock down houses. And so on. In a world governed by regular, orderly natural laws, it is possible for these laws to conspire to intersect with the interests of creatures to cause them harm. When they do so, natural evil will be the result.

There are two serious objections that natural law theodicies need to confront, however. First, one might wonder why God did not create a world with laws that yield less natural evil. After all, would the world have been any worse if the laws were set up so that viruses couldn't occur? Second, aren't there plenty of cases of natural evil which could be eliminated without undermining the regularity of the laws of nature to such an extent that our freedom would be disabled? Would preventing one major hurricane undermine the possibility of my exercising my free will? If not, shouldn't God prevent one or two (or ten) more hurricanes? Let's consider these in turn.

Could the laws of nature have been changed to yield a world that has a substantially better overall balance of good than our world? To show that such a better world is possible, we would need to describe a regular, law-like world which (a) contains goodness of the sorts (either the same sorts or equivalent or better sorts) and amounts found in the actual world and which (b) contains substantially less natural evil than the actual world. There are two problems with trying to offer such a description. First, as we saw when considering the fine-tuning design argument in chapter 5, there is good reason to think that there is not much room for maneuver in the way the laws and constants of the world are structured. If the universe is going to be capable of supporting life, it will have to be governed by laws and constants similar to those we find in the actual world. Second, even if a better set of laws could be specified, it is doubtful that we could know this. Knowing such a thing would require knowing how changes we propose to certain laws and constants would impact not only the natural evils we are trying to prevent, but other laws of nature and the goods and evils that arise from their mutual interactions. It is unreasonable to think we could unscramble such things and thus unreasonable for us actually to believe that the laws could be changed to yield a better world with less natural evil.

The second objection is more formidable. If law-like regularity in the world exists in order to allow free creatures to use their free choice, then any natural evils which could be eliminated without eliminating that good result would be gratuitous. And yet it seems that there are many such evils. Even if God could not prevent such evils by systematically altering the laws that hold in our universe, he could at least do it by miraculous intervention. The evils of kidney stones or ingrown toenails seem candidates for such elimination.

The theist might respond that God already does miraculously intervene to prevent some such evils. That answer is not sufficient, however, since the critic wants to know why *even more* such evils are not prevented. The only answer available to theist is that natural evils serve as necessary conditions for a variety of good ends, and that some of them are just unknown.

Soul-making theodicies

The theodicies considered so far regard evil as a consequence of free choice, or as a by-product of necessary conditions for free choice. Other theodicies treat evil as a necessary condition for goods of different sorts. For example, many theistic traditions regard the earthly life as an arena in which people make choices for the sake of cultivating moral and spiritual growth. If the world were filled with perpetual pleasure and satisfaction we would never experience the growth that can only come from real suffering, hardship, and defeat. As a result, some theists propose that God allows for evil in the world so that we can cultivate virtues of outweighing goodness that could not otherwise be cultivated.

It is easy to think of some such virtues. We could not become charitable unless there were people in need. We could not become courageous unless there were real dangers to be confronted. And so on. More than that, we could not become lovers or friends without the ability to choose and lose our friends and loved ones. All of these cases highlight the fact that one of the important goods in our world is that it provides an arena for *soul-making*, or character building. And this important good requires that the universe contain some evil.

This theodicy, pioneered by the second-century Christian thinker Irenaeus and defended in the twentieth century by philosopher John Hick, stipulates that four conditions must be in place for soul-making to occur. First, there must be creatures capable of choosing between good and evil. Second, those creatures must be placed in an environment that allows free choices to be carried out. Third, the environment must contain challenges to one's character of a sort that allows for both virtuous and non-virtuous responses. And finally, creatures must have sufficient opportunities to respond to make character building possible.

Soul-making theodicies must confront a couple of important objections. The most serious one is this: many sorts of moral and spiritual growth envisioned in soul-making scenarios require only that there be *apparent* evils in the world. For us to develop the virtues of charity and courage there need not be any *actual* need or *actual* peril; it only needs to seem that there is. We could be hooked up to a *Matrix*-like virtual reality machine that gives us a simulation of being confronted with evil, and as long as we are none the wiser, real soul-making can still go on. Wouldn't such a world be preferable? Daniel Howard-Snyder has responded to this criticism as follows:

> However, if God were to set up a world in which there was only illusory evil to which we could respond in the formation of our character, something of

immense value would be missing. No one would in fact help anybody else; and no one would be helped. No one would in fact be compassionate and sympathetic to another; and no one would receive compassion and sympathy ... No one would in fact praise or admire their fellows for pursuing noble ends in the face of adversity; and no one would receive such praise and admiration. No one would in fact satisfy their admirable aims and desires; and no one would be their recipient. No one would in fact generously give of their time, their talents or their money to the poor; and no one would receive generosity from another. In short, if every opportunity for a virtuous response were directed at illusory evils, each of us would live in our own little "world," worlds devoid of any genuine interaction and personal relationships.[9]

While some evils might be avoided in such a world, the cost of avoiding them would be to further take away many of those aspects of the world that we take to be the most valuable: our interactions of love and friendship with others.

The Evidential Argument part 2: the "Distribution Argument"

As mentioned earlier there is more than one way of formulating the Evidential Argument from evil. The Direct Argument took as evidence the existence of particular instances of evil which, as far as we can make out, occur for no good reason. A second and more recent form of the Evidential Argument takes as its starting point the general *pattern* or *distribution* of evil. In other words, the inspiration for this argument comes not from considering a case of apparently pointless evil and concluding that there is probably no God. Rather it is consideration of the apparent fact that evil befalls the virtuous and the wicked in at least equal measure, and pain and pleasure do not seem to be distributed in ways that accord with merit or desert.

The Distribution Argument has been developed in detail by Paul Draper. Draper asks us to consider two rival hypotheses which might be cited to explain the pattern or distribution of pleasures and pains that we find among human and non-human animals. He designates this observed pattern "O." The two explanatory hypotheses are *Theism* (*T*) and the *Hypothesis of Indifference* (*HI*). The Hypothesis of Indifference is the claim that "neither the

---

[9] "God, Evil and Suffering," in Michael Murray (ed.), *Reason for the Hope Within* (Grand Rapids: Eerdmans, 1999), p. 99.

nature not the condition of sentient beings of earth is the result of bene-volent or malevolent actions performed by nonhuman persons."[10]

When we try to assess the credibility of two competing hypotheses we do it by considering the relevant evidence and then asking ourselves: are things more likely to be this way if Hypothesis 1 is correct or if Hypothesis 2 is correct? If we think that things are more likely to be as they are if Hypothesis 1 is correct than if Hypothesis 2 is correct, then it is more reasonable to believe 1 over 2.

Draper thus asks us to consider the question: would we expect things to be the way O describes them to be if T or if HI were the case? Draper thinks it is fairly obvious: it is more likely that things would be as O describes them if HI were the case, for two reasons. First, when we set aside pleasure and pain that seems to have biological value for organisms, there is no connection between the remaining types of pleasure and pain and moral goods that are taken to be central in theism (like justice and virtue). If theism were true we would expect this biologically irrelevant pleasure and pain to have some connection with helping people to do good or shun evil. They don't. Second, if HI were true we would expect that biologically irrelevant pleasure and pain would rather be a mere by-product of the systems that produce biolo-gically relevant pleasure and pain, and indeed this is exactly what we find. As a result, given the relevant evidence, it seems that HI is much more probable than T. And thus is it more reasonable to accept atheism than theism.

The first thing to note about this argument is that it may fall prey to worries like those we considered above when discussing noseeum argu-ments. In this case, we are asked to decide the likelihood of T given O. However, if the skeptical theists are right, we shouldn't put much confi-dence in our judgments about such things. In light of the considerations they raise, we might think it best to conclude that we are just not in a good position to say much about what the distribution of evil would look like if theism were true.

The second thing to note about this argument is that it differs from the Direct Argument in some telling ways. In the Direct Argument, if we have reason to think that some evil is gratuitous, then we have reason to think

---

[10] "Pleasure and Pain: An Evidential Problem for Theists," in Daniel Howard-Snyder (ed.), *The Evidential Argument from Evil* (Bloomington: Indiana University Press, 1996), p. 19.

atheism to be true. In the Distribution Argument, we are supposed to focus our attention on one narrow range of phenomena and ask which of two competing explanatory hypotheses best accounts for those phenomena *alone*. What the argument does not tell us is whether those phenomena are the only, or even the most relevant, phenomena in deciding between the competing hypotheses. Thus, even if the Distribution Argument succeeds, we may still be a long way from anything like a full-blown argument for atheism.

To see why this matters, consider an example: imagine you are outside Wrigley Field in Chicago and out come thousands of fans in the wake of a game against the Reds. All the fans with Cubs hats look sad, while all the fans with Reds hats are smiling and cheering. You would conclude that your observations favor the following hypothesis: the Reds beat the Cubs. But now imagine you notice a bunch of those happy Reds fans holding a newspaper announcing that the star Cubs pitcher has just been signed by the Reds. Because of this you are led to wonder: are the Reds fans happy because they won the game, or because they signed the star pitcher, or both? What should you think about who won the game given the totality of your evidence? Well, nothing really. There is another perfectly reasonable explanation for the evidence of the happy Reds fans and the distraught Cubs fans which has nothing to do with who won or lost. Those distraught looks might be caused by the pitcher changing teams.

Likewise, if we focus our attention simply on the distribution of pleasure and pain, we may conclude that *HI* is more reasonable that *T*. But perhaps other evidence is more relevant. For example, perhaps the evidence of the sort we saw in chapter 5 in favor of theism. Or perhaps the explanations for the existence of evil that we saw in considering the theodicies above. As a result, this argument at best provides only one piece of a complicated puzzle when it comes to the reasonability of belief in atheism.

The Argument from Hiddenness

Critics of theism point to evil as a telltale sign that there is, after all, no God. While the evidence may or may not support that conclusion, others have argued more recently that there is another telltale sign that provides even more potent evidence against the existence of God: the reality of divine hiddenness. The potent critic of theism, Freidrich Neitzsche, acerbically put the argument this way:

A god who is all-knowing and all-powerful and who does not even make sure his creatures understand his intention – could that be a god of goodness? Who allows countless doubts and uncertainties to persist, for thousands of years, as though the salvation of mankind were unaffected by them, or who, on the other hand, holds out the prospect of frightful consequences if any mistake is made as to the nature of truth? Would he not be a cruel god if he possessed the truth and could behold mankind miserably tormenting itself over that truth? – But perhaps he is a god of goodness notwithstanding and merely *could* express himself more clearly! Did he perhaps lack the intelligence to do so? Or the eloquence? So much the worse! For then he was perhaps also in error as to that which he calls his "truth," and is himself not so very far from being the "poor deluded devil"![11]

The argument for atheism from hiddeness has been developed most thoroughly and carefully in a recent book and series of articles by philosopher John Schellenberg.

Schellenberg's argument

The simplest version of Shellenberg's argument looks like this:

6.17. If there is a God, he is perfectly loving.
6.18. If a perfectly loving God exists, reasonable non-belief does not occur.
6.19. Reasonable non-belief does occur.
6.20. No perfectly loving God exists.
6.21. Therefore: there is no God.

Schellenberg argues that since premise 6.17 is true by definition and premises 6.20 and 6.21 follow from the earlier premises, the only controversial claims in the argument are premises 6.18 and 6.19. Schellenberg also thinks that we should have a high degree of confidence in 6.19. Undoubtedly there are some people whose refusal to believe in the existence of God arises out of simple failure to consider the evidence, or even out of a stubborn refusal to entertain the idea. But it seems that there are some who have looked at the evidence very hard and are just unconvinced. These people seem to provide good evidence in favor of premise 6.19.

---

[11] Friedrich Nietzsche, *Daybreak*, trans. R. J. Hollingdale (Cambridge: Cambridge University Press, 1982), pp. 89–90.

That leaves premise 6.18. What should we think of it? Schellenberg claims that this premise too is practically obvious. Most theistic religions hold that ultimate human fulfillment is found by entering into a deep, personal relationship with God. As a result, if God is truly loving, it is reasonable to think that God would seek to do whatever would be necessary to get his creatures to a place where such a relationship would be possible.

What conditions would be necessary to do this? Coming up with a detailed list might be difficult. But such a list is not necessary for the purposes of developing the Argument from Hiddenness. All that we need to show in order to make this argument work is that *one* necessary condition of such a relationship is that God *make his existence known* to creatures in such a way that the only way they could fail to see it is if they were blameworthy in some way. It seems indubitable that person A cannot enter into a deep and personal loving relationship with person B unless person A knows that person B exists! For this reason, we should expect that God would make his existence known to us in a way that rules out the possibility of reasonable non-belief.

One of the first things that should strike us about Schellenberg's argument is the way in which it parallels one of the versions of the Argument from Evil. In formulating our initial version of the Logical Argument from Evil we considered the claim that "If there were a God, there would be no evil." That initially plausible premise had to be surrendered because, as we saw, there is no way of ruling out, right from the start at any rate, that God might have some very good reasons for permitting some evils. As a result, that initial claim was revised to yield the more plausible claim: "If there were a God, there would be no evils except those God had a morally sufficient reason to permit."

That should lead us to wonder whether or not premise 6.18 of this argument might need similar revision. That is, we might likewise think that there is no way of ruling out, right from the start, that God has some very good reason for allowing some people to experience, at least for a time, an apparent absence of evidence of God's existence. If that's right, then premise 6.18 should be surrendered in favor of the more plausible:

6.18.*   If a perfectly loving God exists, reasonable non-belief does not occur, unless God has a morally sufficient reason to permit the occurrence of such reasonable non-belief.

This then requires us to revise premise 6.19 of his argument as follows:

6.19.*   At least some reasonable non-belief occurs for no good reason.

Schellenberg thinks that 6.19* is true. But it is hard to have much confidence in it. The reason for this is, in the end, the same reason that it is hard to have any confidence in the claim that some evils are pointless. It looks like we can only justify belief in such claims through noseeum inferences. But noseeum inferences are notoriously suspect in contexts like this – i.e. contexts in which we have good reason to doubt that our cognitive faculties are up to the task of detecting the items that we fail to see. And in the present case, as before, we have good reason to think that the relevant noseeum inferences will be bad ones. Since God's goodness and knowledge would infinitely exceed our own, we can't be sure that we have any real grasp of the full range of goods that God might want to bring about in creation. Moreover, we have no reason to think that we are in any position to understand the connection between divine hiddenness and whatever outweighing goods such hiddenness might be aimed at securing. For these two reasons critics think we should reject the noseeum inferences offered in defense of 6.19*.

Schellenberg considers this objection to his argument and offers two lines of response.[12] First, he argues that, contrary to the claims made above, noseeum inferences *do* pass the tests in this case. On Schellenberg's view, if permitting hiddenness serves any sort of good at all, those goods would be (or would likely be) goods for *us* (that is, us human beings) and thus it is "unlikely that they, or their relation to evil

---

[12] There is a third response that he has insisted on recently that we will not treat here. The response is to argue that whatever reasons we had to accept 6.18 initially are themselves good reasons for rejecting the idea that there might be some unknown reasons for God to permit some reasonable non-belief. In other words, when we accepted the premise initially we implicitly committed ourselves to the claim that there are no reasons that would justify a loving God in permitting reasonable non-belief. Any subsequent attempt to make appeal to such unknown reasons would amount to a covert attempt to reject the earlier accepted premise 6.18 without really proposing any actual grounds for doing so. But rejecting a premise in this fashion is simply to beg the question. Schellenberg makes this argument in "The Hiddenness Argument Revised (II)," *Religious Studies* 41 (2005), pp. 300–1. Of course, this response collapses once we realize that no one should immediately accept 6.18 any more than they should be inclined to accept that claim that "If there were a God, there would be no evil." The only claim we can be reasonably inclined to accept is 6.18*.

[such as hiddenness], should be impossible for us to grasp."[13] If this is right, then if we don't see any connection between divine hiddenness and certain greater goods for human beings, we can conclude that there is no good reason for hiddenness. We have, after all, looked in the right place, and we would have seen the goods we were looking for if they were there.

Unfortunately, this reply contains three undefended and highly controversial assumptions. We can unearth these by considering three questions. First, why should we think that the goods at which hiddenness aims would have to be human goods? Why does Schellenberg think that the outweighing goods are not goods of another sort, say, goods that contribute to an overall better universe? He does not say. Second, why should we think that, even if hiddenness does aim at human goods, we would be aware of all the human goods that God wants for us to experience? Some of these goods might, for all we know, be unimaginable goods, such as goods that we are able to experience only in the afterlife. Finally, why does Schellenberg think that, if hiddenness is aimed at bringing about known goods, it would be obvious to us what the connection between hiddenness and those goods would be? For all we know, certain painful experiences we undergo contribute to our developing outweighing virtues in the distant future, and the connection between those experiences and that virtue would be impossible for us to understand before or after the fact. The same, it seems, is true, for all we know, with the evil of hiddenness.

It seems, then, that the Argument from Divine Hiddenness suffers from one of the same difficulties raised by skeptical theists for the Argument from Evil. What if the noseeum worries raised by the skeptical theist could be sidestepped? What if we had reason to think that, if there were reasons for God's permission of the sort of hiddenness we find in our world, we would know what at least some of those reasons are? In that case, the theist would need to offer one or more theodicies aimed at explaining why God permits divine hiddenness to occur in some cases, and for some periods of time.

"Theodicies of hiddenness" attempt to show outweighing goods for which hiddenness might be a necessary condition. We will look at two types of hiddenness theodicy here.

---

[13] *Divine Hiddenness and Human Reason* (Ithaca, NY: Cornell University Press, 1993), p. 90.

Theodicies focused on the goods of free choice or soul-making

As noted earlier, certain conditions must be in place in order for morally free creatures to be able to exercise their freedom in morally significant ways. For example, the world must be governed by regular and orderly laws of nature. Here is a second condition: the world must be set up in such a way that free creatures often have real incentives for doing both good and bad actions. The reason for this is that we cannot be free to choose between alternative courses of action unless we have some incentive or desire to choose each alternative. We can see this by considering ordinary cases of coercion. If a mugger sticks a gun in your back and offers you a "choice" – "Your money or your life!" – it seems fair to say that there really is no choice here at all. Although you probably won't really want to give your wallet to the mugger, you will almost certainly have no desire whatsoever to be shot dead. Moreover, there is virtually no chance that you would *acquire* such a desire. But if that is right, then choosing death by gunshot cannot really be said to be a genuine, live option for you. As a result, the mugger isn't giving you a "free choice" between two alternatives. He is forcing you to hand over your wallet.

What we learn from this is that if the world does not contain incentives for us to choose both good and evil actions, then we are not going to be able to form desires for both courses of action and, as a result, we will not be truly free to choose between the two courses of action. There is more than one way that such dual incentives can be eliminated from our world. One way would be for God to set up the world so that we are subjected to coercive threats to behave morally at all times. We can imagine God setting up the world in such a way that we are followed around by the equivalent of moral highway patrolmen at all times, ready to pounce on us whenever we make a morally evil choice. Under such conditions, any incentives for doing evil would be eliminated or at least overwhelmed by the presence of the moral police, and we would be psychologically unable to choose evil.

Such freedom-undermining conditions could be established in other ways as well though. For example, God making his existence clearly and powerfully known to us might have the same impact as the moral patrolmen. Some have argued that this need to prevent pervasive coercion is one reason why God must remain hidden at least to the extent that his existence is not as obvious as a patrol car following us on the highway.

We might take this account one step further. If the soul-making theodicy is correct as an explanation for (at least some) evil, there will be reason to accept this theodicy for hiddenness as well. A soul-making world is a world where we not only have the freedom to choose between good and evil alternatives, but also a world in which we use such free choices to become people with good or evil characters. In this way, morally significant free choice is an instrument that we use to come to have morally significant characters. If the world were characterized by pervasive coercion entailed by the presence of God, such soul-making would be impossible.

Critics of this theodicy have argued that it fails for two key reasons. First, they note that there are many religious folks who are completely convinced of the existence of a God who watches over their every move and who yet seem to be capable of doing both good and evil. Given this, it is hard to believe that God becoming evident to someone undermines the possibility of genuine freedom. Second, Schellenberg argues that even if human beings were subject to coercive pressure of this sort, they would still be able to choose between two morally significant alternatives: choosing to do good *out of a sense of duty* or *merely out of a sense of fear* of divine punishment. Doing the first would be morally good and indeed vastly morally superior to the second. Human beings in these circumstances would face genuinely distinct moral choices and as a result soul-making would be possible for them after all.

Neither of these criticisms is clearly fatal however. It may be true that some people are capable of firmly believing in the existence of God without being coerced into a loss of freedom, since some people are simply more indifferent to threats of this sort than others. With regard to the second criticism, it is not at all clear that we can choose between acting on the different sorts of motives that Schellenberg imagines; nor is it clear that, if we could so choose, we could also know that we have made such a choice. Imagine that, in a spirit of holiday good will, you decide to drop a one hundred dollar bill in the bucket of the Salvation Army volunteer standing outside your local Wal-Mart. As you step out of your car with the bill in hand, the Salvation Army worker sees you coming. He is getting to the end of a long, cold, and frustrating day of ringing the bell with only a few dollars in contributions to show for it. Seeing you coming, he assumes that you are another self-indulgent Wal-Mart customer about to go into the store and blow another hundred dollars on senseless trinkets. As you arrive at his bucket, his anger finally boils over. He pulls out a gun, holds it to your head, and says, "Drop the bill in the bucket!" Stunned, you quickly drop the bill in the bucket and run.

Later, you reflect on the event. Why did you drop the bill in the bucket? At the moment you had two possible motives on which you could have acted: charity and fear. But on which one did you actually choose to act? In the end, you might think that you really didn't have much choice. You might realize that the concern for your own safety ran so high at that moment that you simply couldn't have decided to act merely on the motive of charity once the gun had been pulled. Of course, *maybe* it was possible for you to act on the motive of charity rather than fear. But even *if* that was possible, how could you know after the fact which motive was in reality the one you acted on? It is worries of this sort that can at least make us skeptical that freedom that allows for soul-making would survive in a world in which God makes his existence plain and obvious to us.

Theodicies focused on the good of filial knowledge

Paul Moser argues that God remains hidden to some creatures because failure to hide would prevent those creatures from coming to know God in the proper way. Moser's argument hinges on a distinction between two types of knowledge of God: (1) *propositional* knowledge that God exists, and (2) *filial* knowledge of God. The first is simply the belief that God exists. The second is a much deeper knowledge that consists of one's "humbly, faithfully, and lovingly standing in a relationship to God as our righteously gracious Father."[14] According to Moser, God's perfectly loving character requires that He promote and facilitate not just our propositional knowledge of God, but also our filial knowledge of God.

Propositional knowledge is a necessary condition for filial knowledge, but on its own it can prove detrimental to one's relationship with God. Simply knowing "that God exists" in the way that we know any other true proposition about the world objectifies and trivializes God and his purposes. Not only is this an evil in itself, but those with mere propositional knowledge might respond to God with an indifferent, hateful, impersonal,

---

[14] "Divine Hiddenness Does Not Justify Atheism," in M. Peterson and R. VanArragon (eds.), *Contemporary Debates in Philosophy of Religion* (Malden, MA: Blackwell Publishing, 2004), p. 49.

or presumptuous attitude. Since God wants nothing more than for us to lovingly respond to him, he will not promote propositional knowledge except in so far as this is a component of our filial knowledge of him.

So why hasn't God bestowed upon us the means to know him *filially*? That is, why does he remain hidden with respect to *this* type of knowledge? Moser claims that in order for one to know God filially, he or she must turn towards God in a "morally serious" manner. We cannot respond to God in the appropriate loving manner unless we are open to moral transformation – distancing ourselves from our material and selfish values. Further, we cannot know God in a filial way unless we recognize him as Lord and Father. According to Moser, if we open our hearts to God in this way, then God will make himself known to us through his morally transforming love. This love is the "*cognitive* foundation for genuine filial knowledge of God," and when one possesses it, one is unable to deny God's existence and all-loving character.

Schellenberg argues that this response fails since there are clearly individuals who fully seek God in the way that is required for filial knowledge and yet have neither it nor propositional knowledge. One might, of course, raise doubts about how Schellenberg could know that there are such individuals. Moser further responds that even if there are such cases, we can presume that God is waiting for his "appointed time" to bestow the grace of filial knowledge in such cases, and that there is no way to show that this filial knowledge will not be forthcoming.

Conclusion

At the end of the last chapter we saw that even if there are seemingly good arguments for the existence of God, those arguments might be undermined if we were in possession of very powerful arguments against the existence of God. If an eyewitness claims to have seen you robbing a convenience store yesterday in Miami, that constitutes pretty good evidence that you committed the crime. But if 500 people, including numerous television and newspaper reporters, watched you win the gold high-diving medal in China that same day, the force of that earlier "good evidence" would quickly vanish.

Are the arguments against the existence of God that powerful? Some think so. However, as we have seen, these arguments rely on assumptions that are open to some serious challenges. How serious those challenges are is a matter for each of us to decide.

It is common for students, at the end of reading a pair of chapters like this, to throw up their hands in despair. "If the experts can't agree on what the evidence shows, how am I to decide?" That is a good question. Here is a good answer: use the same critical reasoning skills that you use when you making judgments about which candidate to vote for in an election or when deciding which car is the best one to buy. In both of those cases you will be exposed to arguments for and against each alternative. But this need not, and in most cases does not, throw you into paralysis. Instead, you decide which factors are the most compelling by your lights, and you proceed accordingly. We advise you to do the same here. Setting aside your preferences and biases, take a look at the various arguments and assess them for yourselves. Which seems most plausible? When you come to an answer to that question, you will have formed a reasoned and reflective judgment about a matter of no small importance.

Further reading

Adams, Marilyn, *Horrendous Evils and the Goodness of God* (Ithaca, NY: Cornell University Press, 1999).

Adams, Robert and Marilyn Adams (eds.), *The Problem of Evil* (New York: Oxford University Press, 1990).

Bergmann, Michael, "Skeptical Theism and Rowe's New Evidential Argument from Evil," *Noûs* 35, pp. 278–96.

Hasker, William, "The Necessity of Gratuitous Evil," *Faith and Philosophy* 9 (1992): pp. 23–44.

Hick, John, *Evil and the God of Love* (San Francisco, CA: Harper & Row, 1978).

Howard-Snyder, Daniel and Paul Moser (eds.), *Divine Hiddenness* (Cambridge: Cambridge University Press, 2002).

  The Evidential Argument from Evil (Bloomington, IN: Indiana University Press, 1996).

Plantinga, Alvin, *Good, Freedom, and Evil* (Grand Rapids: Eerdmans, 1977).

Swinburne, Richard, *Providence and the Problem of Evil* (Oxford: Clarendon Press, 1998).

Van Inwagen, Peter, *The Problem of Evil* (Oxford: Oxford University Press, 2006).

  "The Magnitude, Duration, and Distribution of Evil: A Theodicy," *Philosophical Topics* (1988), pp. 67–8.

Part III

Science, Morality, and Immortality

7 Religion and science

In 1615 Galileo was reeling from the first round of public condemnation of his view that the earth was on the move. Despite the traditional position of the Roman Catholic Church that the earth sits motionless in the center of the heavens, Galileo's observations convinced him that it was not so. Nonetheless, Galileo regarded himself as a devout Christian and, as a result, he was keen to find a way to reconcile his religious commitments with his newfound scientific discoveries. His way of doing so was to conclude that the Bible does not in fact teach what Church authorities claimed. In fact, in his view, the Bible did not aim to teach scientific truths at all. In Galileo's words:

> Since the Holy Ghost did not intend to teach us whether heaven moves or stands still, whether its shape is spherical or like a discus or extended in a plane, nor whether the earth is located at its center or off to one side, then so much the less was it intended to settle for us any other conclusion of the same kind . . . I would say here something that was heard from an ecclesiastic of the most eminent degree: "That the intention of the Holy Ghost is to teach us how one goes to heaven, not how heaven goes."[1]

The connection between science and religion is, of course, not simply a historical curiosity but also one of substantial contemporary importance. This is most evident in the United States, where battles continue to be fought primarily by Christians arguing that the Biblical account of cosmic or biological origins stands in conflict with the reigning scientific orthodoxy. These debates, however, are not uniquely American but are being carried on publicly in China, Russia, Israel, and in numerous other Middle Eastern countries.

In order to know how to think about the connection between science and religion we need first to have some idea about what science is. Like most

---

[1] "Letter to Grand Duchess Christina of Tuscany," http://www.fordham.edu/halsall/mod/galileo-tuscany.html. Last accessed December 3, 2006.

other topics treated by philosophers, this one is enormously contentious. But since we need to start somewhere, we can begin with a very minimalist characterization: *science is the collective judgment of professional scholars who aim to explain the workings of the natural world through empirically testable theories.* Of course, science could as easily (and appropriately) be characterized as a certain sort of activity, or practice, or discipline; and a variety of other characterizations might do as well. But for present purposes we think of science primarily as a (perhaps rather loosely defined) body of belief or doctrine, for the most significant points of contact between science and religion will lie in the domain of belief and doctrine. In particular, there will be significant points of contact between religious claims and scientific claims made by scientists as a result of their inquires.

Three views on science and religion

There are three ways in which religion and science (understood in the way just described) might relate to one another: inevitable conflict, independence, and potential-but-not-inevitable conflict. In what follows we will consider each of these modes of relating in turn.

Inevitable conflict

According to this first view, the claims of religion and the claims of science are locked in conflict in such a way that only one or the other can survive. This so-called "warfare" model of the relationship between science and religion was especially popular in the late nineteenth and early twentieth centuries, though defenders of it continue to the present day. It is reflected in the remarks of the Nobel prize-winning biologist E. O. Wilson, who wrote as follows:

> Acceptance of the supernatural conveyed a great advantage throughout prehistory when the brain was evolving. Thus it is in sharp contrast to biology, which was developed as a product of the modern age and is not underwritten by genetic algorithms. The uncomfortable truth is that the two beliefs are not factually compatible. As a result, those who hunger for both intellectual and religious truth will never acquire both in full measure.[2]

---

[2] E. O. Wilson, *Consilience: The Unity of Knowledge* (New York: Viking, 1999), p. 262.

For defenders of the warfare model, there is something about the very definitions of science and religion which require that the two conflict in principle.

Some defend this model in ways that rely on contentious definitions of science or religion. For example, some claim that religion consists of beliefs drawn from purported divine revelations, held entirely on the basis of authority. Science, on the other hand, consists of beliefs justified by sense experience and the scientific method. That alone would not be sufficient to generate principled conflict. After all, it is always possible that science and religion both propose some of the *very same claims* for our acceptance. Conflict is inevitable only when we add to this characterization of science the claim that *the only justifiable beliefs* about the natural world are those that arise from sense experience and the scientific method, or when we add to the characterization of religion the claim that no belief about the natural world held on the basis of religious authority can ever be revised on the basis of empirical evidence. On the first view, to accept the teaching of the Bible or the Koran about the natural world would be anti-scientific while, on the second view, to accept the deliverances of experience and the scientific method when they contradict our cherished understanding of revelation is to be anti-religious. On either view, one source of scientific truth necessarily trumps the other. One can win only at the other's expense.

Others defend the inevitable conflict model simply because they think it is the most fair and straightforward way of interpreting the actual history of the relationship between science and religion. Religion says the earth is flat; science proves that it isn't. Religion says the earth is immobile; science proves that it both orbits the sun and rotates on its axis. Religion says that the universe is less than 10,000 years old; science proves it to be 14 (or so) billion years old. Religion says human beings are directly created by God; science proves human beings are naturally descended from earlier primates. And so on.

While the inevitable conflict model still persists in popular discussions of the relationship between science and religion, it is easy to see that it has fatal flaws. The first flaw is that it characterizes science and religion in ways we should not accept. Even if the scientist were to accept that the only way to justify scientific beliefs is through sense experience and application of the scientific method, nothing from the domain of science justifies the scientist in the claim that *science alone* provides us with justified beliefs about the natural world. First, such a claim is a claim about the justification of human beliefs and, as such, is a claim about the natural world. But there is no reason to think that this epistemological claim is or even could be justified by sense experience and the application of the scientific method. As a result, this characterization of science is self-defeating. The characterization of religion is equally flawed since religious revelations do not claim that the only justified beliefs about the natural world come from revelation. Furthermore, even if they did, the only justification for such a claim the religious believer would have for this claim would be circular (since we would be trusting the authority of the revelation in accepting its claim that it is the only authority).

The second flaw is that it grossly mischaracterizes the history of the relationship between science and religion. While it is true that some of the more widely discussed cases of conflict between science and religion were resolved through religious believers reinterpreting their tradition in light of scientific discoveries, this is not the only way such conflicts are resolved. For example, in the middle part of the twentieth century, the reigning view in cosmology was the "steady state" model of the universe. On this view the universe is beginningless and thus infinitely old, a claim that runs contrary to the teaching of the Abrahamic religions. While Christians, Jews, and Muslims were uncertain about how this conflict would be resolved, a number of religious thinkers were convinced that the scientific evidence favoring a beginningless universe must be flawed and would eventually be shown to be misleading; and indeed they were correct.

Here is a case, then, in which a conflict between science and religion was resolved by science retreating and adopting a position more congenial to a religious perspective. Of course, scientists did not retreat from the steady state model *because* it was incompatible with religion. Scientists are beholden to revise their views in light of their best understanding of the empirical evidence. Nonetheless, this case shows us just one somewhat recent instance in which conflict between science and religion was resolved and in which religion did not simply back down and revise its claims.

Independence

At the other end of the spectrum are those who argue that science and religion can live in a state of peaceful coexistence because they are

independent of one another in ways that prevent conflict. There are different ways of developing models of this sort. One is to argue that science and
religion cannot overlap because they treat *distinct domains of objects*. For
example, one might hold that religion concerns only supernatural reality
while science is confined to describing and explaining the natural world. On
this view, religion relies on revelation or religious experience to inform us
about the existence of God or of angels or of an afterlife, while science,
relying on sense experience, informs us about what the natural world
contains and why natural things behave as they do. Alternatively, one might
argue that religion concerns only one's experiences of religious reality in
one's life while science concerns the objects of our sense experience. The
famous twentieth-century German theologian Rudolf Bultmann, for example, argued that while religious revelations often make specific claims
about the natural world, these claims are religious only in so far as they
bear on ways in which human lives are transformed by theological modes of
conceiving of human existence and meaning. Thus religious revelations are
not really *about* the natural world, even though they sometimes appear to
be. Thus when we read "God said 'Let there be light,' and there was light"
the text is not affirming truths of cosmology, but rather telling us that God
is the creator and sustainer of all that is.

A second way to develop this model is to argue that science and religion
differ not with respect to their *objects* but with respect to their *methods or
aims*. On this view, science and religion may sometimes discuss the same
objects, contrary to the view described above, but the methods used are
distinct and the results are thus appropriately non-overlapping. For example, someone adopting this model might argue that the job of science is to
determine what things the natural world contains and how those things
behave. The task of religion, on the other hand, is to explain how God's
providential purposes play out through the workings of the natural world.
As a result, methods and aims will be different in these two areas. Science
employs empirical observation and empirically testable theories to explain
what there is, and the causal mechanisms that explain why those things act
as they do. Religion, on the other hand, uses religious revelation or religious
experience or both to discover the purpose and meaning of the happenings
in the natural world.

This second version of the Independence model has been defended by the
notable evolutionary theorist Stephen J. Gould. According to Gould, science

and religion represent distinct "magisteria" (i.e. sources of teaching authority) in such a way that "science covers the empirical realm, answering questions like: what is the universe made of (fact) and why does it work that way (theory). The magisterium of religion, on the other hand, extends over questions of ultimate meaning and moral value."[3] While the magisteria might discuss a common object or topic – cloning, for example – the methods and aims will be different. Science uses theory construction and experimentation to determine how cloning does (or might) work. Religion uses philosophical theorizing or appeals to authority to determine the moral boundaries in our use of cloning technology. Moreover, science will focus on the purely physical aspect of cloning – the sorts of questions that can be investigated by the disciplines of biology and chemistry, for example – whereas religion will focus on the moral and existential aspects. As a result, science and religion are, for Gould, Non-Overlapping Magisteria and he designates his view with the acronym "NOMA."

For Gould's position to be tenable, two claims would have to be true:

7.1. Religion makes no natural or empirical claims (even if religious texts do).
7.2. Science can make no claims concerning supernatural reality or morality.

Unfortunately, neither of these claims is very plausible. Let's consider them in turn.

The first claim holds that religion makes no claims either about the natural world or indeed about anything else that is subject to empirical discovery. Yet, when a Muslim affirms that Mohammed ascended bodily into heaven, or the Christian affirms that Jesus rose from the dead, they are indeed making just such claims. Likewise, any time a religious believer affirms that something happens in the world (creation, turning water into wine, parting seas) as a result of direct divine intervention, they are claiming to explain why things in the world behave in a certain way. But for Gould, claims about what the world contains and why it behaves as it does are outside the magisterium of religion. Thus, if Gould is right, we would be forced to say that Muslims and Christians are not entitled to hold beliefs of this sort at all, or at least that they are not entitled to hold these beliefs as

---

[3] Stephen Jay Gould, *Rocks of Ages* (New York: Ballantine Books, 1999), p. 6.

"religious beliefs." However, Gould has given us no reason to accept either of these claims aside from his own definitions of what counts as religion.

The second claim holds that empirical observations of the natural world can tell us nothing about the domain of morality or the supernatural. Even if this claim is right concerning morality, there is no reason to think it true when it comes to the supernatural. As we saw in chapters 5 and 6, many arguments for and against the existence of God take as their starting point facts that we come to know through empirical observations. If, for example, we discover that the universe exhibits a sort of fine-tuning that is best explained by appeal to a non-natural intelligent designer, then empirical evidence has direct implications for religious belief.

Potential conflict

As a result, Gould's view that science and religion are incapable of conflict seems to ignore some important areas of overlap. Science does seem to make claims that in principle could contradict religious claims and vice versa. It is best, then, for us to acknowledge this potential for conflict and to examine cases of purported actual conflict one at a time. Does the existence of pain and suffering in the world give us good reason to deny that there is a God? Does the fact that the universe had a beginning in time give us good reason to accept that there is a God? Does paleobiology give us good reason to think that human beings descended naturally from lower primates instead of being specially created by God? And so on.

Religious believers who admit the possibility of such conflict will then find themselves in the position of having to *balance* the strength of the evidence in favor of their scientific beliefs against the strength of the evidence in favor of the conflicting religious beliefs. Once this balancing act is complete, the religious believer will be faced with one of four options:

 (i) Reject their religion
 (ii) Reject their interpretation of the religious data
(iii) Reject the evidence of their senses
(iv) Reject their interpretation of the sense data

In each case where the claims of science and religion are in apparent conflict, religious believers must thus choose between these options. Must it be the case that one answer is always best? The case of Galileo should make it plain that the answer is no. If we have very good reason to think that a text is indeed divinely inspired, and if we have reason to think that the revelation can only be understood in one way, then, if the scientific data contradict revelation, I can either reject the science or reject the religion. But there is no simple rule can applied that will make it clear which option is the more rational one.

As a result, the most plausible view is one that falls in the middle of the spectrum, namely, that some religious claims have the potential for conflicting with the claims of science, but not all do. In what follows, we consider some of the most important purported points of contact between science and religion.

Science and the credibility of miracles

It is commonly thought that there is something about modern science that makes belief in the miraculous strange or improper. This thought is expressed not only by naturalistic scientists, but even by contemporary theologians. For example, Rudolf Bultmann famously said of belief in miracles:

> It is impossible to use the electric light and the wireless and to avail ourselves of modern medical and surgical discoveries and at the same time to believe in the New Testament world of spirits and miracles. We may think we can manage it in our own lives, but to expect others to do so is to make the Christian faith unintelligible and unacceptable to the modern world.[4]

What is it about the world of modern science and technology that makes belief in miracles untenable? How could electric lights and the wonders of surgery lead us to reject the idea that God causes miracles?

Many philosophers and theologians point to the arguments made by the eighteenth-century Scottish philosopher David Hume as providing the most powerful reasons to reject either the credibility or the possibility of miracles. In Book X of his *Enquiry Concerning Human Understanding*, Hume offers arguments of two different sorts. Arguments of the first sort are aimed at showing that there is something about the *justification of beliefs* that rules out the reasonability of belief in the reality of miracles in all cases. Arguments

---

[4] "New Testament and Mythology," cited in Hans Werner Bartsch (ed.), *Kerygma and Myth* (New York: Harper Torchbook, 1961), p. 5.

of the second sort are aimed at showing that even if belief in the reality of miracles could, under ideal circumstances, be reasonable, any evidence we actually have that miracles occur or have occurred is tainted in a way that makes belief in those miracles in fact unreasonable for us. While both sorts of arguments are worth considering, arguments of the second sort involve an examination of the integrity of historical evidence for the occurrence of particular miracles that is more appropriate to the domain of history than philosophy. As a result, we will focus our attention on arguments of the first sort.

Humean arguments for the unbelievability of miracles

It is common for us to use the word "miracle" to refer to strange, uncommon, or fortuitous events. Rapid recoveries from illness, escapes from near brushes with death, strokes of luck at cards, are often referred to as miracles. And no one – not even Hume – denies that we can reasonably believe that strange or fortuitous events of that sort occur. What Hume and others think we cannot reasonably believe is that there are *real* miracles. While there is disagreement over what it takes for an event to count as a *real miracle*, Hume's characterization is quite common and, indeed, central to his argument. So we will start with that characterization. In Hume's words, a miracle is "a transgression of a law of nature by a particular volition of the deity, or by the interposition of some invisible agent." For Hume, then, an event counts as a miracle only if it satisfies two conditions: first, the event must violate or "transgress" a law of nature, and second, the event must be caused by a supernatural agent.

What would it take for an event to transgress a law of nature? To answer this question we will first have to know what a law of nature is. This issue is itself a vexing and disputed one in the philosophy of science. For our purposes we can again stick with Hume's definition and then modify it later if the need arises (and indeed it will). On Hume's view a *law* is that which is "established by firm and unalterable experience." The "law of gravitation," for example, is a description of how massive bodies attract that is confirmed by repeated and consistent experiences. When I drop my pen, it falls to the ground. And it just never happens otherwise.

With these details in place we are now in a position to consider three Humean (or Hume-inspired) arguments for the unreasonability of belief in miracles. Let's call these the Balance of Evidence Argument, the Wrong Laws Argument, and the Merely Anomalous Event Argument.

The balance of evidence argument

On Hume's definition, a miracle is an event that does not fit the patterns of our "uniform experience." This places the person confronted with a purported miracle in a dilemma. Should she accept the evidence of repeated past experiences that the law is true, or should she rather accept the evidence that some event has occurred which violates this law? Hume argued that given the weight of our past experience, it is our duty to maintain our belief in the well-established law and to *reject* the claim that the apparently "law-transgressing" event occurred. We might summarize this argument as follows:

7.3. Jones's evidence that a miracle has occurred either comes from the testimony of others or from his own sense experience.
7.4. Nothing is a miracle unless Jones has repeated sensory evidence against its occurrence (i.e. the sensory evidence which supports the supposedly violated law).
7.5. Repeated sensory evidence is always stronger than both testimonial evidence and evidence from singular experiences.
7.6. Thus, Jones always has better evidence that no miracle occurred than he has that some miracle occurred.
7.7. A rational person always "proportions her belief to the evidence."
7.8. Thus, Jones cannot rationally accept that a miracle has occurred.

Initially this argument might strike us as attractive. Who would think it reasonable to accept a claim on weaker evidence at the expense of a claim resting on much stronger evidence? No one, of course. Nevertheless, premise 7.5 seems suspect. Is it really true that singular experiences and testimony always yield weaker evidence than repeated past experience.

Clearly they don't. If they did, then we would be rationally obligated to reject the occurrence of any singular event that does not conform to past patterns of our experience. But we don't do this. In 1986, the Air Force Academy and Notre Dame football teams met for the twenty-seventh time. Notre Dame had won all twenty-six previous meetings. Past "uniform experience" would have led anyone to expect Notre Dame to win again.

But they didn't. If we followed Hume's advice to accept the weight of past uniform experience over evidence from singular experiences, we would have to disbelieve the apparent outcome of the game (as some Notre Dame fans did). But surely it is irrational to think that Notre Dame won the game just because they had won the other games in the past.

Such a principle would not only be problematic for scorekeepers at record breaking sports events; it would also be problematic for scientists confronted with evidence challenging long-held scientific theories. Any long-held scientific theory is long held because the predictions made by the theory are confirmed through repeated, uniform experience. Yet many such theories ultimately proved to be false when later experiments upended certain other predictions. If Hume were right, such experiments and their results would have to be rejected since they amount to nothing more than single experiences which don't cohere with past uniform experience.

The Wrong Laws Argument

Some have thought that this is not the most charitable way to read Hume's arguments against miracles.[5] They claim he should be understood to argue as follows:

7.9. Miracles are events which transgress a true law of nature.

7.10. When Jones encounters (through experience or testimony) an event that transgresses a law of nature (as he understands the laws), Jones must decide whether the event transgresses a true law of nature, or whether instead the event shows that his beliefs about the laws of nature are just mistaken.

7.11. It is always more likely that Jones's beliefs about the laws of nature are mistaken than that he has encountered an event that transgresses a true law of nature.

7.12. A rational person always proportions his belief to the evidence.

7.13. Thus, if Jones is rational he should conclude that the seemingly miraculous event indicates mistaken beliefs about the laws of nature rather than the occurrence of a miracle.

---

[5] For an excellent discussion of Hume's arguments, see Alan Hájek, "Are Miracles Chimerical?" *Oxford Studies in Philosophy of Religion* 1 (2007).

Like the first argument, this second one is aimed at showing that we are never rationally entitled to believe that an event is genuinely anomalous. And since all miraculous events are anomalous, we are never entitled to believe that an event was miraculous.

This argument seems to be in better shape than the Balance of Evidence Argument because the controversial premise in this argument – premise 7.11 – seems far more plausible. How could Jones have any confidence that his encounter with a seemingly law-transgressing event is not better explained by his having *mistaken beliefs* about what the true laws of nature are? In fact, given our limited experience and ignorance about the laws of nature, we should be *very* slow to conclude that any event is truly law-transgressing.

These sorts of doubts become especially pronounced as one learns more and more about the strange and marvelous events that the laws of nature are capable of explaining without any supernatural intervention. We know, for example, that events thought miraculous by less scientifically sophisticated societies in the past have since been shown to be the result of purely natural causes. This consistent pattern of finding out that seemingly miraculous events have purely natural causes should at least lead us to pause when we are told of, or think we have witnessed, a miracle.

Still, when trying to determine whether or not an event we encounter counts as a miracle, one will often have more information available than simply that the event transgresses a principle that one assumes to be a law of nature. To see this we might imagine that the Biblical story of the Exodus is true. Imagine that you are one of the Hebrews standing on the eastern banks of the Red Sea after it has closed over the armies of Pharoah, securing your safe passage from Egypt. According to the Wrong Laws Argument, it would be more rational for you to assume that the events you witnessed were consistent with the laws of nature rather than miraculous violations of those laws. But surely this is mistaken. In this case, there is a great deal of *indirect evidence* that tips the balance in favor of the claim that a genuine miracle occurred. Of course, it is *possible* that the events just witnessed were the result of ordinary law-like processes. But it would be such a colossal coincidence for these events to unfold *naturally* (i.e. non-miraculously) in just the way necessary to allow our escape, that it would be unreasonable to believe that this is in fact what happened.

In addition to the importance of indirect evidence there is one other consideration that might lead us to accept that an apparent miracle is genuinely anomalous and not merely believed to be so because of mistaken beliefs about the laws if nature. If after many years of concerted scientific investigation one were to conclude that a particular event is not caused by any known law of nature, and further that the event seems to be one that would not be explicable even on any imaginable reconfiguring of the laws of nature, this too would constitute sufficiently good reason to accept that an apparent miracle was truly anomalous.[6]

The Purely Anomalous Event Argument

There is another way to show that belief in miracles is unreasonable, namely, showing that it is always unreasonable for us to think that an event in fact has a *divine cause*. We might argue as follows:

7.14. For an event to count as a miracle it must be both anomalous and divinely caused.

7.15. An anomalous event is one which is *not caused* by natural things using their natural powers.

7.16. But once we conclude that an event is anomalous in this way, we must consider two possible ways of explaining its occurrence, namely, that it was caused by some *supernatural thing using supernatural powers* or that it was *not caused at all*.

7.17. It is always more reasonable to conclude that an anomalous event is uncaused rather than supernaturally caused.

7.18. Thus, for any anomalous event, it is more reasonable to conclude that it is uncaused rather than supernaturally caused.

7.19. Thus it is never reasonable to believe that an anomalous event is divinely caused.

7.20. Thus, it is never reasonable to believe that a miracle occurred.

The most controversial premise in this argument is 7.17. There are two ways that one might defend it. The first is by appeal to simplicity. Philosophers, scientists, and other who use theoretical explanations agree that when all other things are equal, we should prefer explanations which are simpler. We need not detain ourselves here over *why* philosophers, scientists, and others think that, though we will return to that question shortly. Instead,

---

[6] In fact, Hume seems to recognize as much in the same footnote of the *Enquiry* where he provides his definition of a miracle.

we can note that once we see that accepting simpler explanations over more complex explanations is indeed rational, we should conclude that premise 7.17 is true. It is much more complex to hypothesize the existence of supernatural agents as a way of explaining anomalous events than it is to hypothesize no cause at all. Thus, we should always prefer to deny that there was a cause than to assume that there was a supernatural cause.

The second way to defend premise 7.17 is by arguing that no-cause explanations are preferable because such explanations are *natural extensions* of our ordinary ways of explaining other natural events. As we saw earlier in chapter 5 when discussing the multiverse explanation for cosmic fine-tuning, explanations of this sort, all other things being equal, are to be preferred to unique or unusual explanations.

Notice that both of these defenses of premise 7.17 rely on the fact that no-cause explanations have certain merits that should lead us to accept them over supernatural explanations, *all other things being equal*. But as we saw in the case of the Wrong Laws Argument, even if this is true, there *could* be cases where the indirect evidence makes all other things unequal. If we encounter an anomalous event in a context where indirect evidence seems to point to a supernatural cause, then no-cause explanations become correspondingly less plausible.

Consider the above example of the parting of the Red Sea again. Without taking any stand on the historicity of the event, we can still note that *if* we were present for the occurrence of the event, none of us would think it more plausible that this event is to be explained by no-cause rather than a supernatural cause. While supernatural causes might seem to be more complex and a less natural extension of our modes of scientific reasoning, in this very context it seems highly plausible that the event was caused by a supernatural agent looking to rescue the Israelites. To believe otherwise would be to believe that the event was a coincidence of monumental proportions. While it might indeed be such a coincidence, we are no more entitled to believe that it was than we would be to believe that it is a mere coincidence when my opponent in poker draws royal flushes all night. While it could be a coincidence, the reasonable person would suppose him to be cheating.

A Humean-style argument for the impossibility of miracles

In examining the Humean arguments for the unbelievability of miracles we have assumed a certain definition of miracles and laws. Miracles are transgressions of the laws of nature, and laws are universal generalizations established by firm and unalterable experience. Hume thought that conceiving of miracles and laws in this way made rational belief in miracles impossible. As we have seen, it is difficult to defend that claim. However, one might think that belief in miracles falls prey to another and perhaps more serious problem, namely, that miracles described this way are *impossible*. To see why, consider another universal generalization that seems to be "established by firm and unalterable experience": human bodies dead for three days stay dead forever. Most Christians think, of course, that at least one human body that was dead for three days did not stay dead forever – the human body of Jesus. These Christians think that three days after Jesus' death, the miracle of the Resurrection occurred, and unaltered experience was altered. The law was transgressed. A miracle occurred.

Or did it? Recall that a miracle is a violation of law of nature. A law of nature is a true universal generalization of some sort.[7] However, once our "law-breaking" event occurs, this universal generalization is no longer *universal*. There is now at least one event, the resurrection of Jesus, that does not follow this general pattern. As a result we should conclude that the only thing our supposed law-breaking event can do is *show the law to be false* and not *break* the law. Once the body that was dead for three days comes back to life, it is simply no longer true that firm and unalterable experience establishes that human bodies dead for three days stay dead forever. The result of all of this is that supposed miracles can never do what miracles must do, namely, *break* or *violate* laws. Thus, according to this argument, miracles cannot occur. We might formalize this argument as follows:

7.21. Miracles are violations of laws of nature.

7.22. Laws are true, universal generalizations.

7.23. If an event occurs which does not fit the general pattern described by the law, then the law is not true after all, but false.

7.24. Thus, any event which appears to violate a law instead only shows the law to be false.

7.25. Thus, there really can be no such thing as a law-breaking event.

7.26. Thus, there really can be no such thing as a miracle.

---

[7] Not *every* universal generalization is a law. There are no gold mountains, for example; but, though that is a true universal generalization, it is not a law of nature. But, on the Humean view, every law of nature is some sort of universal generalization.

Admittedly, this argument looks suspicious. We can imagine someone impatient with such an argument reasonably reacting by saying: "I don't care what any philosopher says, if someone dead three days comes back to life then a miracle has occurred and that's that."

There is indeed something suspicious about this argument, and it reveals to us something of fundamental importance when thinking about laws and miracles. On the assumptions we have made so far, laws are to be thought of in terms of regularities, and miracles are to be thought of in terms of violations of those regularities. If that is as far as we go, we will be forced to accept this argument and its conclusion.

However, reflecting on this argument further should show us that there is a better way to conceive of miracles than as violations of laws of nature. A more satisfying conception is rather something like this: an event (ultimately) caused by God that cannot be accounted for by the natural powers of natural substances alone. Conceived of this way, miracles don't violate laws of nature but rather involve the occurrence of events which cannot be explained by the powers of nature alone. When dead bodies come back to life it is a miracle because the molecules that make up the corpse lack the powers necessary to generate life. When water instantaneously turns into wine, it is a miracle because water molecules do not have the power to change into wine on their own.

Characterizing a miracle in this way is not new. In fact, it is the definition of a miracle we find in the works of historic theistic philosophers like Thomas Aquinas and Gottfried Leibniz. Once we adopt this definition of a miracle the above argument collapses since both of the key premises turn out to be false. Premise 7.21 is false since miracles need not involve any violations of laws. Laws tell us how natural things work – what they can do by force of their own powers. If an event occurs that exceeds their powers, no law is *broken*. Instead, something has happened that has exceeded the laws. Premise 7.22 is also false since laws are not true universal generalizations, but true descriptions of what lies in the powers of natural substances.

Conclusions: miracles and science

So what can science or empirical evidence tell us about miracles? We might be tempted at this point to say: nothing! But this would be too hasty. What science might show us is that some events that we once thought were miracles – events we once thought exceeded the powers of natural substances – are not miracles after all. Perhaps we used to think that thunder and lightning were miracles. Science has shown us that they are not. Perhaps people once thought volcanoes and meteor strikes were miracles. Science has shown us that they are not. So, science is relevant in so far as it can show us that something we thought was miraculous was not.

Science has its limits as well, however. First, science cannot show us that an event *is* miraculous. To make that inference we would first have to agree that the event in question is not and likely will not be explicable in scientific terms, and we will have to judge that the indirect evidence indicates a divine cause. Second, science cannot tell us that miracles are *impossible*. The reason for that is that science can only tell us what natural things can do through their natural powers. Beyond that, science must remain silent.

Contemporary interfaces between science and religion

Though some have argued that the practice of science undermines the reasonability of belief in all miracles, this claim is overstated. There are, however, other cases where there is much greater potential for interplay between science and religion. In some cases science and religion seem to be at odds with one another, whereas in other cases it appears that they are mutually supportive. Let's consider these in turn.

Science challenges religion: a case study

When people think of the relationship between science and religion, most first think of the battles waged in politics, the courts, and the media over evolution. Since the Scopes' trial in the early twentieth century, the issue of evolution has been a persistent topic of public dialogue, especially in America. Those inclined to a more literal interpretation of the early chapters of the biblical book of Genesis argue that it teaches that the universe was created in a form quite similar to its current form, including stars, planets, and the various types of organisms we now find, within six twenty-four-hour periods, 6,000–10,000 years ago. This picture contrasts starkly with the picture offered by cosmologists, geoscientists, and biologists, who argue that the empirical evidence indicates that the universe is roughly 14 billion years old, the earth approximately one third as old as that, and life on earth having existed for just short of four billion years. In addition, our best science indicates that the various types of organisms found in our world were not separately and specially created, but rather came into existence from a common ancestor by means of variation and natural selection through many trillions of generations.

For this conflict to arise, defenders of the "young universe" position must make some crucial assumptions. First, they must assume that biblical revelation does not err when it comes to making assertions about the contents or workings of the natural world. Second, they must assume that the particular narrative in question does in fact make assertions of this sort. Critics have argued that both of these claims are at least open to question.

Regardless of the stance that one takes on those two questions, religious believers who think that the teachings of revelation are in conflict with evolution are faced with a challenge. Although we do not intend to answer that challenge here, what we learned earlier at least gives us a recipe for doing so. In this way, the evolutionary challenge can provide a case study for the way in which scientific challenges can be resolved.

Religious believers must first acknowledge that the word "evolution" is commonly used to designate a variety of scientific positions. Alvin Plantinga argues that, in the broadest sense, "evolution" encompasses five distinct theses:

(T1) The Ancient Earth Thesis: The thesis that the universe and the earth are billions of years old.

(T2) The Progress Thesis: Life has moved from simple unicellular organisms to complex multicellular organisms over time.

(T3) The Common Ancestry Thesis: All terrestrial life shares a common ancestor.

(T4) Darwinist Thesis: The mechanisms that account for the diversity and complexity of life are those identified by evolutionary scientists: random variation and selection, genetic drift, gene flow, and so on.

(T5) Naturalistic Origins of Life Thesis: Life on earth arose through purely naturalistic processes.

Critics of evolution take issue with one or all of these theses because they interpret biblical passages as teaching that they are false. These critics argue that scientists have misunderstood or mishandled the empirical evidence that they use to support the theses of evolution and thus that they have fallen into error. However, such critics must also acknowledge that in the same way that our scientists must interpret the *empirical evidence* to come to scientific conclusions, religious believers must interpret the *evidence of revelation* to come to their religious conclusions. In the same way that scientists can be mistaken in the conclusions that they draw from the empirical data, religious believers must remain open to the possibility that they have mistakenly interpreted the revelatory data.

Thus, for the religious believer, the conflicts between science and religion will involve balancing evidence against evidence: the empirical evidence favoring scientific claims against the revelatory evidence favoring theological claims. The Christian critic of evolution might look at the five theses above and conclude that the empirical evidence favoring those theses decreases in strength as one goes down the list. The evidence for an ancient earth seems quite strong, while the evidence for the naturalistic origins of life is, in fact, virtually non-existent. This then needs to be balanced against the evidence of revelation. How clear is it that the Bible teaches that the earth is young, or that God directly intervened in the cosmos to bring about life?

It is important to keep two things in mind when it comes to this balancing act. The first is that the relevant evidence is likely to change over time. Scientific hypotheses that at first seem unlikely, later come to seem well-supported, while apparently well-confirmed hypotheses are later overthrown. Can the same be said when it comes to revelatory evidence? It can. To provide one simple example, we can imagine a religious believer learning that a certain idiom used by biblical writers signals something entirely different from what one thought. If we were to discover, as many claim we have discovered, that the Genesis creation narrative represents a type of ancient mythological literature which all ancient readers would have understood to be something other than literal cosmic history, that should incline contemporary interpreters to become doubtful of the claim that the early chapters of Genesis are intended to teach cosmology. As we learn more about the stylistic, linguistic, and literary forms employed by the authors of sacred texts, our understanding of what they reveal can and does change.

The second thing to keep in mind is that even though the empirical and revelatory evidence can change, this does not mean that there will always be an escape route available when science and religion clash. There may well be cases in which a purported revelation clearly teaches something that is contradicted by extraordinarily well-confirmed scientific theories. In that case, the religious believer might decide that the apparent contradiction is in fact a real one. She must then conclude either that the sacred texts of her tradition teach falsehoods, or that science has erred despite the strong empirical evidence.

Can science support religion?

Far from seeing science as a perpetual threat to religion, some scientists and philosophers argue that scientific discoveries provide evidence for the truth of many religious claims. In chapter 5, for example, we saw that the evidence that the universe came into existence in the finite past and evidence of cosmic fine-tuning can be used to argue for the existence of a supernatural designer.

In addition to evidence of that sort, others argue that the scientific method itself presupposes certain truths which only make sense on the assumption that the universe is designed by a supernatural mind. Let's consider one example. When scientists are weighing the merits of a theory there are a number of factors to be considered and one of those factors is simplicity. Why do scientists favor simpler theories over more complex ones? The answer, we would have to think, is that simpler theories are, all other things being equal, *more likely to be true*.

We can imagine two teams of scientists performing an experiment which yields a data plot that looks as follows:

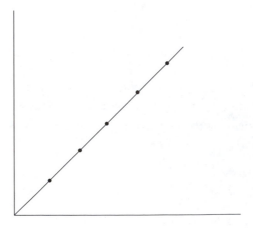

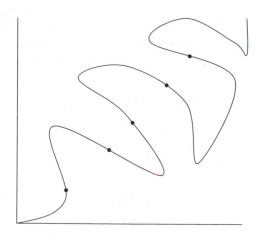

We can imagine that each of the two lines that connect the points on our two graphs represent two different "explanations" for the data. Which one do you think is more likely to be correct? The first, of course. And why? Because it is simpler, and simpler theories are more likely to be true. And now we come to our question: why do we think *that*? Why should we think that the simplest curve or theory will more likely make for the *correct* explanation?

In the end, only two explanations seem plausible. The first is that evolutionary forces have wired us so as to favor simpler explanations over more complex ones. Perhaps the lesser amount of mental computing power needed to understand, render, and remember simpler curves and theories inclines us to accept them (since evolutionary pressures generally favor processes that use available resources economically). The problem with an explanation of this sort is that, if it's right, then we favor simpler theories over complex ones not because the former are more likely to be true, but rather because they are *more efficient from an evolutionary standpoint*. Once we admit this, however, it is hard to see why we should think that our theoretical faculties are aimed at truth. As we saw in chapter 4, what is important from an evolutionary standpoint is survival and reproduction; and so what we have most reason to believe on the supposition that our cognitive faculties are the products of blind evolutionary forces is just that our cognitive faculties are well-suited for producing theories that will enable us to accomplish those two goals. But for purposes of facilitating survival and reproduction, all we really need to get from our scientific theories is the ability to predict and control our environment. False theories can do this just as well as true ones; and it seems quite natural to suppose that our penchant for simpler theories has arisen in us not so much because simpler theories are likely to be true, but because simpler theories (so long as they get their predictions right) more greatly and quickly facilitate the enterprise of controlling our environment. In sum, then, if our preference for simpler theories is the product of evolutionary forces, then whereas we are normally accustomed to thinking of science as a way of finding out the truth about how the world works, it now looks as if we ought to conclude instead that it is simply an effective way of coming up with useful heuristics that help us reproduce and pass on our genes in the most efficient way.

But our tendency to favor simple explanations over more complex ones might be explained in another way. One of the hallmarks of rational beings is that they act, or at least *try to act*, by the simplest means to achieve their ends. If I want to walk from the dining room to the kitchen, I walk through the opening in the wall between them rather than climbing out the window, shimmying up the downspout, sliding down the chimney and cutting through my living room. That is, I don't do that if *all* I want to do is get from one place to the next. If that is all I want, I take the simplest path. Analogously, it would be reasonable to think that if the universe were supernaturally designed, it would operate in accordance with laws and theories that are simpler, all other things being equal. As a result, if a designer were to create our universe in accordance with the standards of reason, it would be reasonable for us to use simplicity as a standard for choosing between competing explanations in just the way that scientists in fact do. Furthermore, simplicity is a factor we would look for in a theory because, if this way of thinking were correct, simpler theories would indeed be more likely to be true.

This provides us with one sort of argument that the underlying assumptions of the scientific method make more sense if theism or some other view that implies supernatural design is true than if those views are false.

A controversial case of scientific support of religion: intelligent design

In the last decade a small group of scientists and philosophers have argued that science supports religion in one further way. Like cosmologists who point to universal fine-tuning as evidence for a cosmic designer, these philosophers and scientists claim that facts from the realm of biology provide evidence that life is the result of intelligent design.

Defenders of so-called Intelligent Design Theory, or IDT, adopt a two-pronged approach to the topic of design detection. We might call these the *theoretical* and the *applied* prongs. On the theoretical side, defenders of IDT point out that design detection is something we do routinely. Show someone a picture of an ordinary cliff face and another of Mount Rushmore and ask them which is designed. The answer will be easy and obvious to everyone: Mount Rushmore shows clear and evident signs of design, the ordinary cliff face does not. What is it about Mount Rushmore that tips us off to the fact that it was designed? Or we might ask more generally, what makes us think something is designed rather than not?

Theoretical intelligent design

The most prolific theoretician for IDT, William Dembski, argues that we infer design through an intuitive three-step process of reasoning that he calls the "explanatory filter." When we come across a structure, process, or event (or, let's say more simply, "a thing") that we want to explain, we first ask ourselves whether or not that thing was the inevitable (or nearly inevitable) outcome of the workings of the laws of nature. If so, we conclude that it is explained in terms of law and we stop.

If we conclude that the thing is not explainable in terms of law, the next step is to consider whether or not the thing occurred by *chance*. We can conclude that the thing occurred by *chance* if it is *simple*, or *unspecified*, or both. What does that mean? A thing is simple if it is not complex. Imagine that you come down the hall towards your classroom one day and find two Scrabble tiles laying on the floor spelling out the word "an." Now you know that this occurrence was not inevitable given the sheer force of the laws of nature. But you have no reason to conclude that this word was placed there by design either. Someone might, for all you know, have been carrying the game and accidentally allowed a couple of tiles to fall out. The pattern here is too simple for you to conclude that this was anything other than chance.

Still, the existence of mere complexity is not enough to rule out an explanation in terms of chance. If you come down the hall and find a string of tiles that spell out AJFBAIREHFNAKDJNBWEIGFNAKHA the sequence is complex, but it is also gibberish. You should probably conclude that this sequence arose from chance as well. Someone spilled a pile of tiles and then never cleaned them up. But if you see tiles on the floor that spell out "Welcome to class" things are different. Here you can be sure that chance is not the right explanation because the pattern is complex, and complex in a special way. That *special way* is something that Dembski refers to as "specificity." "Specificity" is hard to characterize succinctly, but for our purposes we can say that a complex thing has specificity if it conforms to a pattern that makes sense even in advance of our seeing it (a pattern like *being a grammatical English sentence*).

Dembski argues that this explanatory filter functions in our everyday practices of detecting design. In addition, detecting design through detection of specified complexity is the method used by paleontologists trying to distinguish artifacts from mere natural objects, and by scientists searching for extra-terrestrial intelligence who need to distinguish meaningful signals from "merely random" ones. Before we go on to look at how IDT advocates apply this theory to biology it is worth noting that the theoretical question they raise represents an interesting philosophical puzzle that deserves serious scrutiny. IDT theorists are right that we do seem to be able to quickly and unreflectively detect design, and it is worth asking what features of things we pay attention to in making these judgments. Perhaps it is non-law-produced-specified-complexity, as Dembski claims, perhaps not. But whatever the case may be, the question is a serious one that deserves serious attention.

Applied intelligent design

The theory behind IDT is then *applied* to certain cases in biology where we find specified complexity which is not, they argue, explained as the inevitable outcome of natural laws. Notice that to defend successfully the claim that specified complexity implies design requires showing two things: (1) that specified complexity can't be explained in terms of "law," and (2) that the structure or process actually exhibits specified complexity.

The most widely discussed version of this "applied" argument has been developed by biologist Michael Behe. First set forth in his highly controversial book *Darwin's Black Box*,[8] Behe argues both that certain processes and

---

[8] Michael Behe, *Darwin's Black Box* (New York: Free Press, 1998).

structures that he labels "irreducibly complex" could not have come to be through natural Darwinian processes (and thus that they are not explained by Law), and that those processes and structures exhibit specified complexity (and thus are explained by Design rather than Chance). Let's consider the two parts of the argument in turn.

For Behe "irreducibly complex" processes and structures (ICs) are complexes "composed of several well-matched, interacting parts that contribute to the basic function, wherein the removal of any one of the parts causes the system to effectively cease functioning."[9] Behe's favorite illustration of irreducible complexity is the mousetrap. Mousetraps consist of five parts (a base, a spring, a "whacker," a cheese-holder, and a catch that holds the whacker until the mouse bites the cheese). Take away any of those parts and it seems clear that the mousetrap cannot work.

Irreducibly complex structures might come into existence in a number of ways. But Behe argues that there is *one* way that ICs *cannot* come into existence. Specifically, they cannot come into existence by a gradual process in which there are increases in complexity accompanied by increasingly more efficient function. The reason for this should be obvious. Since any simpler version of the IC will be *non-functional*, the IC structure cannot evolve by increasing in complexity and functionality over time. As a result, we can be sure that a story such as the following one would have to be false:

> In the early seventeenth century, mouse-catching technology was quite primitive. Mousetraps from this period, for example, consisted simply of a base and a whacker. In the eighteenth century inventor U. R. Cawt added two additional parts to the mousetrap, a catch and a cheeseholder. While these mousetraps vastly outperformed their predecessors, they were no match for the twentieth-century model developed by I. Ga Chu who added the spring.

We know this is false because these supposed less effective predecessors would not have worked at all. They could not have been early versions of the mousetrap since they could not have performed the mouse-trapping function.

In the same way, since evolution occurs by means of organisms, and subsystems of those organisms, evolving through increasing complexity and improved functionality over time, no IC structure could possibly evolve. This would not raise any problems for Darwinism if there were no ICs in

[9] Behe 1998, p. 39.

the biological world. The problem, Behe argues, is that there are numerous irreducibly complex structures found in organisms. Thus if his argument is correct, Darwinism will be unable to account for ICs. And since it appears that Darwinism is the only law-like process that could account for the existence of organisms and their structures, we are forced to conclude that these ICs cannot be explained in terms of Law.

Of course, this only takes us halfway. Showing that something is not explicable in terms of Law does not show that it is to be explained in terms of Design. As we saw, there is a third alternative: chance. Are ICs in the biological world more reasonably thought to be the result of chance or design? Behe and Dembski both argue that the correct answer is design since a set of interacting parts working together to perform a specifiable and beneficial function clearly exemplifies that special indicator of design: specified complexity.

The "applied" argument thus claims to show that in biology intelligent design must have played a crucial role. None of this shows that Darwinism or standard evolutionary theory is wrong. Most advocates of IDT are willing to admit that standard Darwinian explanations are likely to be correct when it comes to explaining a wide range of biological phenomena. It only goes wrong when it gets too greedy and tries to explain the origins of all organisms and biological structures. Some of those structures will have to be explained by appeal to design.

Problems with intelligent design

Initially this applied argument seems to have a good deal of plausibility. But the argument faces some serious objections. We will consider the two most serious ones here. The first objection focuses on the notion of irreducible complexity itself. Behe's claim is that irreducibly complex structures cannot perform their function with a mere proper subset of its parts. One of his favorite examples is the blood clotting cascade. In human beings, for example, this cascade involves dozens of proteins and enzymes which interact in a way that insures both that we stop bleeding when we are cut, and that our blood does not clot so readily that we are in danger of it turning to Jello in our veins. Is this system irreducibly complex as Behe maintains?

It may be that simpler systems would be non-functional if everything else were held constant. The problem is that ancestor organisms or their environments, or both, might have been different in ways that allowed subsystems to perform the clotting function. Critics have noted that human beings, unlike many other organisms, need circulatory systems that operate at high pressures. To pump the blood through our large bodies and to pump it uphill through our five or six-foot frames, we need lots of pressure. This in turn requires a complicated and fine-tuned blood clotting process. If our ancestors were smaller or not so tall, they could get by with much simpler blood clotting cascades. For example, our ancestors could clot their blood the way other smaller organisms that are alive today do. In those cases, blood clots when certain sticky white cells in the bloodstream cling to the margins of the open wound until they form what amounts to a dam.[10]

If, through random variation, a more complicated blood clotting mechanism were to arise which allowed descendents with larger, faster, stronger bodies to live and thrive, these organisms would benefit. Further generations could get larger still, until we arrive at the point where the descendents are so large, and have blood pressures so high, that they can no longer clot blood using sticky white cells. For them the complex blood clotting mechanism is now the only one that will do the trick.

Under such conditions it might seem to us that no subset of the more complex mechanism could perform the function of clotting blood. And in one sense no subset could do that – for the particular organism that has this more complex mechanism here and now. But if the ancestors were different in certain crucial ways, then a subset of the parts might well suffice. To show that a system is IC in such a way that it could not have evolved from simpler states, we would have to show that the ancestor organisms and their environments were sufficiently similar to our own that no subset of the parts of the current IC structure could perform the needed function back then. Behe has not shown us anything like that.

The second objection argues against Behe's claim that if IC structures evolved, they must have done so through increasing complexity and func-tionality over time. He argues that this is impossible because any structure of lesser complexity could not have performed the function *at all*. Even if it is true that no subset of the ICs parts could perform the function currently performed (call that function "F"), perhaps the subset of parts performed some *other* function which was important in the survival and reproduction of the ancestor (we can call the function of the subset of parts "G"). If the subset

---

[10] See Kenneth Miller, *Finding Darwin's God* (New York: Harper Perennial, 2000), pp. 155–6.

performed some useful function in the ancestor, it would continue to be passed along from generation to generation, and when the final piece of the IC structure evolves, the new function F would emerge as well. If evolution sometimes unfolds this way, then we will find IC structures that arise from subsets of parts which performed different functions for the ancestors.

Critics sometimes point to the evolution of the mammalian ear as an example. The mammalian ear contains three bones which transmit vibrations from the eardrum to the inner ear. We now know that two of these three bones were originally part of the rear of the reptilian jaw. As mammals evolved, those reptile bones decreased in size and moved into a position that allowed them to transmit sounds instead. Bones which once performed one function, now came to perform an entirely new function. In the same way, it might be supposed that structures which once performed function G in our ancestors has since been modified in such a way that it can now perform function F. If so, then it will be true that the current structure is irreducibly complex. But it will be false that there is no way for Darwinism to account for its evolution.

Two final challenges to religion from science

In the preceding sections, we have considered a variety of challenges that might be raised for religious belief from science. In this last portion of the chapter we will consider two final challenges that some take to be the most potent and general challenges available.

Religion has nothing to explain

> The "know-nothings," or fundamentalists, are . . . honest. They are true to history. They recognize that until recently one of religion's main functions was scientific: the explanation of existence, of the universe, of life. Historically, most religions have had or even been a cosmology and a biology. I suspect that today if you asked people to justify their belief in God, the dominant reason would be scientific. Most people, I believe, think that you need a God to explain the existence of the world, and especially the existence of life. They are wrong, but our education system is such that many people don't know it.[11]

[11] Richard Dawkins, from *The Nullifidian*, December 1994.

With these words, Oxford biologist Richard Dawkins raises a challenge to religion that a number of scientists and philosophers regard as potent. The argument is that belief in supernatural entities was once justified when unexplained phenomena required an explanation, and gods and spirits were the only available candidates. As science has progressed, those phenomena have been progressively explained in naturalistic terms. Indeed, in Dawkins' view, there are no longer any phenomena which cannot be explained by appeal to purely natural entities and processes. Once we lose all of the justification we ever had for supposing that gods exist in the first place, we are obliged to give up belief in those things. And this means that those who hang on to belief in supernatural entities hold those beliefs irrationally. We might formalize the argument as follows:

7.27. The only potentially good reason anyone ever had for believing in supernatural entities was the existence of phenomena that could not be explained otherwise.

7.28. All phenomena that we formerly thought were explained by the activity of supernatural entities have now been explained in purely naturalistic terms.

7.29. Thus there are no longer any good reasons for believing in the existence of supernatural entities.

7.30. We should thus reject belief in supernatural entities.

Although this argument seems to enjoy popular support, it is not a good argument. In fact, what we learned in chapters 4 and 5 gives us good reason to deny both premises 7.27 and 7.28. While some theists and other religious believers might have believed in gods and spirits simply as a way of explaining otherwise unexplained natural phenomena, many more did not and do not. Instead, many hold these beliefs on the basis of religious experiences of the sort discussed in chapter 4.

What if someone thinks that religious experience does not justify religious belief and further that religious beliefs are not properly basic? Should that person find this argument convincing? She should not. The reason should again be clear from what we have already seen in chapter 5. There we saw that there are all sorts of phenomena that science has not explained and for which supernatural explanations seem quite plausible. For example, the apparent fine-tuning of the cosmos for life is a phenomenon which is plausibly explained in terms of supernatural design. Of course, natural explanations are available for such fine-tuning (the possible existence of multiple universes, for example). But there is some reason to think that supernaturalistic explanations are indeed preferable.

Finally, we should notice that if someone believes in the existence of super-natural entities as some sort of explanatory hypothesis, empirical phenomena might be only one sort of phenomena they are aiming to explain. Some theists think that theism is the best explanation for the fine-tuning of the cosmos for life, but they can also think that it provides a comprehensive explanation for other facets of their larger worldview. For example, they might take theism to provide the most satisfying explanation for the existence of objective moral truth and obligation. They might think theism is the best explanation for the existence of human immaterial souls. They might think that theism best accounts for hope for the prospect of immortality, and so on. Explanatory hypotheses need not be narrowly focused on explaining empirical phenomena. If theism provides a satisfactory foundation or ground for these other beliefs, that too can count in its favor. As a result, premise 7.29 is equally unsatisfying.

Evolutionary psychology and religious belief

Over the last decade a new challenge to religious belief has emerged from the domain of evolutionary psychology. Evolutionary psychology is a field of study which aims to understand the way in which evolutionary pressures in the past have shaped human cognition and behavior. And since religious beliefs and practices are pervasive across human times and cultures, this gives us reason to think that religion did not spread (in the way that folk tales do) but is in some way "wired into" our human cognitive machinery. It is easier to imagine how such evolutionary explanations would unfold if the traits to be explained provide obvious adaptive advantages. But in the case of religious belief and practice, the trait seems almost to harm fitness. Thus, religion is a Darwinian anomaly – it is found across times and cultures, and yet seems to lead people to believe things that are very strange and to behave in ways that seem to harm their reproductive success (taking vows of celibacy, giving time and resources to religious activities, and so on). Evolutionary psychologist Scott Atran describes what we might call the evolutionary "problem of religion" as follows:

> Religion is materially expensive and unrelentingly counterfactual and even counterintuitive. Religious practice is costly in terms of material sacrifice (at

least one's prayer time), emotional expenditure (inciting fears and hopes), and cognitive effort (maintaining both factual and counterintuitive networks of beliefs).[12]

A number of theorists have now turned their attention toward explaining the "evolutionary problem of religion."

Initially there seems to be something odd about evolutionary explanations for belief. Belief is the sort of thing that we each acquire individually based on our distinctive experiences, history, and reasoning. It is true that when we think of individual beliefs it is hard to imagine how evolutionary pressures could explain them. But while appeal to our evolutionary history might not be able to explain why we have specific token beliefs, it might be able to explain belief formation at a more general level. For example, it seems likely to be useful to appeal to evolution when we try to explain why we have *cognitive equipment that allows us to form sensory beliefs when our sense organs are stimulated in a particular way*. If there were some corresponding evolutionary explanation for the fact that we have the cognitive equipment that *leads us to form religious beliefs (and practices) when stimulated in a particular way*, then we would likewise have an evolutionary explanation for our religious beliefs.

There are various different evolutionary accounts of religion currently on offer, but they all seem to agree at least on this: the human mind has a cluster of cognitive tools that collaborate in predictable ways to generate religion as a cross-cultural phenomenon. These tools lead us to form beliefs in unseen agents as the causes of natural events which appear to have no immediately identifiable cause. The unseen agents violate what appear to be innate cognitive expectations we have about agents (that they are not invisible, for example). Furthermore, because of the way our cognitive faculties are structured, these "minimially counter-intuitive (or MCI) agents" are highly likely to be remembered and discussed, thus making them also likely to become targets of our communal interest. In addition, because of their unique character, we are naturally led to generate stories about them. For example, we are inclined to suppose that the unseen agents have special powers which might allow them do things that natural agents are unable to do – for example, to know our thoughts, or to know what people are doing when they are alone and nobody else is watching. In this

[12] Scott Atran, *In Gods We Trust* (Oxford: Oxford University Press, 2002), p. 6.

way, the unseen agents possess "strategic information" from which we might benefit or through which we might be harmed. This makes them attention grabbing and worth trying to please or placate through activities such as devotion or ritual.

An assessment of evolutionary models of religious belief

Do evolutionary models of religious belief challenge the truth of religious belief? Many evolutionary psychologists think so. In their view, this empirical research shows us that religious belief is a trick played on us by evolutionary forces. But such models do not, on their own, show this. The first reason they do not show this is that it is not at all clear that these accounts are correct. Taken on their own terms, the explanations seem to leave us with some unanswered and puzzling questions. The most pressing of these concerns the account of the way in which MCI ideas become the object of religious attention and devotion. Critics of this view have pointed out that there are many MCI ideas that are never seen as anything but fictional and so never become the object of religious attention: the Tooth Fairy and Santa Claus are two such examples. If their accounts are attempts to explain why certain ideas become religiously significant, they owe us an account of why these ideas are not. At this point, no plausible response to this question has yet been offered.

However, even if these evolutionary accounts are ultimately vindicated, they do not, on their own, undermine the truth or justification of religious beliefs. The first reason for this is that we are not entitled to draw conclusions about the truth or falsity of a belief merely by considering the origin of that belief. The famous scientist Friedrich Kekule is reputed to have come to believe that a certain molecule (benzene) has a ring structure because of a dream he had of a snake biting its tail. This is not a good reason for holding beliefs about chemistry, but it is no reason to think that the belief is *false*. Arguments which attempt to draw conclusions about the truth or falsity of a belief because of its origin thus fail because they commit a fallacy of reasoning known as the *genetic fallacy*. Likewise, to conclude that religious beliefs are false because of their evolutionary origins would be equally fallacious.

What is more, there would be something odd at least about concluding that a belief is false because evolutionary pressures have given us a predisposition to come to have it. It seems reasonable to think that evolutionary pressures have disposed us to form perceptual beliefs like "There is a computer in front of me," when our retinas are stimulated in just the ways that they are stimulated when we sit in front of our computers. Should this make us skeptical of such beliefs? Surely not. Evolutionary forces can dispose us to have ideas, but it might well dispose us to have ideas that are true, and even *because they are true*.

We can imagine an evolutionary scientist saying at this point: "Now hold on a minute. Evolutionary pressures might dispose us to form beliefs about our environment on the basis of vision because *those* beliefs are *true*. They do that because organisms that have a way of coming to true beliefs about their physical environment survive, while those that don't come to such beliefs will not survive. That is how we can be sure, or at least reasonably believe, that evolution has not "tricked us" about these beliefs. But when it comes to religious or supernatural belief, there is no reason to think that evolutionary forces would favor true over false beliefs, and so no reason to accept such beliefs."

There are various problems with this line of reasoning. The first is that it is hard to defend the idea that evolutionary forces would succeed in selecting for the formation of true beliefs about our environment. (We discussed this in some detail at the end of chapter 4.) The second is that even if our imaginary scientist is right about the role evolutionary pressures play in giving us true beliefs about our environment, there is no reason to think that evolutionary pressures would lead us to false beliefs concerning religious reality. We can see this by hypothesizing that theism is true, and that God created the world in such a way that biological complexity and diversity evolves in much the way evolutionary scientists believe. The theist might then look on these evolutionary accounts as providing us with a description of the way in which God configured evolutionary history to make belief in supernatural reality easy or natural for us. If that is the way things really are, then our coming to believe that there is supernatural reality is something that leads us to true belief because those beliefs are true.

Conclusion

Science and religion represent two ways in which human beings claim to know things about reality as a whole. While science focuses largely on the natural world, science can and does have implications for what supernatural reality is or can be like. Similarly, while religion has much to say about the nature of supernatural reality, almost all religions make claims about natural reality as well. As a result, science and religion are positioned to engage each other. There is no way to know from the outset whether that engagement will be friendly or hostile. As we have seen, the history of the engagement of these two domains has shown us both sides. Religious believers will continue to be in a position of having to negotiate the connections between these two domains of belief and scientists will need to remain unprejudiced and open-minded about the potential religious implications of their discoveries and findings.

Further reading

Barbour, Ian (ed.), *Religion in an Age of Science* (San Francisco: Harper & Row, 1990).

Barrett, Justin, *Why Would Anyone Believe in God* (Lanham, MD: AltaMira, 2004).

Dembski, William and Michael Ruse, *Debating Design: From Darwin to DNA* (Cambridge: Cambridge University Press, 2004).

Earman, John, *Hume's Abject Failure: The Argument Against Miracles* (New York: Oxford University Press, 2000).

Houston, J., *Reported Miracles: A Critique of Hume* (Cambridge: Cambridge University Press, 1994).

Miller, Kenneth, *Finding Darwin's God* (New York: Harper Perennial, 2000).

Murphy, Nancey, *Theology in an Age of Scientific Reasoning* (Ithaca, NY: Cornell University Press, 1990).

Plantinga, Alvin, "Games Scientists Play," forthcoming.

Polkinghorne, John, *Belief in God in an Age of Science* (New Haven: Yale University Press, 1998).

Ratzsch, Del, *Battle for Beginnings* (Downers Grove, IL: InterVarsity Press, 1996).
  Science and Its Limits (Downers Grove, IL: InterVarsity Press, 2000).
  Nature, Design and Science (Albany, NY: SUNY Press, 2002).

Shanks, Niall, *God, the Devil, and Darwin: A Critique of Intelligent Design Theory* (Oxford: Oxford University Press, 2004).

Swinburne, Richard (ed.), *Miracles* (New York: Macmillan, 1989).

8   Religion, morality, and politics

It is commonly believed that morality is importantly and fundamentally connected with the existence of God. The remark, famously (if not quite accurately) attributed to Dostoyevsky, that "without God, all is (morally) permissible," captures a view shared by many devout religious believers and many atheists as well. Indeed, such a view reflects the majority opinion within Western philosophy throughout most of its history.

The belief in an intrinsic connection between morality and the existence of God explains, among other things, the historical proliferation of arguments for theism based on various types of moral facts. Aristotle, St. Thomas Aquinas, Leibniz, Kant, and many others believed and argued that there is something about morality that simply makes no sense unless there is a God. Yet, despite its widespread appeal, the belief in such a connection is not at all widely endorsed by contemporary moral philosophers. Most contemporary moral philosophers are quite content with the idea that morality can be explained entirely in naturalistic terms. As a result, much less attention has been paid to the connections between religion and morality in philosophy over the last hundred years.

There is more than one reason for this shift. The most important of these is that many moral philosophers have become increasingly doubtful that morals belong in the domain of objective fact. As William Lycan has observed, "Moral facts are right up there ... in the ranks of items uncordially despised by most contemporary philosophers."[1] If moral claims derive their truth and authority merely from human preferences or desires then we can explain everything that needs to be explained about morality simply by appealing to facts about human minds, their contents, or their

---

[1] William Lycan, *Judgement and Justification* (Cambridge: Cambridge University Press, 1988), p. 198, quoted in Charles Taliaferro, *Contemporary Philosophy of Religion* (Malden, MA: Blackwell Publishers, 1998), p. 193.

activities; as a result, appeals to God or to other supernatural entities would be rendered superfluous. It is thus fitting to begin this chapter by assessing the reasons that have been offered for thinking that morality is not objective.

Ethical objectivism and ethical subjectivism

Philosophers commonly draw a distinction between objective and subjective claims. Objective claims are claims like *George Washington was the first president of the United States*, *1 + 1 = 2*, and *the Earth has four moons*. The first two of those claims are objectively true, while the third is objectively false. Objective claims are characterized by two distinguishing marks:

(i) They are not mere expressions of taste, desire, or attitude.
(ii) They have absolute truth values – that is, they aren't merely "true for so-and-so" or "true in this or that culture" (whatever exactly those "true for" expressions might mean).

Subjective claims on the other hand lack these features. So, for example, to say that vanilla is better than chocolate, that soccer is boring, or that it is bad to belch out loud after a good meal is *not* to say something that is straightforwardly true or false. Rather, it is to say something that is, we might say, "true for you" but maybe not true for someone else. What does it mean to say that a sentence is true for you? Plausibly, all it means is that the sentence in question merely expresses your attitudes or preferences rather than making an assertion about some fact in the world. (Note, in this connection, that a sentence *about* your attitudes, preferences, or tastes – e.g. a sentence like "Sally prefers chocolate" – *would* be an objective claim, since it would assert an alleged fact about the world and would, therefore, have a truth value. Thus, the difference between objective and subjective facts isn't that the latter *depend* on human attitudes and preferences, as some are inclined to say. For, after all, the truth of "Sally prefers chocolate" is wholly dependent on human preferences – namely, Sally's. Rather, the difference is that subjective claims do nothing more, really, than *express* human attitudes or preferences.)

The distinction between objective and subjective claims can be applied in the ethical domain as well to provide us with two broad views concerning morality. Let's call these views *moral objectivism* and *moral subjectivism*.

Discerning whether or not there is any important philosophical connection between religion and morality will first require that we come to some conclusion on the question of whether or not moral objectivism or moral subjectivism is more plausible. If subjectivisim is more plausible, there will be little or no connection. Moral claims will be dependent for their truth on the beliefs, desires, and decisions of human beings and will amount to nothing more than a form of human convention. If objectivism is true, however, a number of important philosophical puzzles arise. For example, if moral claims are objective, then there must be some mind-independent facts which make these moral claims true. But what sorts of facts might these be? On first inspection, ordinary non-moral facts seem incapable of grounding the truth of these objective moral claims and this might incline us to think that supernatural facts will have to be called in to fill the role.

Of course, such questions are out of place if there are good reasons to think that moral claims are, in the end, subjective. What reasons are there to favor such a view? In what follows we discuss two arguments for subjectivism.[2]

Two arguments for subjectivism

The most common argument for moral subjectivism starts by pointing out the vast diversity of moral beliefs across times and cultures. It is no surprise to learn that different cultures accept widely divergent moral beliefs. Some cultures affirm the moral acceptability of slavery, infanticide, theft, genital mutilation, ritual rape, and so on (while others disagree). Likewise, some cultures affirm the moral goodness of truth-telling, humility, equal rights for all persons, beneficence, and so on (while others disagree). Given this diversity of moral belief it seems hard to believe that moral claims are objective, such that for each of them there is a *single right answer* when it comes to questions about their truth or falsity. As a result, moral subjectivism is true.

A second argument against moral objectivism arises out of an *epistemological* concern. Moral facts seem quite unlike the sorts of non-moral facts with which we are acquainted. Most of what we know we seem to know

---

[2] The following arguments are derived from J. L. Mackie, *Ethics: Inventing Right and Wrong*.

either by way of some sort of experience (usually sensory experience, but maybe religious experience as well) or by analyzing our concepts. It is easy to see how we can come into contact with the sorts of facts investigated by science, and it is likewise easy to see how we could come into contact with facts about how our concepts are related to one another. But how could we possibly come into contact with *moral* facts? How could we possibly *discover*, say, that it is wrong to own slaves or good to help the poor? We don't go digging in the dirt to discover these truths; and we can't discover them simply by analyzing the meanings of the terms we use. Thus, the sorts of facts with which morality seems to deal are *weird* – so weird, in fact, that it is hard for many philosophers to believe that they exist.

Assessing the arguments for subjectivism

The first and most common argument is also the least compelling of the two. The mere fact of moral disagreement comes nowhere close, on its own, to settling the question of whether moral claims are objective or subjective. To see why, we have only to note that there has been widespread disagreement about all sorts of obviously objective claims. Does the earth stand still or orbit the sun? People disagreed – even bitterly. But there is only one right answer. What this shows is that even though in some cases disagreement occurs because the claim at question is subjective, in other cases it occurs because someone is just wrong.

Likewise, the question of whether moral claims are subjective is not settled by the further fact that moral disagreement is very hard to resolve. Students often note that the difference between moral claims and, say, the claim that the earth orbits the sun is that there is no *proof* (scientific or otherwise) for the former sort of claim, but there is for the latter. There is no *publicly available evidence* to which we can point to resolve the disagreement. But the same is true of a wide variety of clearly objective claims as well. What did Julius Caesar have for breakfast on the day of his death? What was the most often-read book in the famed Library of Alexandria? No one will ever know; and if people were to take views on these questions, there would be no evidence on the basis of which we could ultimately resolve the disagreement. But that fact goes no distance whatsoever toward showing that these claims are subjective. In fact, the idea that they are merely subjective is flatly absurd.

How do we know, then, whether a claim is objective or subjective? We have to consider it in light of the two distinguishing marks identified above. Is it reasonable to think that it is an expression of individual preferences or attitudes? Is it plausible to think of it as the sort of claim that is neither absolutely true nor absolutely false, but merely "true for so-and-so" at any given time? If the answer to both questions is yes, then we have reason to think that the claim is subjective. Knowing, for example, that the claim in question is one for which we could have no publicly available evidence, or about which people might interminably disagree, might give us some insight into these questions; but it hardly settles them.

Consider, then, how all of this might work with respect to a particular moral claim, such as "Genocide is immoral." Is this claim an expression of individual preferences or attitudes? Is it merely true for us, but not for others? It seems highly plausible that the answer to both questions is no. To see why, consider what a "yes" answer would mean. If we were to answer yes to the first question, we would be committed to thinking that if an individual or group of individuals *valued* genocide, then it would for that very reason *be moral*. Surely this is wrong-headed. Genocide is wrong for everyone, not just for us and people who share our preferences and attitudes. If anyone thinks genocide is morally commendable (or takes genocide to be desirable) they are not simply different from us, they are drastically and frighteningly morally mistaken (or corrupt, or both). For the same reason, a "yes" answer to the second question is equally unacceptable. If "genocide is immoral" can be true for some people and false for others, then we are committed to the claim that some people *rightly* see genocide as perfectly morally permissible (perhaps even morally *commendable*). Again, such a position is surely incredible. Any theory on the nature of morality which leads us to conclude that genocide (or slavery, or human sacrifice, or ritual rape) might be morally permissible or commendable should, for that very reason, be rejected. Indeed, if such a consequence were not a sufficient reason to reject a theory of morality, it would be hard to know what would be.

The second argument for the conclusion that moral claims are subjective is also problematic. It turns on the idea that moral facts are unique – very different from the sorts of non-moral facts with which we are most familiar. Since it is hard to see how we could have access to such facts, moral facts are declared strange and, on that basis, we are advised to disbelieve in them.

But this way of reasoning simply ignores a wide range of facts that seem no less "strange" than moral facts but which few people are willing to dismiss simply on the basis of their strangeness.

Moral claims are a species of *normative* claim. That is, they express norms – they tell us what we *ought* to do. But there are other kinds of normative claim as well. For example, when we talk about what it is to be rational, we talk, among other things, about what sorts of beliefs are justified or unjustified, warranted or unwarranted; and in so doing, we are talking about what beliefs we think *ought* to be held or rejected in light of certain kinds of evidence. When we are injured – with a torn muscle, or a detached retina, say – we naturally speak as if the relevant part of our body is not functioning as it *ought* to function. Disease is sometimes thought of in terms of malfunction: when we are ill, our bodies are not as they ought to be. None of the "oughts" here are moral; but they are normative nonetheless. But whatever problems arise for grounding our knowledge of normative moral claims will equally arise for grounding our knowledge of these other normative claims. If moral claims are strange, then so are their epistemological or physiological counterparts. Yet, relatively few of us will be willing to jettison the idea that there are norms of rationality or physiological norms on account of their strangeness. Thus, it is hard to see why we should think that moral claims have a *special* sort of strangeness that makes them, more than these other sorts of claims, candidates for rejection.

The two central questions

Our short discussion of objectivism and subjectivism does not consider the full complexity of the arguments for and against each view, but it does indicate that it is by no means clear that ethical subjectivism is the best or only option. If we embrace ethical objectivism, two questions immediately arise, and these two questions are arguably the central problems for ethical objectivism. These questions will occupy our remaining discussion of the connection between religion and morality.

The first question is: what explains the truth of moral claims? If moral objectivism is true, then there are moral facts (like *its being wrong to torture small children for fun*) and moral properties (like goodness, wrongness, and so on). But where do these facts come from? What explains why one moral property rather than another is exemplified by an act or circumstance? Are these just brute features of the universe, or are they brought about by something? Moral objectivists owe us some answers here.

The second question is: even if moral claims are objectively true, why should we care about them? Those who are new to philosophy or to moral theory often find this question baffling. Isn't there something about morality, they wonder, which makes it automatically important to us? When someone points out the fact that some action you are considering is immoral, and you acknowledge that she is right, doesn't this alone give you a good reason not to do it? We all seem to think that the answer is yes. There is something quite absurd about saying, "I realize that it is entirely immoral to do X; but, really, I have no reason not to do it." And yet, this fact itself is puzzling. Why does morality have this seemingly intrinsically motivating character? Why does it seem not to be a rational option for you to declare that you simply don't care about morality?

To grasp fully what is at stake here it is important that we get clear about what ethical claims are and about what distinguishes them from other sorts of claims. What makes something an ethical claim? Beyond being objective (an assumption for the purposes of this discussion), ethical claims have at least three distinguishing features: (i) they are action guiding; (ii) they apply universally; and (iii) they render us worthy of moral blame when we violate them and moral praise when we follow them. Others might be identified as well, but these three will suffice for present purposes.

What does it mean to say that moral claims are universal? One thing it means is that they prescribe actions (or states of character) as good or bad for us regardless of our interests in those actions or states. Not all action-guiding claims are like this. If you want to win the 5km race next year, you should train a few times each week. But the "should" in that sentence is action guiding only on the supposition that you want to win the race. If you don't care about running or winning the race, it is not true that you should train a few times a week. The "should" we find in moral claims is different. If you admit a certain moral claim to be true, "You should not steal" for example, you can't escape the action-guiding force of the claim by saying that you don't really care about being moral. Unlike other sorts of action-guiding claims whose force is only *conditional* or *hypothetical*, moral claims have a force that is universal or, in the language of moral philosophers, *categorical*.

In addition, ethical claims, unlike other action-guiding claims, are action guiding in such a way that once we understand or appreciate their moral character, we take ourselves to have not only *a* reason to do them, but *sufficient reason* to do them. When you consider performing an action, there are all sorts of reasons for and against it that might weigh in the balance. If an action will advance your career, enrich your fortune, make your friends and family members happy, and so on, then there is some reason for you to do it. But these reasons can be overridden by other reasons that are outweighing. When we make practical decisions we are continually forced to weigh these competing reasons against one another. Sally wants to advance the happiness of one of her children by paying for her to have very expensive bagpipe lessons. But she also wants to send the child to college. And if these goals come into conflict, one will have to take priority. If the only way to provide bagpipe lessons is to give up saving for college, Sally might think that it is just tough luck for bagpiping. She might regard saving for college as more important. Thus, for her, one set of reasons – those that favor college – are overriding. And so, given her value structure and her circumstances, she *ought* to forgo the bagpipe lessons in favor of saving for college.

For Sally, the reasons she has for saving for her child's education override her reasons for wanting to provide bagpipe lessons. But the college-related reasons could be overridden as well. Thus, it might turn out that, given her value structure, if her circumstances were to change in some way, then she ought *not* to save for college. In the case of morality, however, *nothing* overrides. That is part of what is unique about morality. When moral reasons oblige us to do a certain action, or to refrain from a certain action, other non-moral reasons must take a back seat. Moral reasons are in this way *intrinsically overriding*. Thus, for example, even though Sally might be willing to sacrifice a lot to send her child to college (and might justifiably do so), if there is a conflict between sending her child to college and fulfilling her moral duties, there is no question of what she ought to do: no matter what her circumstances, and no matter what her preference structure, she ought to fulfill her moral duties. If the only way to provide for her child's college education is for her to sell narcotics or embezzle money from her employer or rob a bank, tough luck for college. She ought not to do those things, even if she very much wants to and, furthermore, would have to in order to achieve her other goals. The fact (if it is a fact) that Sally values bank-robbing (say) and has to engage in it in order to achieve her ends goes no distance whatsoever toward justifying her actions. We all recognize that morality makes demands on us that cannot be trumped by considerations of personal gain, pleasure, or happiness. If the choice is between one of these and the demands of morality, then moral demands prevail.

The above discussion was aimed at helping us appreciate the force of the second of the two central questions for which we will seek answers below. That second question was: why should we care about morality? None of this discussion goes any way towards answering this question. But perhaps now we can see more clearly what it is asking. When we consider the way in which we take morality and its demands to work, one thing that is evident is that it seems to have this categorical and intrinsically overridding grip on us. What could explain this fact?

The grounds of objective morality

The first of our two questions is: what explains the truth of moral claims? Before we move to consider answers to this question, it important to note that objective moral claims come in more than one variety. Because of this we might expect that there will be more than one type of ground for moral claims. For example, moral philosophers commonly insist on a distinction between claims concerning *the good* and claims concerning *the right*. Claims of the first sort tell us what sorts of things are worth pursuing: it is good to learn a foreign language, tell the truth, and give your life to helping the poor. But notice that these three examples of good things fall into three very different categories. The first – learning a language – while good, still falls short of counting as a *moral* good. The third – giving your life to serve the poor – counts as a moral good. But doing such a thing requires a sacrifice that most of us think goes way above and beyond the call of duty. We might say that it rises to the level of a moral good, but goes well *beyond* what you are obligated to do. Philosophers call actions of this sort *supererogatory* acts.

The second example, however, truth telling, seems to be both a moral good *and* an obligation. Goods that fall into this category make up what philosophers call "the right." Things that are *right* are moral goods that have a special hold on you, because you are *obligated* to pursue them.

In what follows we will consider four arguments that God is in some way required to ground the truth of objective morality. Some of these arguments apply specifically to the good, while others apply to the right.

Laws imply a law-giver

Many theists are fond of an argument, frequently cast in the form of a slogan, declaring that since all laws require law-givers, *moral* laws require a *moral* law-giver. Surely, the argument continues, moral law-givers are intentional, deliberate agents. Thus, some intentional, deliberate moral agent exists, and is the ground of objective moral truths.

The problem with the argument, of course, is that the underlying premise (or slogan) is false or question-begging. There are all sorts of law-like or normative principles that seemingly have no need of a law-giver to explain their truth: laws of nature and laws of mathematics, for example. It is hard to see why the Commutative Law or the Laws of Thermodynamics require a law-giver.

Furthermore, even if the theist can show that contingent laws, like the laws of nature, do require a law-giver, it is hard to see how the same case might be made when it comes to mathematical laws. Unlike natural laws, mathematical laws are necessary truths – truths that could not be otherwise no matter what. If that is right, then these laws seem to be true in a way that is not dependent on anything else, including the acts of any law-giver. Since moral truths seem also to be necessary truths, we have reason to think that these truths do not depend on the acts of a law-giver either. As a result, the general claim that laws require a law-giver seems unsustainable.

Necessary truths require a necessary being

While it might be true that necessary truths wouldn't depend for their truth on the act of a law-giver, it may be too hasty to conclude that there can be no explanation at all for necessary truths. In fact a number of theists have argued that moral claims are necessary truths but that their truth is somehow explained by some sort of special, non-natural ground. Since the various parts of nature exist contingently and are arranged as they are contingently, those things cannot serve to ground necessary truths. Nor could necessary truths obviously be grounded in divine commands since at least some of these might also be contingent. But that doesn't mean that necessary truths can't be grounded in other kinds of special, supernatural facts. And so those who think that necessary truths stand in need of some sort of ground or explanation will naturally insist that the grounds for necessary truths are precisely such special, supernatural facts.[3]

The seventeenth-century German philosopher Gottfried Leibniz defended the necessity of moral truths, arguing that they must thus have grounds of the same sort as other necessary truths, namely, necessary states of the divine intellect. In rejecting the extreme voluntarism of Samuel von Pufendorf, Leibniz writes:

> Neither the norms of conduct itself nor the essence of justice depends on [God's] free choice, but rather on eternal truths, or objects of the divine intellect ... Justice follows certain rules of equality and proportion which are no less grounded in the immutable nature of things and in the divine ideas than are the principles of arithmetic and geometry.[4]

This argument rests on a number of assumptions, some more controversial than others. It is at least moderately controversial that necessary truths require non-natural grounds. It is a necessary truth that nothing can be both entirely red and entirely green at the same time. Yet it is hard to see how the truth of this claim depends in any way on some sort of non-natural ground.

More controversial is the claim that moral truths are necessary. But note that even if we grant these controversial claims, it is not at all clear that the grounds for necessary moral truths must be God or the divine nature or intellect. Many philosophers have accepted the claim that necessary truths require exotic, non-natural entities as grounds, but not all of them have thought that they must be grounded in or explained by the activity or character of a divine being. Plato and his followers, for example, hypothesized the existence of non-natural entities or "forms" which play the grounding role. Why, then, must we conclude that the grounds for necessary moral truths are some divine reality as opposed to these more austere, Platonic forms? This argument offers no answer to this question.

---

[3] Contemporary defenses of this view have been offered by Richard Swinburne, *The Coherence of Theism* (Oxford: Clarendon Press, 1977), and C. Stephen Layman, *The Shape of the Good* (Notre Dame: University of Notre Dame Press, 1991).

[4] Gottfried Leibniz in *Opera Omnia*, Louis Dutens (ed.), Geneva, 1768, Volume IV, iii, p. 275.

Good requires a paradigmatic standard of goodness

Historically, a number of philosophers argued that any property which a thing could have to greater and lesser degrees must have a perfect exemplar. The best way to understand the underlying argument is by way of an example. Suppose a professor asks her class to take out a piece of paper and to draw a circle. Each student grabs a pen or pencil and draws something roughly round. After looking at each paper the professor says, "Those look good, but no one has drawn a shape that is perfectly circular; try again." So, they try again. Does anyone draw a perfect circle the next time? Probably not, though the shapes are probably getting closer to the ideal of perfect circularity. Close to the *what*? The ideal – perfect circularity. What exactly is this thing that everyone is trying to get their circle to resemble? It seems as if there must be *something* that they are trying to approximate when they draw their circles. After all, it would be odd if there were *nothing* that they were trying to approximate. How could one try to approximate nothing?

Reasoning of this sort inclines some philosophers to think that properties which can approximate an ideal to a greater or lesser extent require some really existing perfect instance of that ideal. St. Thomas Aquinas, for example, famously argued this way in one of his arguments for the existence of God:

> The fourth way [to argue for God's existence] is taken from the gradation to be found in things. Among beings there are some more and some less good, true, noble and the like. But "more" and "less" are predicated of different things, according as they resemble in their different ways something which is the maximum, as a thing is said to be hotter according as it more nearly resembles that which is hottest; so that there is something which is truest, something best, something noblest and, consequently, something which is uttermost being; for those things that are greatest in truth are greatest in being ... Now the maximum in any genus is the cause of all in that genus; as fire, which is the maximum heat, is the cause of all hot things. Therefore there must also be something which is to all beings the cause of their being, goodness, and every other perfection; and this we call God.[5]

---

[5] *Summa Theologica*, Fathers of the English Dominican Province (trans.), Christian Classics, 1981, I Question 2, article 3, response.

The premises of this argument have proven notoriously difficult to defend, relying on a number of underlying claims which are widely rejected. This includes the central claim of the argument: when we encounter cases of properties that admit of greater and lesser degrees there must be some really existing perfect instance of that property. In fact, Aquinas' own example in the passage seems to reveal the problem quite strikingly. He argues that since things are more or less hot, there must be something that is maximally hot. But, of course, there is no such maximally hot thing (no matter what your friends say about their favorite Hollywood star).

It is also worth noticing that even if we accept the premises of Aquinas' argument, at best we can conclude that there is "something which is the maximum" with respect to goodness. What would this "something" be and what would it be like? It *could* be that it is a personal being which exemplifies goodness perfectly, and in that case, the "something" would at least have one of the central properties that theists attribute to God. But why think that perfect goodness would have to be *personal*?

Robert Adams has recently attempted to answer this question. According to Adams, excellence and moral excellence are best thought of as resemblance relations (like the relation between the students' circles and "perfect circularity") between things and Maximal Goodness.[6] What sort of thing would Maximal Goodness be? Adams argues that it would have to be personal:

> Theists have sometimes tried to infer the personality of the supreme Good from the premise that persons, as such, are the most excellent things that we know, from which it is claimed to follow that the supremely excellent being must be of that sort. A more cautious line of argument begins with the premise, harder to deny, that most of the excellences that are most important to us, and of whose value we are most confident, are excellences of persons or of qualities or actions or works or lives or stories of persons. So if excellence consists in resembling or imaging a being that is the Good itself, nothing is more important to the role of the Good itself than that persons and

---

[6] Robert Adams, *Finite and Infinite Goods* (Oxford: Oxford University Press, 1999). This component of the view is primarily defended in the first section of the book, pages 13–130. As one might expect, since resemblance is such a slippery affair Adams needs to, and does, provide a more refined view. In particular, he holds that moral excellence is a species of value excellence generally where the latter is to be understood as "resembling God in a way that could serve God as a reason for loving the thing" (p. 36).

their properties should be able to resemble or image it. That is obviously likelier to be possible if the Good itself is a person or importantly like a person.[7]

Adams' argument depends on two controversial claims that we can only mention here. The first is the claim that excellence is to be thought of as a relation. The second is that moral excellence is best understood as a relation to a Maximally Excellent Person. As we noted earlier, followers of Plato, to pick one example, have been content to understand excellence as a relation between things and "forms." Does the Maximally Excellent thing need to be personal in order to play this relational role? Perhaps.

Moral obligation requires (personal) imperatives

Our first three arguments aim to show that the truth of claims about what is good can be explained only by the existence or activity of a divine being. Our fourth argument focuses specifically on the way in which God might be necessary for grounding claims about what is *right*.

Some philosophers argue that claims about the right must be grounded in something over and above whatever grounds claims about the good. Something, they argue, must serve to distinguish when goods rise to the level of the moral and when they go so far as to become supererogatory. Not all philosophers agree that there must be an extra fact which explains why some actions are both good *and* obligatory. For example, someone might deny that there are any supererogatory acts because they think we have an obligation to perform *every* good action. Surely these obligations would be merely *prima facie* (literally "at first glance") obligations. Since there are so many good things that you could do at any one time you would, at any given time, have numerous and conflicting obligations. Your *ultima facie* or "all things considered" obligation would then be to do that which is best among those competing obligations. So if it is best that you give all of your time, money, and energy to serving the needs of the poor, you would, on this view, be obliged to do that.

For those who think that some additional grounds are needed, is there any reason to think that divine command is an especially good ground? Robert Adams argues that it is. He writes:

[7] *Ibid.*, p. 42.

> The most important distinction between the right, or obligation, and the good, in my opinion, is that right and wrong, as matters of obligation, must be understood in relation to *social* contexts, broadly understood, but that is not true of all the types of good with which we are concerned. The beauty of a scene or the badness of a pain can be understood in abstraction from any social setting . . . If I have an obligation on the other hand, I believe it can only be in a personal relationship or in a social system of relationships.[8]

Adams points to two facts about obligation that he thinks weigh strongly in favor of his view. First, obligatory actions are actions that we *care* about performing. That is, if someone agreed that a certain action was indeed obligatory but then shrugged it off by saying "But I don't care about that," we would suppose that they did not really understand what it means to be obligated to do something. This feature of morality was discussed earlier, when we noted that the demands of morality apply universally, whether we want them to or not.

What is it about obligatory acts that could explain this intrinsic motivational feature? Adams argues that the most plausible answer is that obligations are imposed on us only by way of the demands of a *system of social relationships*. According to this "social theory of obligation" an obligation to perform an action consists of "being required . . . by another person or a group of persons to do it." How does this explain the motivational force of obligations? The answer is that the motivational force arises because we value the social relationships we find ourselves in. Complying with an obligation is thus "an expression of my valuing and respecting the relationship."[9]

Second, there are close and important connections between the notions of obligation and guilt. When you fail to perform an action that you are obliged to perform, you are guilty; and guilt carries with it two important connotations. First, we usually tie our use of the word "guilt" to wrong actions that did or might have harmed *some person*. Second, we usually associate guilt with *being alienated* from other people. For this reason we often seek forgiveness from others when we commit a wrong as a way of being "freed" from guilt.

Both of these features argue strongly in favor of the notion that obligation involves demands imposed in a social context. The obvious question to

---

[8] *Ibid.*, p. 233.   [9] *Ibid.*, p. 242.

ask at this point is: why think that the social context involves God? Won't purely human social contexts suffice to establish moral obligations? For Adams, the answer is no, and for reasons we have already considered. If obligation is reduced to demands made by actual human communities, then obligation would lose its *objective* character. The obligation not to commit genocide cannot be undone simply because a human social community changes its demands. However, if obligation arises through the social demands imposed on us by God's commands, this strong notion of the objectivity of moral obligation can be preserved.[10]

Moral motivation and religion

The second central question about the nature of objective morality was this: why should we care about being moral? Unlike the theoretical question of how to *ground the truth* of moral claims, this question concerns the distinctly practical matter of motivation.

There are, of course, many different answers to the question of why we ought to care about morality. Plato, for example, presses for the view that to be a virtuous person – to be, in other words, the sort of person who habitually behaves morally – is to be a psychologically healthy person. Immoral behavior promotes vice and therefore causes disease in the soul. Thus, we should care about behaving morally for exactly the same reason we care about (say) exercising or eating a healthy diet: it promotes our health and makes us better off. In a similar vein, the three main theistic religions are often interpreted as recommending that we care about morality as a means of achieving some sort of reward or avoiding some sort of punishment in the afterlife. And, of course, there are many others.

Our goal in this section, however, is not to canvass the variety of answers that have been offered in the historical and contemporary literature to the question of why we should care about morality. Rather, given that our topic is *religion* and ethics, we want to focus our attention on an argument for the conclusion that belief in God *makes a difference* in whether we care about morality. As we shall see, if this argument is sound, then theists have greater reason to care about moral behavior than non-theists have.

---

[10] *Ibid.*, p. 248.

The argument we shall consider is a reconstructed version of an argument offered by Immanuel Kant. According to Kant, the possibility of living the moral life would be diminished or extinguished unless we were to accept belief in theism.[11] Robert Adams reconstructs his argument as follows:

8.1. It would be demoralizing not to believe that there is a moral order of the universe.

8.2. Demoralization is morally undesirable.

8.3. Therefore, there is a moral advantage in believing that there is a moral order of the universe.

8.4. Theism provides the most adequate theory of a moral order of the universe.

8.5. Therefore, there is a moral advantage to accepting theism.[12]

Adams tells us that, by "demoralization," he means "a weakening or deterioration of moral motivation."[13] Likewise, to say that something provides a "moral advantage" is to say that it provides us with motives – additional motives that we otherwise would not have – that encourage or help to sustain moral behavior. Thus, the conclusion amounts to the claim that theists have greater moral motivation – and so greater reason to care about moral behavior – than non-theists.

Note, however, that the first premise can be understood in at least two different ways, depending on how one understands the term "moral order." On the first, "universalistic" reading, to say that the world has a moral order is to say that the world is set up so that "morally good actions will probably contribute to a good world-history."[14] On the second "individualistic" reading, to say that the universe has a moral order is to say that our universe is set up so that those who act virtuously ultimately become happy. Thus, we arrive at the following two understandings of 8.1:

8.1.* It would be demoralizing not to believe that morally good actions will probably contribute to a good world history.

---

[11] Such arguments seem to be at work in Kant's *Religion Within the Bounds of Reason Alone*.

[12] Robert M. Adams, "Moral Arguments for Theistic Belief," in *The Virtue of Faith* (Oxford: Oxford University Press, 1987), p. 151.

[13] *Ibid.*, p. 151.   [14] *Ibid.*, p. 151.

8.1.**   It would be demoralizing not to believe that morally good actions will lead to one's own ultimate happiness.

Suppose we read 8.1 as 8.1*. The argument then suggests that if you believe that your performing a good action ultimately contributes to the overall goodness of the universe, then good action takes on a greater measure of importance for you. Likewise, if you believe that things will ultimately turn out badly no matter what you do, or that the long term effects of your action are just as likely to lead to bad ends as good ones, you will likely feel discouraged or ambivalent about doing the right thing.

However, read in this way the argument seems vulnerable to at least two objections. First, 8.1* seems rather dubious: it is not clear that it really makes much practical difference to an individual that his action will contribute towards an overall good world history. Of course, we might well care in the abstract about contributing to a good world history. But the point here is that it is hard to imagine being demoralized simply by the thought that particular moral acts of ours make little or no difference to the global good. Second, the argument neglects the fact that the universe might exhibit a moral order (in the sense given by 8.1*) even if there were no theistic deity. Consider, for example, the view held by many sects of Buddhism and Hinduism that global moral order is maintained by means of karma. Those who are virtuous in this lifetime, but who still fall short of the ideal of enlightenment, are reincarnated in the next life in a better condition while those who are vicious are reincarnated in an inferior condition. This "karmic management system" seems to play the same role as God does in Kant's picture. So, while we might be able to conclude from Kant's argument that proper moral motivation requires belief in some sort of entity or process which ensures universal moral order, perhaps a non-theistic being or even purely impersonal process would suffice equally well.

Suppose, on the other hand, we replace 8.1 with 8.1**. This version of the argument initially appears more promising, since it plays on the more powerful motive of our own self-interest. But there is something strange about the argument under this reading as well. The argument encourages us to think this way: "Unless I think that acting morally will ultimately be good for me, I won't act morally. So, I should start to believe that acting morally will indeed ultimately be good for me." Is it sensible to reason in this way? Consider how such reasoning works in the abstract: "Unless I think that doing X is good for me, I won't do X. So, I better start believing that X is good for me." Such reasoning makes sense if we *already have* good reason to do X, but not otherwise. (To see this, substitute in for X "hitting myself in the head with a brick" and note that the reasoning is just silly.) But if I *already have* good reason to think that X (acting morally, in the case of our argument) is good for me, then this argument is superfluous.

Adams suggest a further motivational argument which he sketches as follows:

> It is widely thought that moral judgments have an action- and preference-guiding force that they could not have unless everyone had reason to follow them in his [or her] actions and preferences. But there has also been widespread dissatisfaction with arguments purporting to show that everyone does have reason always to be moral . . . It is plausibly assumed, however, that virtually everyone has a deep and strong desire for his own happiness. So if happiness will in the long run be strictly proportioned to moral goodness, that explains how virtually everyone does have an important reason to want to be good.[15]

Thus, since this commonly held feature of morality is more likely to be true if theism is true than not, this feature of morality provides a reason to believe in theism.

This argument has a few controversial premises. But more importantly for our purposes, it seems to fall prey to the objection that afflicts other arguments above, namely, that while this feature of morality might require appeal to something beyond those things we find in ordinary nature, it does not necessarily require an appeal to theism. So, for example, it appears that once again an appeal to a system of "karmic management" (whether actually religiously grounded or not) will fit the bill just as well as theism.[16]

---

[15] *Ibid.*, p. 158.

[16] We should note, however, that some have argued that belief in karma actually *undermines* moral motivation. Moreover, it has also been argued that the idea of a karmic management system is utterly implausible apart from the supposition that there is some organizing mind in charge of the administration of karmic rewards and punishments. So, in the end, appeals to karmic management might not do as well as theism in solving the problem of moral motivation (they might simply make it worse); or, on the other hand, they might be untenable apart from theistic belief. See, in this vein, Paul Edwards, *Reincarnation: A Critical Examination* (Amherst, NY: Prometheus Books, 2001), and Robin Collins, "Eastern Religions," in Michael Murray (ed.), *Reason for the Hope Within* (Grand Rapids: Eerdmans Press, 1999).

Divine command theories of the right and the good

In Plato's famous dialogue *Euthyphro*, Socrates engages Euthyphro in a discussion of his plan to prosecute his own father for an unintentional killing. Socrates is puzzled by Euthyphro's confidence in his moral condemnation of his father in light of the moral ambiguities of the case. Perhaps in order to shake Euthyphro's confidence, Socrates poses a challenge to the view of moral uprightness or "piety" that Euthyphro endorses. On Euthyphro's view, piety is "that which is loved by the gods."

Socrates then asks the question: is the pious loved by the gods because it is pious, or is something pious because it is loved by the gods? Contemporary philosophers call Socrates' question and the dilemma that it spawns "The Euthyphro Dilemma." The Euthyphro Dilemma is of interest to us because, as we have seen, many philosophers think, like Euthyphro, that important ethical claims depend on facts about God in some essential way. If that is right, these philosophers will also need to give us a response to the Dilemma.

Consider the Euthyphro Dilemma as it arises in a theistic context with respect to morally good actions. Thus: are morally good acts good because they are loved by God, or does God love them because they are good? As with any dilemma, this one presents us with two alternatives, each of which seems to have fatal consequences.

Suppose we accept the second horn of the dilemma. On this view, something counts as good simply in virtue of its being loved by God. But this view faces three very serious problems. We can call them the *contingency problem*, the *non-objectivity problem*, and the *anything goes problem*. First, the claim that good actions are good because the gods love them seems to make truths about goodness objectionably contingent. If nothing prevents God from loving things that are different from what God actually loves, then goodness can change from world to world or time to time. This is obviously objectionable to those who believe that claims about morality are, if true, necessarily true.

Second, it casts doubt on the notion that morality is genuinely objective. If moral claims can sensibly be regarded as expressions of divine tastes or preferences, why not similarly regard them as sometimes expressing our tastes or preferences as well? What is it about God that *privileges* his tastes, so that what he loves or hates becomes good or bad *for everyone*? It is, one might think, rather difficult to see any reason for privileging divine tastes over creaturely tastes; and so if we think that morality depends in part on what the gods love, it seems we should also think that it depends in part on what we love too – in which case it seems to be merely subjective.

Third, and most worrisome, however, is the fact that on this view (as applied to *the good*) we are forced to admit that if God were to love something that we now regard as morally reprehensible – torturing innocents, for example – then such an action *would become good*. Since the love of God determines the standards of goodness, his loving such torture is all it takes to make that action good. And this seems wrong. We are inclined to think that no matter what God thinks about torturing innocents, such an action is paradigmatically wrong. In fact, when we engage in moral theorizing, we typically think that when a moral theory entails consequences like this, such entailments are fatal for the theory.

On the other hand, the second horn of the Dilemma is similarly problematic. If God loves good actions because they are good, rather than the other way around, then it seems that God's sovereignty and independence are threatened. There is something – the standards of moral goodness – over which God is *not* sovereign. God is bound by the laws of morality instead of being their establisher. Moreover, God *depends* for his goodness on the extent to which he conforms to an independent moral standard. Thus, God is not absolutely independent.

What shall we say about this dilemma? Suppose we embrace the first horn of the dilemma. *Theological voluntarism* is the view that good and evil are entirely dependent on what God wills and nothing else. Medieval philosopher Jean de Gerson put the view straightforwardly as follows:

> Nothing is evil except because prohibited [by God]; and nothing is good except because accepted by God; and God does not therefore will and approve our actions because they are good, but they are therefore good because he approves them. Similarly, they are therefore evil because he prohibits and disapproves of them.[17]

Similar remarks can be found in the works of the Roman Catholic philosopher Peter d'Ailly and Protestant theologian Martin Luther.

---

[17] Jean de Gerson, *On the Spiritual Life of the Soul*, Reading I, Corollary X, cited in William Wainwright, *Religion and Morality* (Burlington, VT: Ashgate Publishing, 2005), p. 74.

Thus baldly stated, it is hard to see how one might avoid the three pitfalls that we identified earlier. But there are ways of supplementing one's voluntarism that seem to provide the resources for doing so. For example, one might insist that God's preferences are freely formed, but also necessary. Thus, in chapter 1 we considered the suggestion that God's freedom might be compatible with his inability to sin. If that is right, then God's freedom might also be compatible with his being unable to *command* anything other than what he has commanded. (One might even think that the two inabilities are connected: God cannot sin for the same reason he cannot command differently – namely, it is part of his very nature to love kindness, abhor cruelty, and so on.) If this is right, then one has a voluntarist position (facts about moral goodness might depend on divine commands) but one can easily avoid both the contingency objection and the anything-goes objection. The concern about objectivity remains; but here one might respond by saying that divine tastes and preferences are relevantly different from human tastes and preferences. The latter do not provide objectivity, one might say, precisely because (unlike God's) they are neither necessary nor objectively authoritative.

Alternatively, we might try to embrace the second horn of the Dilemma. In the preceding sections of this chapter we already have considered views which give God a central role in morality and which implicitly contain ways of resolving the Dilemma. For example, Robert Adams' theory of goodness holds that goodness does not depend on what God loves or wills even though goodness is centrally connected to the being of God. On that view, goodness of a thing (or action or state of character) depends on the ways in which that thing *resembles* God. This, then, seems to be a way of maintaining that God *loves* good things because they are good without committing oneself to the claim that facts about goodness or moral standards or the like are *independent* of God. Moreover, the threat to God's sovereignty is mitigated because nobody feels a burden to say that God is sovereign over his very nature.

Note, however, that, though this view might well explain what makes morally good acts *good*, it does not obviously have the resources to explain what makes them *obligatory*. And so the Euthyphro question arises once again: are morally good acts *obligatory* because they are commanded by God? Or are they commanded by God because they are obligatory? The former suggestion seems to fall prey to the same problems that plague the first horn of the original Dilemma. On the other hand, the latter question simply raises the question of *why* morally good acts are obligatory. After all, not *all* good things are obligatory. It might be good to give all your money to the poor. It is not obviously obligatory that you do so. Thus, some story would have to be told about what makes (certain) morally good acts obligatory; and, moreover, the story would have to avoid the pitfalls associated with the second horn of the original Dilemma.

One might try to solve this problem by telling a story about moral obligation that parallels the story about moral goodness – grounding it somehow in God's essential nature. Doing so would allow one to avoid the problems associated with the second horn of the original Dilemma (threats to sovereignty and independence); but it is very hard to see *how* this could be done. Notably, Adams himself embraces voluntarism at this point.

Recall that earlier in this chapter we said that Adams thinks that moral obligation (unlike moral goodness) *is* dependent on divine commands. Pursuing certain goods and avoiding certain evils becomes obligatory for us only in so far as those things are commanded by God. However, because the commands are issued by a *loving* God, there are certain things that even God could not command. For example, because torturing innocents is intrinsically bad, God could never command us to do it, and even were God to do so, the command could not obligate us since we can never be obligated to do something that is intrinsically evil.

The trouble with this view, however, unlike the voluntarist position described earlier in this section, is that it avoids the contingency problem and the anything-goes problem apparently by saying that some obligations depend on divine commands whereas others do not. For it looks as if we will be obligated to refrain from torture *regardless* of what God commands, simply because torture is inherently bad. But if that is right, then it is hard to see why God's commands should be relevant to any other (universal) obligation either.[18]

---

[18] Obviously God's commands will be relevant to *some* obligations. For example, the Hebrew Bible tells us that God commanded Jonah to prophesy to the Ninevites. Presumably *that* obligation is wholly dependent on God's command. But it is not a universal obligation. (The rest of us don't have to go find Ninevites and prophesy to them.)

Religion and public discourse

It will come as no surprise to any reader that conflicts over the relationship between religion and politics are widespread and serious. Whether it is American judges trying to determine the appropriate relation of church and state, theocrats in Iran aiming to establish an "authentically Islamic state," or factions in Northern Ireland or Southern Lebanon struggling to determine the rights and roles of religious minorities and majorities, the confusion concerning the role of religion in matters of the state is important in a way that is hard to overestimate.

Of course, philosophical theorizing about the relationships between religion and politics is not a new phenomenon. In early modern Europe religiously inspired wars flared repeatedly in ways that threatened to destabilize the entire continent. These persistent conflicts increased the sense of urgency among philosophers and political theorists who sought defensible philosophical grounds for establishing stability and peace. Then and now, two issues are of paramount importance. The first concerns the question of whether it is good for the citizens of a state to tolerate those who hold religious beliefs and engage in religious practices that conflict with their own. Throughout modern history states have engaged in a variety of intolerant practices aimed at forcibly converting, killing, or exiling those who dissent from the majority (or otherwise officially sanctioned) state religion. Many in early modern Europe sought to stem such practices by arguing that sound moral and political reasoning demands religious toleration. The second issue concerns the role that religious views or concerns should be allowed to play in the governance decisions in liberal democracies. In this section of the chapter we will examine both of these issues.

Religious toleration

To most in the West, the claims that the state is to be tolerant of religion and religious diversity, and that religious sects and religious individuals are to behave with tolerance towards one another, border on truisms. But such ideas are not and have not been universally shared. On what grounds then can a stance of religious toleration be defended? There are two general types of arguments for toleration, one pragmatic and the other epistemological.

The seventeenth-century British philosopher John Locke argued that states are required to tolerate religion and religious diversity because the interests of the state extend only to "procuring, preserving, and advancing" the "civil interests" of citizens. Religious organizations, on the other hand, are voluntary associations in which people engage in "the public worshipping of God, in such a manner as they judge acceptable to him, and effectual to the salvation of their souls."[19] Thus for Locke, the state is obliged to be tolerant of all forms of "public worshipping" as long as it does not interfere with the civil interests of any citizens of the state.

Locke's view does not give religious organizations unfettered freedom. For example, a religious organization would not be permitted to engage in activities like human sacrifice or illegal drug use, even for religious purposes. In addition, the state might block religious individuals from engaging in actions that harm their own civil interests. The state might, for example, use coercive means to force someone to accept a life-saving blood transfusion even if his or her religious community regards that form of treatment as religiously objectionable. Still, this leaves religious individuals and communities with a great deal of latitude in their religious activities.

While Locke's position has some initial appeal, critics have noted that it is not likely to persuade people who are not already in favor of state-sanctioned tolerance. Many (Islamic theocracies, for example) hold that it is just wrong to think that the role of the state is limited to advancing "civil interests." They will argue rather that states are constituted to procure, preserve, and advance the interests of the whole person, including distinctively religious interests such as obedience to God's commands or the salvation of the citizen's eternal souls. Locke's position lacks resources to convince such critics.

In the same work Locke offers another pragmatic argument that state tolerance of religious diversity is essential since the only alternative would be (a) to purge religion from the state or (b) to enforce religious conformity. However, doing either of these things would require that the state exercise its coercive powers to change citizen's religious commitment – commitment which, in Locke's words are "inward persuasions of the mind." But, Locke continues, coercive force is simply unable to change minds. Beliefs are not

---

[19] John Locke, *A Letter Concerning Toleration*, in G. and J. Rivington (eds.), *The Works of John Locke* (Oxford, 1824), Volume 5, pp. 10–13.

under our voluntary control and so threats and violence cannot do anything to bring about this result.[20] States must thus adopt a posture of toleration towards diverse religions.

While Locke is right that we do not have direct voluntary control over our beliefs, this does not entail that coercive force cannot change minds in other ways. Pascal, for example, argued that if we do not believe that Christianity is true, but nevertheless think that there are good practical reasons to accept it, the prudent thing to do is to adopt various Christian practices – church attendance, Bible reading, and so on – with the intention of generating such belief. If these indirect mechanisms sometimes succeed, this might be enough reason for the state to take it upon itself to coerce citizens to engage in religious practices and rituals in order to bring about the change of belief that Locke thinks is impossible. In light of this, Locke's second pragmatic argument in favor of tolerance also seems to fail.

In addition to these pragmatic arguments, philosophers have offered a number of epistemic arguments in favor of tolerance. These arguments share in common the idea that accepting or acting on intolerant policies will always involve relying on beliefs that are *uncertain* in some way or other, because they are doubtful on their own, or at least *more* doubtful than beliefs that support policies of tolerance. The seventeenth-century French philosopher Pierre Bayle, for example, argued that any principle that comes from revelation and which conflicts with the "clear and distinct notions of natural light" must be rejected as false. Bayle thinks that religiously intolerant policies all run afoul of this test and thus that any religious believer who holds such a policy is rationally obligated to give it up.

Advocates of intolerant policies will not likely be persuaded by such arguments. Bayle's argument depends on the claim that state sponsored coercion of belief is obviously immoral. But those who commend intolerant policies might well respond that their coercive tactics are not immoral after all since they are aiming to protect people from serious evils such as eternal damnation. It is not clear that this impasse can be resolved.

Immanuel Kant offered a quite different epistemic argument for tolerance. Kant held that full moral conscientiousness requires that we only act on moral principles that we are certain are true. However, those who practice extremely intolerant policies are surely acting on policies of which they

---

[20] *Ibid.*, p. 11.

cannot be certain. Kant considers an especially extreme case in which a heretic is condemned to death for his beliefs. In this case, he contends:

> That it is wrong to deprive a man of his life because of his religious faith is certain, unless . . . a Divine Will, made known in extraordinary fashion, has ordered it otherwise. But that God has ever uttered this terrible injunction can be asserted only on the basis of historical documents and it is never [absolutely] certain. After all, the revelation has reached the [executioner] only through men and has been interpreted by men . . . it is at least possible that in this instance a mistake has prevailed.[21]

Kant's argument hinges on the claims that we must act only on moral principles which we hold with certainty, and that God could never reveal to us any moral principle that could rise to that level. Even if the second claim is true, however, it is hard to see why one would accept this very strong first claim. It might be that it is wrong for you to act from moral principles which you have not thought about at all, or in which you have little confidence. But a requirement of certainty seems too strong.

Perhaps a weaker version of Kant's argument would suffice according to which, when we come across a purported revealed divine command that seems to contradict a moral principle that appears certain to us, it is immoral for us to act on that command. So, when you take a Biblical passage to recommend that you use coercive force to gain converts – something which otherwise seems quite wrong – you should refrain from acting on it (at least in part because the justification for your belief about the command would seem to be outweighed by the certainty you have concerning the moral principle).

Unfortunately, critics of tolerance will not likely be convinced by this argument either. First, even if Kant is completely correct, there are all sorts of intolerant policies that would not violate moral principles that seem otherwise obvious. While murdering heretics might be obviously objectionable, excluding dissenters from one's community, or certain privileges in the community, is not. Furthermore, critics are likely to think that biblical texts and their interpretations have a very high degree of warrant for us. When they do, they will be able to outweigh even moral principles in which one has a good measure of confidence.

---

[21] Immanuel Kant, *Reason Within the Limits of Reason Alone* (New York: Harper and Row, 1960), p. 175.

The role of religious belief in liberal democracies

While on the one hand defenders of liberal democracy have argued for policies that are tolerant towards religion and religious diversity among their citizens, a number of recent liberal theorists have argued, on the other hand, that the role of religion in civil matters must be severely constrained. Democracies are founded on the notion that citizens of the state can engage in collective decision making, and that this decision making imposes obligations on all citizens that can be backed by coercive enforcement measures. Still, we all recognize that this decision-making power by the majority is not entirely unconstrained. The majority, for example, does not have the authority to enact policies which violate the fundamental rights of citizens. Even if, for example, the majority wants to use all blue-eyed citizens as slaves or as unwilling subjects in medical experiments, they lack the authority to make and enforce such policies.

Are there any other limits on the authority of the democratic majority aside from these fundamental rights of individual citizens? Some think so. For example, imagine that the majority decides that every car manufactured and sold in the state must be black. When polled, all of the citizens who voted for the new policy explain their decision by saying that they voted for it just because they like black cars. Are these permissible grounds on which to make policies that govern everyone, even those with different preferences? It hardly seems so. After all, why should the simple preferences of the majority come to have legal force over you, someone who really dislikes black cars? While not a very serious matter, something about this governance arrangement seems unjust.

Cases like this have led some political theorists to argue that when citizens are acting in their role as policy decision makers, they are obligated to make those decisions only on certain sorts of grounds. John Rawls argues that, at least when it comes to the most central aspects of state policy, what Rawls calls "questions of constitutional essentials and questions of basic justice," citizens are obliged to make decisions "in terms each could reasonably expect others might endorse as consistent with their freedom and equality."[22] More specifically, Rawls claims that in justifying our decision making "we are to appeal only to presently accepted general beliefs and

---

[22] John Rawls, *Political Liberalism* (New York: Columbia University Press, 1993), p. 218.

forms of reasoning found in common sense, and the methods and conclusions of science when these are not controversial."[23]

The reason for these constraints is apparent. If citizens are allowed to make decisions on the basis of reasons that each *could not in principle* reasonably expect others might endorse, then the results of these decisions might be unjustly coercive in the way the policy about black cars would be. Decision making in liberal democracies must take place by appeals to such "public reasons" in order to provide a shared public basis for political justification and authority.

Such restrictions, however, have a straightforward and important consequence: since religious beliefs are justified by *private* reasons (appeals to religious experience, religious authorities, or "faith") those beliefs would not be permitted to play a role when citizens are engaged in making decisions, at least when it comes to the central issues Rawls identifies. However, this constraint extends beyond religious belief. Rawls argues that citizens are not permitted to invoke any "comprehensive doctrine" when engaged in civil decision making about constitutional essentials and matters of basic justice. As a result, one can no more appeal to one's Marxist views than one can appeal to one's Mormon views. Citizens with religious (or Marxist, or . . .) convictions are, of course, welcome to defend policies that are motivated by their religious commitments, but only when those policies can *also* be supported by sufficient public reasons. In fact, in some of his most recent work on the topic, Rawls even allows that religious citizens could argue for civil policies on the basis of private reasons as long as sufficient public reasons are offered in support of the appropriate policy "in due course."[24]

What should we think of these restrictive positions? Rawls emphasizes the importance of theoretical agreement for just and stable societies while minimizing the role of disagreement and compromise to the point where the Rawlsian ideal seems to become unrealistic. In real states there will be wide divergence of opinion when it comes to what counts as a "good reason" or a reason "each could reasonably expect others might endorse." Many religious believers might think that their religion is rationally supported and that their reasons are ones others might endorse. Others will

---

[23] *Ibid.*, p. 224.
[24] John Rawls, "The Idea of Public Reason Revisited," in *The University of Chicago Law Review* 64 (1997), p. 783.

disagree. How then can we settle, on the Rawlsian picture, which reasons are admissible? No easy answer suggests itself.

Paul Weithman argues that such difficulties render the Rawlsian ideal unworkable. As a result, he proposes that citizens are obligated to advocate for policies when they can offer reasons favoring the claim that the policies would be genuinely good for the state. However, because there will be widely differing conceptions of what counts as a good or accessible reason by various constituencies, we cannot expect or mandate that the reasons offered will be seen as good or accessible by everyone. This may, Weithman notes, make some citizens "resent being offered reasons they regard as inaccessible, but it would be a mistake to cite their resentment as evidence that those who offered them the inaccessible reasons have violated some moral obligation."[25] Thus, according to this view, citizens in liberal democracies do not violate their duties as citizens when they choose to engage in decision making on the basis of religious reasons that they can articulate and use to show how such a policy would, by their lights, be good for the state.

Conclusion

In this chapter we have looked at the connection between religion and two central normative areas of thought: morality and politics. In the domain of morality we have seen that appeals to God or other forms of religious reality might be useful in providing answers to two crucial questions in moral philosophy: What grounds the truth of moral claims? and Why be moral? While religion might help provide answers to these questions, it is worth pointing out that other moral systems might as well. One question we have not considered (at least in any detail) here is: Does theism provide resources for answering these questions that is superior to other, non-religious moral theories? This is an eminently worthwhile question, but one that goes beyond what we can address here.

We also have considered two important questions about the connections between religion and politics: Are there reasonable grounds for promoting a policy of religious toleration? and What role, if any, should religious commitments be allowed to play when citizens act as political agents?

---

[25] Weithman 2002, p. 135.

Interestingly (though perhaps this is not surprising from those who know what to expect from philosophers!) the seemingly obvious answers are not so easy to defend. The available arguments for toleration all seem to rest on principles that defenders of intolerance are unlikely to accept. In addition, the arguments that religious reasons should be excluded from the political domain, while widely endorsed by political theorists, either seem to exclude too much or too little.

Further reading

Adams, Robert, *Finite and Infinite Goods* (Oxford: Oxford University Press, 2002).

Audi, Robert, *Religious Commitment and Secular Reason* (Cambridge: Cambridge University Press, 2000).

Eberle, Christopher, *Religious Conviction in Liberal Politics* (Cambridge: Cambridge University Press, 2002).

Helm, Paul (ed.), *Divine Commands and Morality* (Oxford: Oxford University Press, 1981).

Murphy, Mark, *Divine Authority* (Oxford: Oxford University Press, 2003).

Quinn, Philip, *Divine Commands and Moral Requirements* (Oxford: Clarendon Press, 1978).

Rea, Michael, "Naturalism and Moral Realism," in Thomas Crisp *et al.* (eds.), *Knowledge and Reality: Essays in Honor of Alvin Plantinga* (Dordrecht: Kluwer, 2006).

Wainwright, William, *Religion and Morality* (Burlington, VT: Ashgate Publishing, 2005).

Weithman, Paul, *Religion and the Obligations of Citizenship* (Cambridge: Cambridge University Press, 2006).

Wolterstorff, Nicholas and Robert Audi, *Religion in the Public Square* (New York: Rowman and Littlefield, 1996).

Zagzebski, Linda, *Divine Motivation Theory* (Cambridge: Cambridge University Press, 2004).

9 Mind, body, and immortality

Dust you are, and to dust you shall return. So Christians worldwide are reminded every year during the Ash Wednesday liturgy. But according to Christian doctrine, the return to dust is not the end of all things. In the words of the Nicene Creed, "We look for the resurrection of the dead, and the life of the world to come." The Islamic tradition expresses a similar expectation:

> I swear by the Day of Resurrection, and by the self-reproaching soul. Does man think We shall never put his bones together again? Indeed, We can remould his very fingers! Yet man would ever deny what is to come. "When will this be," he asks, "this day of Resurrection?" But when the sight of mortals is confounded and the moon eclipsed; when sun and moon are brought together – on that day man will ask "Whither shall I flee?" No, there shall be no escape. For on that day all shall return to your Lord.[1]

Likewise, the Hebrew Bible predicts a future resurrection,[2] and the thirteenth-century Jewish philosopher-theologian Maimonides lists belief in bodily resurrection as one of the thirteen central principles of the Jewish faith.

Belief in some sort of afterlife is characteristic of most world religions. But is life after death really *possible*? Many philosophers think that it is not. If they are right, then the core doctrines of a great many world religions will have to be either substantially modified or rejected. On the other hand, some have argued not only that life after death is possible, but that we actually have evidence that it occurs. Are these arguments cogent? If so, then perhaps such arguments will provide reason to take theistic belief or some other sort of religious belief more seriously. These are the sorts of

---

[1] *The Koran*, trans. by N. J. Dawood, 2nd edn. (Baltimore, MD: Penguin Books, 1999), p. 412.
[2] See, e.g. Daniel 12: 1–3.

questions that we shall take up in the present chapter. To answer them, however, we must begin with a little stage-setting.

Whether you can take belief in an afterlife seriously will depend on your views on a variety of related topics. First, it will depend on what you think life after death might amount to. Second, it will depend on what you think we are. Are we purely material beings? Are we beings with an immaterial soul? Or are we some other sort of thing? Third, it will depend upon what you think it takes for a person to *survive* some change. Must she retain the very same body? Must there be some sort of unbroken biological continuity between her past states and her future states? We'll begin by exploring these issues briefly; then we will turn to an examination of some of the main philosophical arguments for and against belief in life after death, and of some of the more interesting alleged empirical reasons for thinking that survival after death has actually occurred.

What life after death might be

There are diverse views about what it might mean for a person to survive death. The notion of *survival* implies, at the very least, the continued existence or the return to existence of something. To say that someone will survive death but that absolutely nothing pertaining to her – not even the memory of her name – will ever exist beyond her death is incoherent. The question is, if we do survive death, *what is it*, exactly, that continues in or returns to existence? The different views about what the afterlife consists in may be fruitfully organized around various different answers to this question.

For ease of exposition, let us recast our question so that it focuses on a specific historical person (Julius Caesar will do), and let us label it "The Question":

THE QUESTION: Suppose that Julius Caesar is experiencing or will experience an afterlife. What is it about him that still exists or will return to existence?

Now, many readers will surely want to say that the *obvious* answer to THE QUESTION is "Julius Caesar!" After all, it is quite natural to think that if Caesar no longer exists and never will exist again, then his survival is out of the question. (Imagine Brutus trying to reassure his old friend during the stabbing by whispering in his ear, "Don't worry, my friend; you'll survive this. Well, sure, when we're all done here you'll be dead and you won't ever *exist* again. But my point is, you'll *survive*." Small comfort that would be.)

The trouble with this obvious answer, however, is that it still leaves us wondering what it takes for Caesar to exist after his death. Must his body still exist? Suppose that, after the stabbing, God had simply annihilated Caesar's body. Could *Caesar* nevertheless continue existing? Is, perhaps, the continued existence of his soul – if there are such things as souls – sufficient? And what of the oft-heard suggestion that a person might continue to exist "in our memories"? Is that mere poetic claptrap, or does it highlight a legitimate form of survival? The fact is, poetic claptrap or not, many conceptions of the afterlife posit ways of surviving death that don't involve the continued existence of anything that could sensibly be called *our selves*. It may be tempting to deny that these latter views really count as views according to which we survive death. But, in our view, such conceptions of the afterlife should be dismissed, if at all, by *arguments* rather than by terminological fiat.

So let us, for now, set aside the "obvious" answer to THE QUESTION, and let us focus on four other answers:

ANSWER 1:   Not his body, not his mind, but only an appropriate effect or product of his life, personality, or body.

ANSWER 2:   Only his body.

ANSWER 3:   Only his mind.

ANSWER 4:   Both his mind and his body.

Obviously these answers are not logically exhaustive. For example, "only his left pinkie-toe" is a *possible* answer. But it is not an answer that anybody is likely to take seriously. ANSWERS 1–4 do, however, seem to capture the range of views about the afterlife that *are* likely to be taken seriously. Moreover, it is important to bear in mind that many people embrace mixed views of the afterlife. Some Christians, for example, maintain that, for a time after death, only our minds exist, but later our minds are reunited with our bodies. Many adherents of Eastern religions, on the other hand, maintain that the afterlife for most people consists in the continued existence and re-embodiment of their minds, but that some people escape the cycle of reincarnation and survive in a way that doesn't involve the existence of either their body or their mind but only of an appropriate "trace."

In this sense, then, ANSWERS 1–4 are not exclusive of one another (though, of course, it can't be that more than one of these answers is strictly true of the same person at once).

ANSWER 1 is meant to cover a variety of what might be called *non-personal* and *quasi-personal* conceptions of the afterlife. In Homer, for example, we find an understanding of the afterlife according to which, for most people, surviving death consists in being *remembered* by those who are still alive and in having one's "shade" – a sort of thin, not-fully-personal remnant of oneself – travel to the underworld, sometimes for punishment (as in the famous cases of Sisyphus, Tantalus, and others) but more often just for a rather humdrum sort of continued existence. On the other hand, many other religious traditions teach that what happens to us after we die is something like *absorption* by a cosmic mind or soul. On such views, we do not continue to exist as individuals; but presumably some trace of our personhood or personality lingers in such a way as to contribute, like a drop of water in the ocean, to the overall qualitative character of whatever it is that has absorbed us. In ancient Greece, this sort of view was embraced by the Orphics (the members of a mystery cult oriented around the tale of Orpheus), the Pythagoreans (number-worshipping followers of Pythagoras), some of Plato's followers, and the Stoics. It is also taught in various Eastern religions.

ANSWER 2 doesn't figure prominently into many religious traditions, but it corresponds to a conception of the afterlife that is prevalent in the popular imagination and in a great deal of classic and contemporary fiction. We are all familiar with the idea that one possible, though undesirable, way of surviving death is as an "undead" zombie. But, of course, a zombie is nothing more or less than a re-animated corpse without a mind. To the extent that one thinks that life as a zombie is at least a possible form of afterlife, one will be inclined to take ANSWER 2 seriously.

ANSWER 3 is perhaps the most popular answer. If you believe that some people survive death as disembodied or reincarnated souls, then you embrace ANSWER 3 for The Question specified to those people. And most of the major world religions in both the East and the West teach that at least some people, at least temporarily, survive in this way.

Finally, ANSWER 4 is given by those who believe in *resurrection*. To say that Julius Caesar will be resurrected is to say more than that his mind will exist again in some body or other. It is, rather, to say that his mind will exist again in numerically the same body that he had while alive on earth. That is precisely the difference between resurrection and reincarnation. The resurrected body might be different in various respects. Thus, for example, the Bible reports that, after rising from the dead, Jesus's body, though physical (he ate, and allowed people to touch him) nevertheless had the capacity to pass through walls and to go unrecognized even by close friends. Very different indeed. But it was nevertheless the *same* body – just as your body now is the same body you had when you were born, only quite different in many respects. And Christians teach that just as Jesus's resurrected body was different – better, and "glorified" as the Apostle Paul tells us in 1 Corinthians – so too our resurrected bodies will be different. Thus, though resurrection occurs only if we have *numerically* the same body, it does not at all guarantee that we will have *qualitatively* the same body. And so we would hope! A person who dies painfully as a result of contracting the Ebola virus, for example, would hardly hope to come back to life with qualitatively the same body she had when she died. Even those who die peacefully in old age would surely prefer to be resurrected with bodies far less decrepit than those they died with. And so on.

There are, of course, other *possible* conceptions of the afterlife than those surveyed here. But these are the main ones on offer in the contemporary marketplace of ideas. We turn now to a brief discussion of theories about what we are – theories that will help to determine both our views about whether life after death is possible, and also our views about which of the above answers to THE QUESTION are viable.

Materialism vs. dualism

Materialism is, roughly, the view that nothing exists except for spacetime, material objects and events in spacetime, and the properties exemplified by these things.[3] Theists have traditionally rejected materialism, if for no other

---

[3] Some readers of this text will be familiar with a view in the philosophy of mind called "property dualism," according to which (a) mental properties are supposed to be non-physical properties, and therefore (b) materialism – or, at any rate, what is often called "reductive materialism" – is supposed to be false. Even these readers should be willing to recognize, though, that there is a clear sense in which even property dualists can count as materialists; and it is this sense of "materialism" that we have in mind and aim to capture with our definition.

reason than that God has traditionally been regarded as an immaterial being. Traditional theism, then, is committed either to some form of *substance dualism*, or to some form of *idealism*. Substance dualism is the view that there are two kinds of concrete substances, material and immaterial. Idealism is the view that there are no material substances, but only minds and whatever other immaterial substances there might be.

Moreover, for a long time – at least until the nineteenth century – theists tended largely, though not universally, to endorse the view that we human beings are immaterial things or, at the very least, have an immaterial component. The view, of course, wasn't that our *bodies* or any parts thereof are immaterial. Rather, the view was that what we are, fundamentally, is either an immaterial being (a soul) temporarily housed in a material body, or else a composite whose parts are a material body and an immaterial soul. People who endorse views like this are typically referred to as *mind–body dualists*, since they recognize that minds, whatever they are, are neither material substances, nor properties of material substances, nor events in spacetime. Note, however, that it is possible to be a substance dualist without being a mind–body dualist. One might, for example, believe in the God of traditional theism while at the same time believing that human minds are material things.

You might wonder what the difference is between, on the one hand, saying that a human being is a soul housed in a body and, on the other hand, saying that she is a composite of body and soul. The difference is simply this: on the former view, the person can exist whole and complete without her body; on the latter view, she cannot. It might be that she can exist in a sort of degenerate or severely incapacitated state without her body; but, on this view, so long as a person's soul is disembodied, she will be in some sense incomplete or not fully herself. The former view is typically referred to as "Cartesian dualism," named after René Descartes, one of the view's most prominent defenders. The latter view is commonly attributed to St. Thomas Aquinas. For present purposes, we will characterize that as a form of dualism as well, though for various technical reasons that we won't get into here, there is, in fact, some controversy about that characterization.

In the theistic tradition, then, there has, historically, been a strong tendency toward both substance dualism generally and toward mind–body dualism more specifically. One important reason for the tendency toward mind–body dualism is that this sort of view of human minds seems to fit better with traditional theistic views about the afterlife. It is (relatively) easy to see how one might survive death as a disembodied soul. It is much harder to see how one might survive death if one is *identical* to some physical thing (one's body, or one's brain) that is destroyed when one dies and decomposes. For this reason, then, materialism – which currently dominates the academic world so completely that mind–body dualists are, nowadays, typically mocked rather than engaged as serious dialogue partners – has been seen by many as a threat to traditional theistic belief.

Furthermore, the very intuition that seems to make materialism a threat to belief in immortality in general also seems to pose a threat (independent of the dualism/materialism debate) to belief in resurrection in particular. For, as we have seen, believers in resurrection maintain that – regardless of whether they have an immaterial soul – some day they will be re-embodied in the *very same* body that they have here and now. But if you have already accepted that a material thing that has died and decomposed cannot enjoy any sort of afterlife, then you cannot believe in resurrection. For, after all, if your present body can never live again after it dies, then whatever body you get back on "Resurrection Day" won't be the *very same* body that you had when you died; and so whatever happens to you on that day will not be resurrection but rather some sort of reincarnation.

We now face two questions. First, is it really true that life after death is impossible if materialism is true? Are there, in other words, insuperable obstacles either to resurrecting a body that has died and subsequently decomposed, or to bringing it about that some new body nonetheless constitutes the same material person that was previously constituted by a different body? And, second, are there, in fact, such powerful arguments against dualism that (as is commonly alleged or implied) anybody who accepts it is simply being stubborn or stupid? We will take up the first question at length later on in this chapter. We will address the second question briefly here.

There is, in fact, a lot to be said in favor of materialism. We often talk as if it is true. We fret about our weight, compliment friends on their appearance, and complain when people bump into us. But, of course, if we are immaterial souls, we have no weight, our friends have no appearance, and nobody ever bumps into us. Moreover, there is no denying that our minds are intimately connected with our brains. Damage to your brain damages your mind. Depending on how much of your brain is damaged, you can lose memories, capacities for certain kinds of thought, the ability to speak, or all of these things and more. Put the wrong substances in your blood and your brain malfunctions; and as your brain malfunctions, so too does your mind. All of this is easy to explain on materialism: the mind *is* the brain, or maybe it is like software being run on the brain. It is much harder to explain on dualism. And this is in no small part because it is very hard to see how an immaterial soul could *interact* with a material brain. There's a scene in the movie *Ghost* where Patrick Swayze's character – now a ghost – tries for the first time to kick a can. He can't. And, of course, we can all see the problem right away: he's just not the right sort of thing anymore to interact with the physical world. (The problem gets "solved" in short order in the film; but, as we might expect, the "solution" isn't one that anybody can take with philosophical seriousness.) So, in short, materialism seems to be the best explanation for mind–body interaction and dependence, and it is fairly commonsensical as well.

But does any of this constitute anything approaching a compelling reason for rejecting dualism? Hardly. The fact that we often talk as if materialism is true shows nothing – especially since we often also talk as if it is false. (You look in the mirror and you say "I hate my body." Do we infer that you hate *yourself*? No. Even if you do hate yourself, we typically recognize that hatred as something different from whatever hatred you feel toward your body. So we sometimes talk as if we are distinct from our bodies. Score a point for the dualist. And further examples abound.) Likewise, the fact that mind–body dependence is explained – or even *best* explained, whatever exactly that comes to – on materialism is, at best, only one piece of evidence on materialism's side. It is compelling evidence, however, only if there are no countervailing reasons for accepting dualism.

And theists, at any rate, do have such countervailing reasons. For theists are already committed to the existence of at least one immaterial mind – namely, God. And it would be puzzling, to say the least, if some minds were material and others immaterial. Moreover, just about every theist wants to say that God can interact with the material world. So theists are also committed to the possibility of material things interacting with immaterial things. In other words, the "interaction problem" should be wholly unmotivating for a theist. And the fact is, though it is indeed hard to see why or how an immaterial mind should depend so intimately on the brain with which it is associated, it is also hard to see, in general, how a piece of meat like a brain could do anything at all like experience pains, love other people, or think about unicorns. Consciousness is utterly baffling on materialism. Of course, as is often pointed out, it is not as if dualism by itself *answers* any of the hard problems of consciousness. But theists, at least, are already committed to the idea that at least one immaterial thing *is* conscious and can experience, love, think, and so on. And that, together with the other considerations just mentioned, should, at the very least, create a strong presumption in favor of dualism – a presumption that isn't at all obviously defeated by attention to common ways of talking or to facts about mind–body dependence.

Note that we are *not* here claiming to have provided an argument for dualism. Our aim is much more modest. We aim only to show that, contrary to what is commonly suggested, it isn't obviously irrational to be a dualist. In fact, as we see it, if one is a theist, then dualism should, at the very least, be a serious, live option – even despite the arguments that are commonly offered in support of materialism. If that is right, then even if materialism implies that life after death is impossible, the usual arguments for materialism will pose no real threat to the theist's belief in an afterlife.

People sometimes talk as if science has somehow shown that there is no immaterial soul. But, in fact, science has *shown* no such thing. It can't. Immaterial souls, by their very nature, are inaccessible to science. Thus, saying that science has shown that there are no immaterial souls is like saying that my visual survey of the room reveals that there are no invisible leprechauns in the room. If I'm wanting to show that there are no invisible leprechauns in the room, my eyes are simply the wrong instrument to use for the job. Likewise, scientific methods are the wrong methods to use to show that there are no souls. But the fact is, there are currently no very persuasive philosophical arguments against dualism either. As we noted earlier, dualism is commonly mocked rather than argued against. But here, as is often the case in philosophy, the resort to ridicule is simply a signal that serious *arguments* aren't available. And once that is clear, the ridicule itself starts to look ridiculous.

Survival and identity

We have looked so far at several different conceptions of what it might mean to survive death, and we have also briefly considered the question of what sort of thing we are – material or immaterial. We are now ready to turn to our final stage-setting question: the question of what it might *take* for us to survive death (or any other change).

The answer to this question depends in part on what we are. If we are fundamentally nothing more than immaterial souls, the answer is pretty straightforward: we survive a change if, and only if, our soul survives. Of course, one might then ask, "What does it take for an immaterial *soul* to survive?" But on this question there is rather remarkable agreement. Most philosophers throughout history have seemed willing to believe that, if there are immaterial souls at all, souls survive a change if, and only if, they are not annihilated by God or some other divine being. Non-theistic philosophers, and philosophers who have believed (for whatever reason) that God wouldn't annihilate souls, have tended therefore to say that souls are indestructible. Traditional theists, on the other hand, have typically left room for the possibility that God might destroy some souls at the end of all things.

But one might think that mere soul identity won't be enough for personal identity after all. If your soul survives but loses all of the psychological states that it had, we would be hard pressed to say that *you* survive. This seems to indicate that if you are some substance – a soul or, indeed, any other sort of substance – then, in addition to the survival of the bare substance, some of the properties of that substance must persist as well. And this presents problems not only for the defender of the survival-as-soul-survival view, but also for the defender of materialist and mind–body-composite views of survival as well.

With respect to the latter two views, one might think that, though we are (at least in part) material things, it is only the survival of our *consciousness* (whatever exactly that might mean) that matters for our survival. Or, alternatively, one might think that our own survival depends importantly on the survival of our bodies – in which case one then has to contend with the diversity of views about what it takes for a body to survive change. It is on these issues that the philosophical literature on personal identity has tended to focus.

Let us begin with a thought experiment – a scenario now prevalent in science fiction stories and films.[4] Leap ahead to the not-too-distant future.

---

[4] Among the relevant films are *The Matrix*, *Freejack*, *Abre Los Ojos* (remade as *Vanilla Sky*), and *The Sixth Day*. Among the more well-known novels and short stories are Neal Stephenson's *Snow Crash*, Roger Zelazny's " – For a Breath I Tarry –," Greg Egan's "Dust," and Philip K. Dick's "We Can Remember it For You Wholesale" and "Impostor" (both made into movies – *Total Recall* and *Impostor*, respectively).

It is now possible for computers to interface directly with a human brain. Information can flow freely from one to another; memories (or apparent memories) and skills can be uploaded or downloaded; psychological states – beliefs, desires, emotions – can be perfectly simulated on computers; and entire personalities can be transferred from a brain, stored on a computer, and uploaded back onto a brain. Now, suppose someone makes you the following offer of virtual "immortality": for a rather large fee, you can pay to have your entire mind uploaded into a corporate mainframe. You can come in as often as you like to update what you have stored. And your mind will remain on the mainframe in perpetuity, where it will always be available to be loaded onto a new brain whenever your current body dies. So long as the relevant software continues to exist, and so long as it remains possible to load your mind onto a new brain (be it an organic brain or a synthetic, computer brain), your continued existence will be possible. Not quite *eternal* life, but close enough to it. Or so goes the sales pitch. Would you pay the fee? Again, pretend that this sort of technological development is *really* possible. Would it then offer a way of surviving death?

Many philosophers – most notably the eminent seventeenth-century philosopher John Locke – have thought that what really matters in survival is just a kind of *psychological continuity*. On this view, a person A and a person B count as the *same person* if, and only if, A's psychological states display the right sort of continuity with B's psychological states. What exactly is the right sort of continuity? Well, it's hard to say exactly. After all, your beliefs and desires now are probably very different from the beliefs and desires you had when you were five; your goals are (hopefully) very different; your memories are very different; and so on. So, assuming – as seems right – that the person sitting in your chair right now is the same person as the five-year-old who bore your name so many years ago, it can't be that the right sort of psychological continuity requires substantial overlap of memories and other psychological states. Maybe some overlap is required. At any rate, some psychological continuity theorists have wanted to insist that some overlap is required – so that if A and B share no memories whatsoever, for example, then they are different persons. But what seems more important is a kind of hard-to-specify developmental relationship: A and B are the same person only if A's psychological makeup is connected to B's by a series of stages that looks like the development of a single mind over time. To the extent that there is that sort of continuity (together with the right sort of overlap), advocates of the psychological continuity theory will say that the person with the later mind *is* the same person as the one with the earlier mind.

If this view is right, then the technology described in our thought experiment might well offer a way of surviving death after all. For the psychological connection between the original person and the freshly stored mind will be quite intimate, as will be the connection between the stored mind and the mind of the "newborn" person that results from a post-mortem download.

Unfortunately, however, the view strains credulity. Consider what we would say about a case where a stored mind is loaded onto *two* brains at once. Which of the resulting persons is the same person as the original? There are, of course, only three possible answers: One, both, or neither. The first answer can't be right, since *both* resulting persons have exactly what it takes, according to the psychological continuity criterion, to be the same person as the original. But the second answer can't be right either. For, it seems, x is the same person as y if, and only if, x is a person, y is a person, and x is identical to y. And, of course, it can't be the case that the two *distinct* resulting persons are both, at the same time, *identical* to the original. (The reason, obviously, is that if they are *both* identical to the original then they are identical to one another. For if $x = z$ and $y = z$, then $x = z$.) That leaves the third answer. But if neither person is the same as the original, then it seems as if the right thing to say is just that the psychological continuity criterion is false. For it seems absurd to think that one of the resulting persons *would* have been the same as the original if only the other one had not existed. So, in short, the fact that the psychological continuity criterion allows for cases in which there is a lot of pressure to say that more than one person is the same as the original seems to be a reason for thinking that the criterion is false.

Apart from the truth of the psychological continuity criterion, there seems to be no reason to think that storing a mind on a computer for later use offers a way of surviving death. For if the psychological continuity criterion is false, then presumably more – not less – than mere psychological continuity is required for survival. And for people who do not believe in souls, the natural additional or alternative claim to make is that A is the same person as B only if A's *body* is the same (identical) body as B's. If this view is right, however, then it is possible to survive *death* only if it is possible for a dead body to come back to life. Moreover – and more worryingly – it is possible to survive the destruction or decomposition of your body only if it is possible for one and the same body to be both rebuilt and reanimated after its constituent parts have been scattered.

One might object to this view on the grounds that (intuitively) a person "goes where her brain goes." Thus, for example, you might think that the possibility of surviving the transplantation of your brain into a new body just shows that it's *not* true that A is the same person as B only if A's body is identical to B's body. (For, you might say, your post-transplant body would be *distinct from* your pre-transplant body.) But proponents of some sort of bodily criterion will respond as follows: what happens in the transplant case is just this. Your body is whittled down to the size of a brain; then, upon transplantation, it grows substantially, gaining a variety of new parts. We all know that our bodies can survive the gain and loss of parts. If you receive a heart transplant, for example, we don't say you've received a new body. We just say that you've undergone a change of parts. Likewise, then, in the case where you receive a new head, torso, and legs: your body shrinks substantially and then grows again; but it is the same (identical) body throughout the procedure.

Proponents of this view will still face the difficult question of what it takes for a *body* to survive some change. Must it, for example, retain all of the same parts? If so, then the view would seem to imply that, far from being able to survive death, we can't even survive a shave. If not, well then how many (and which) parts can it lose? Can bodies survive complete disassembly and then subsequent reassembly? If so, what does it take to reassemble a body? Must you use *all and only* the original parts? If so, then which parts count as the "original" parts? Ones you have today? Or ones you had when you were two? Or some others? If not, well then how many parts in the "reassembled" body can be new ones? (Wouldn't a body with *all* new parts just be a new body? On the other hand, isn't it arbitrary to say that, for example, exactly 64 percent of the parts must be original?) These are difficult questions, and trying to answer even some of them in appropriate detail would require several additional chapters. But we raise them just to note that imposing a bodily continuity criterion doesn't by itself solve the problem of figuring out what, in addition to or instead of psychological continuity, is necessary or sufficient for surviving death. In fact, it is only the beginning.

Arguments for and against survival

Having completed our stage setting, we are now prepared to consider some arguments for and against the possibility of post-mortem survival. Our discussion will hardly be exhaustive. Rather, we shall confine our focus to arguments for and against belief in the three most widely endorsed forms of survival: disembodied survival, reincarnation, and resurrection. Moreover, in each case we shall restrict our attention to what we take to be the strongest arguments on each side.

Disembodied survival

As noted earlier, many philosophers and theologians throughout history have endorsed the possibility of disembodied survival. We have already discussed some of the main motivations on either side of the materialism/ dualism debate, and it would take us too far afield to try to discuss more. It should be clear, however, that whatever evidence there is against dualism also counts as reason to believe that disembodied survival is impossible. Likewise, whatever evidence there is in support of dualism will at least open the door to belief in disembodied survival – open the door, but not close the case. The reason it will not close the case is that there might be reason to reject belief in disembodied survival even under the assumption of dualism. And, in fact, many philosophers have thought that there is. This is the issue on which we shall focus in the present section.

Apart from general arguments in support of materialism, the main argument against belief in disembodied survival is one originally developed by David Hume and defended in one way or another by various thinkers since. The argument is simple. In Hume's words:

> Where any two objects are so closely connected, that all alterations which we have seen in the one, are attended with proportionable alterations in the other: we ought to conclude, by all rules of analogy, that, when there are still greater alterations produced in the former, and it is totally dissolved, there follows a total dissolution of the latter.
>
> Sleep, a very small effect on the body, is attended with a temporary extinction: at least, a great confusion in the soul.
>
> The weakness of the body and that of the mind in infancy are exactly proportioned; their vigour in manhood, their sympathetic disorder in

sickness, their common gradual decay in old age. The step further seems unavoidable: their common dissolution in death . . .

Every thing is in common betwixt soul and body. The organs of the one are all of them the organs of the other. The existence therefore of the one must be dependent on the other.[5]

Note that this is an argument from *mind–body dependence*, and *not* an argument from *materialism*. As it happens, neither Hume nor the argument's most well-known defenders are dualists; but everything said here is fully consistent with dualism.

The basic idea, then, is just this:

9.1. Mind and body (or, if you prefer, mind and brain) are *intimately* connected, so that any change in the latter is attended by a change in the former.

9.2. Whenever two things are intimately connected in that way, we should assume that when the one is destroyed the other will be also.

9.3. Therefore we should assume that the mind will be destroyed upon the destruction of the brain.

Hume seems to regard this as an argument against post-mortem survival generally; but it clearly isn't. Suppose, for example, you believe in resurrection. You could then happily grant that the mind is destroyed when the brain is destroyed; but you will go on to insist that, just as the brain will return to existence at the time of resurrection, so too will the mind. Or suppose you believe in reincarnation, and you also believe (a) that reincarnated souls do not exist *between* incarnations, and (b) that the existence of a mind depends – like software, perhaps – on the existence of *a* brain, but not necessarily on the existence of the *same* brain with which it was originally associated. Here again you might happily grant that the mind will cease to exist when the brain is destroyed; but you might still insist that it can come back into existence, housed in a new brain, later on. Thus, strictly speaking (and contrary to what some defenders of the argument – like Paul Edwards – have explicitly argued), the argument tells only against belief in disembodied survival.

But is the argument successful? Should we accept the premises? The first premise is clearly true. Alcohol and drugs alter your brain chemistry; in

---

[5] "Of the Immortality of the Soul," in Richard Popkin (ed.), *Dialogues Concerning Natural Religion and the Posthumous Essays* (Indianapolis, IN: Hackett, 1980), p. 95.

doing so, they affect your mind. Such substances can produce hallucinations, induce confusion, cause or cure depression, relieve or produce anxiety, and so on. Memories, desires, and even entire personality traits can be wiped away by destroying relevant parts of the brain. And the list goes on. Even the most die-hard dualist can hardly doubt that the connection between mind and brain is as tight as premise 9.1 says that it is.

Matters are different with the second premise, however. On the one hand, it is hard to see *why* mind and body should be so intimately connected to one another if the very existence of the one doesn't depend on the existence of the other. (Indeed, it is hard to see why they should be so intimately connected if the mind isn't identical to the brain, or at the very least like software running on the brain.) But it is surely possible for the correlations between changes in the mind and changes in the brain simply to be by-products of the mind's temporary association with the brain. When you stand in front of a mirror, there is a rather tight correlation between changes in your body and changes in the mirror-image. But nobody fears that the destruction of the mirror-image will be attended by the destruction of the body it reflects.

One might respond that the mirror example is defective since there are a great many changes that take place in the body that aren't correlated with changes in the mirror image. A myriad chemical reactions happen inside your body every second without making any discernible difference in your reflection. But we can easily change the example. Imagine a body-scanner that produces an image on a screen that changes in some way every time anything – anything at all – changes in the body that is being scanned. Again, nobody will fear that destroying the image will destroy the body. Moreover, there is no reason to doubt that the destruction of the body could be attended by the persistence of the image. (Suppose the scanner is programmed in such a way that, upon the destruction of the body, the image corresponding to the last living, or fully functional, state of the body is preserved on screen.)

These examples by themselves don't *refute* premise 9.2. For the premise does not say that it is a necessary truth that intimately correlated things pass out of existence at the same time. All it says is that when we find two things so intimately correlated, we *should assume* that the existence of one depends on the existence of the other. The idea, then, is presumably that such correlation is unlikely unless there is a kind of existential dependence.

But why should we believe this in the case of mind and brain? More importantly, why should we believe this if we are not already materialists (as we clearly wouldn't be, if we are taking seriously the hypothesis of *disembodied* survival)? Do we really know enough about what immaterial souls would be like, or about how they might relate to the body, to say whether it is unlikely that there would be intimate correlation between soul and brain without existential dependence of the one on the other? It seems that we do not. Thus, it is hard to see why we should endorse premise 9.2. But without premise 9.2, the argument fails.

The failure of Hume's argument is not by itself positive reason to believe in the possibility of disembodied survival. For the right sorts of positive arguments, one will have to look either to putative divine revelation or to philosophical arguments in support of dualism. But with those arguments in hand, and given the failure of Hume's argument, there seems to be no serious obstacle to believing that disembodied post-mortem survival is a live possibility.

Reincarnation[6]

Reincarnation happens if and when one and the same person returns to life in a body that is numerically distinct from the body she had (or was) when she died. Some believers in reincarnation believe in souls that survive as disembodied spirits between incarnations; others – many if not most Buddhists, for example – do not. Most believers in reincarnation also believe the doctrine of *karma*, according to which the quality and nature of one's later incarnations depends in large part upon one's behavior during earlier incarnations. The doctrine of karma merits extended discussion in its own right. But for purposes here we shall leave that discussion aside.

Unlike belief in disembodied survival, there is more than just philosophical argument to support belief in reincarnation. There is alleged empirical evidence. As early as the sixth century BC, the Greek philosopher Pythagoras is reported to have produced such evidence for his own belief in reincarnation:

---

[6] The discussion in this section is substantially influenced by the works of Paul Edwards listed among the titles for Further Reading at the end of the chapter.

They say that, while staying at Argos, he saw a shield from the spoils of Troy nailed up, and burst into tears. When the Argives asked him the reason for his emotion, he said that he himself had borne that shield in Troy when he was Euphorbus; they did not believe him, and judged him to be mad, but he said he would find a true sign that this was the case; for on the inside of the shield was written in archaic lettering EUPHORBUS'S. Because of the extraordinary nature of the claim, they all urged him to take down the offering; and the inscription was found on it.[7]

Most of us nowadays will dismiss this story about Pythagoras as mere legend. But contemporary research has produced similar evidence for reincarnation that is less easy to dismiss. Two kinds of evidence in particular deserve our attention.

First, there are well-known cases in which hypnotic regression in adults has uncovered apparently suppressed memories of past lives. One of the most famous such cases involved a woman named Virginia Tighe who, in the early 1950s, underwent several sessions of hypnotic regression during which she seemed to recollect details of a past life as a woman named Bridey Murphy in nineteenth-century Ireland. Part of what made the case impressive was the amount of detail in her memories that seemed as if it could not have come from other sources. Summarizing the case, Paul Edwards writes:

> Bernstein [the hypnotist] as well as the others attending the sessions found several of the features of Bridey's responses overwhelmingly convincing. Her Irish brogue [which was present only under hypnosis] seemed entirely genuine. She constantly used strange Irish words and she seemed to possess a wealth of information about nineteenth-century Ireland. One episode which was particularly impressive to them concerned the "Morning Jig," an Irish dance mentioned by Virginia during one of the sessions. Bernstein gave her a posthypnotic suggestion to dance the jig after coming out of her trance. When Virginia came back, after some urging on Bernstein's part, she suddenly "became vibrantly alive" and "her feet were flying in a cute little dance." Then she looked dazed and unaware of what she had done. The episode was doubly impressive because Virginia was known to be a poor dancer. She was also not given to reading books and, according to Bernstein's account, there is no evidence that she had ever engaged in the study of Irish history and customs.[8]

---

[7] Diodorus, X.6.2; quoted and translated in Jonathan Barnes, *The Presocratic Philosophers* (London: Routledge, 1979), p. 110.

[8] Paul Edwards, *Reincarnation: A Critical Examination* (Amherst, NY: Prometheus Books, 2002), pp. 60–1.

Moreover, though the case of Bridey Murphy is one of the most famous, it is hardly unique. There are many documented cases in which hypnosis has turned up detailed apparent recollections of times and places of which the subject allegedly had little or no prior awareness. And many people take such cases as clear empirical evidence of reincarnation. Indeed, a Google search on terms like "past life regression" reveals a small industry devoted to helping people recover details of their past lives through hypnosis.

Second, there is a fairly large body of research by psychiatrist Ian Stevenson, documenting a variety of cases in which children seem to be remembering – on their own and without the aid of anything like hypnosis – details of past lives. The main body of Stevenson's research is summarized in his two-volume work *Cases of the Reincarnation Type*.[9] The cases documented there strongly resemble one another. Here is a fairly striking and representative case:

> *The Case of Samuel Helander*. Samuel Helander was born in Helsinki, Finland, on April 15, 1976. When he was two years old, he began to make some statements and recognitions that suggested he was remembering the life of his mother's younger brother, Pertti Häikiö . . .
>
> Samuel was only about a year and a half old when, upon being asked his name, he said that it was "Pelti." (At that time and for some time later, he could not pronounce the "r" sound of "Pertti.") Attempts to convince Samuel that his name was "Samuel" generally failed; he insisted that it was "Pelti" and later "Pertti" . . .
>
> On looking at [a photograph of Pertti] Samuel remarked that he remembered how a dog had bitten him on the leg. A dog had bitten Pertti on the leg when he was a child of three, but Samuel had never been bitten by a dog and had never been told about Pertti's having been bitten. Nor did the photograph give any clue suggesting that he had been bitten.
>
> On another occasion Samuel noticed a photograph of Pertti as a young child using a walker. He said that the photgraph was of himself and that he had been in the hospital with his legs in plaster. [The photo] showed Pertti using a walker . . . but nothing in the photograph suggested that his legs had been in plaster, as they had been just before the photograph was taken. Pertti's legs had both been fractured in an accident when he was about four years old. When Samuel made his remark about this, he was himself between three and four years old.

[9] Ian Stevenson, *Cases of the Reincarnation Type* (Charlottesville, VA: University Press of Virginia, 1975).

When Samuel saw a photograph of Pentti Häikiö, Pertti's father, he said: "This is my father" ... Samuel also identified several objects that had belonged to Pertti: a guitar, a velvet cordouroy jacket, and an old watch ... When Samuel was taken to the cemetery where Pertti had been buried, he looked at Pertti's grave and said: "This is my grave."[10]

As with the hypnotic regression cases, these cases are thought to lend support to the doctrine of reincarnation because reincarnation is viewed as the best available explanation of the phenomena.

But is it? Unfortunately for those who would like to believe in reincarnation, the answer seems to be "no." The trouble with both the Stevenson cases and the hypnotic regression cases is that plausible naturalistic explanations for the phenomena are usually available, and even when they aren't, the abundance of naturalistic explanations for other cases makes it very plausible to think that, if only we had access to further information, we would find such explanations for the remaining cases as well. Thus, for example, in many of the hypnotic regression cases, we have substantial evidence that the alleged "memories" are not genuine memories at all, but rather invented or recollected stories that incorporate or are based on information gleaned from forgotten sources. There is, therefore, no need to appeal to reincarnation to explain the remarkable amounts of detail in these memories; and the fact that the subject reports no previous awareness of the times or places involved in the memories is readily explained by the supposition that she is suffering from *cryptomnesia* (roughly, a phenomenon wherein the brain fabricates pseudo-memories from forgotten source-material and then represents the pseudo-memories as genuine). Indeed, part of our evidence that cryptomnesia is a good explanation for at least some of these cases is the simple fact that, in some such cases we have actually *identified* the forgotten sources. And this, in turn, makes it very plausible that cryptomnesia is what ultimately explains the other cases – like the Bridey Murphy case – where we cannot identify the forgotten source.

Likewise, independent investigation of the work of Ian Stevenson has turned up methodological flaws in the vast majority of his case studies.[11] It is, of course, possible that the cases are genuine despite the methodological

---

[10] Ian Stevenson, *Children Who Remember Previous Lives* (Jefferson, NC: McFarland, 2001), pp. 73–5.

[11] It would take us too far afield to discuss the problems in detail here; but see the works by Paul Edwards listed in the Further Reading section for discussion.

flaws. But the trouble is precisely that, given the flaws, we have no real reason to think that the cases are genuine. The claim that the reincarnation hypothesis provides the best explanation for these phenomena is believable only if we have no reason to think that flaws in our investigative techniques might be masking the correct explanation. But the presence of so many methodological flaws in Stevenson's work gives us a great deal of reason to think that the correct explanation might be hidden from us. Moreover, the fact that such flaws are present in the vast majority of his cases makes it hard to take seriously the reincarnation hypothesis in the few cases that aren't manifestly flawed. Perhaps whatever explains the other cases also explains those.

So it would appear that neither hypnotic regression nor the sorts of spontaneous memories investigated by Stevenson lend any real support to the doctrine of reincarnation. This is surely bad news for advocates of the doctrine of reincarnation; but, on the other hand, it goes no distance toward showing that that the doctrine is false. Nevertheless, the doctrine does seem to face problems. It is to a consideration of these that we now turn.

The two oldest and most important objections to belief in reincarnation were both raised by the third century Christian philosopher Tertullian. The first is the so-called "population problem." As it is usually raised, the objection is that the doctrine of reincarnation is inconsistent with population growth. In order to defend the inconsistency claim, however, it is necessary to appeal to additional views that typically but don't necessarily attend belief in reincarnation. For example, consider this view:

REBIRTH   Every human birth is the rebirth of a soul that once lived as a human being here on our planet.

If REBIRTH is correct, or if it could plausibly be seen as *essential* to the doctrine of reincarnation, then the inconsistency would be manifest. If the starting population of human beings is n, and REBIRTH is true, then at any given time the population of human beings cannot possibly be more than n. There simply would not be enough souls to go around.

The trouble for the objector, however, is that there is no good reason to suppose that REBIRTH is essential to the doctrine of reincarnation. That doesn't mean that the objection is useless as it is standardly formulated. For, after all, even if REBIRTH (or something relevantly like it) isn't an essential part of the doctrine of reincarnation, it might well be an essential part of some widely endorsed religious view that incorporates belief in reincarnation. And if it is, then the population problem will tell against that religious view. But if what is desired is a general objection against belief in reincarnation, then the population problem as it is standardly formulated will not do. Perhaps there are ways of reformulating it so that the problem is more generally applicable; but if so, it is hard to see how.

The second objection is more serious. The problem, in short, is that whereas all newborn human beings *seem*, unlike Winnie the Pooh, to have very young – indeed, brand new – infant minds, or souls, this is not at all what we would expect if the doctrine of reincarnation were true. If the soul of every baby is in fact a soul that has lived once, or many times, before in different bodies, why aren't babies more like adults? Indeed, one might expect that, more often than not, parents would give birth to children who could share with *them* a great deal of advice and life experience. Moreover, despite the fact that the phenomenon of recollecting past lives isn't entirely rare and isolated, it is, at any rate, quite a bit less frequent than we would expect under the assumption that the doctrine of reincarnation is true. Why don't more of us remember our past lives if, as believers in reincarnation maintain, *all* of us in fact lived different lives in the past? Remarkably, this objection has not received nearly the sort of attention that one might expect from believers in reincarnation. (Paul Edwards comments in his discussion of the objection that it is "little less than scandalous that no reincarnationist has ever attempted to reply to this argument."[12])

In closing our discussion, it is worth noting that some views about what we are will exacerbate the concerns just raised, and other views are outright inconsistent with the doctrine of reincarnation. Versions of materialism that say that we are identical with our bodies (or with some part thereof, such as the brain) fall clearly into the latter category. And versions of materialism according to which our minds are like software for the brain seem to exacerbate the worries raised in the second objection. For if the mind is like software, it is very hard to see any sense in which the "mental program" of an infant could be seen as a "reincarnation" of the mental program of a now-dead adult. Thus, any argument that supports either of these two materialist views will count against the doctrine of reincarnation as well.

---

[12] *Reincarnation: A Critical Examination* (Amherst, NY: Prometheus Books, 2002), p. 223.

Resurrection

In this, our final section, we turn to a discussion of resurrection. As noted earlier, the difference between reincarnation and resurrection is just the difference between acquiring a new body that is numerically distinct from whatever body one had before, and returning to life in (or as) the numerically same body that one had (or was) before.

Belief in resurrection is a central element of the Christian tradition; and the Christian hope of resurrection is explicitly anchored in the resurrection of Jesus of Nazareth. Not surprisingly, then, one way of defending belief in resurrection has been to offer historical arguments for the reliability of the New Testament (which records not only the resurrection of Jesus but also several other resurrection miracles performed by Jesus and his disciples) and for the truth of the claim that Jesus did in fact rise from the dead. The strongest versions of the latter argument typically take the form of an inference to the best explanation. Christians begin by citing a variety of largely uncontested historical facts – that Jesus died as a result of crucifixion; that, upon his death, his disciples despaired and lost hope; that, shortly after despairing and losing hope, his disciples had experiences that they took to be experiences of the risen Jesus; that these experiences transformed them into bold proclaimers of Jesus' message and of his resurrection; that the resurrection message was preached in the very city (Jerusalem) where Jesus was crucified; that, as a result of the belief that Jesus rose on Sunday, the disciples – mostly devout Jews, used to worshipping on Saturday – changed their regular day of worship to Sunday; (somewhat more controversially) that the tomb in which Jesus had been buried was found empty very soon after his death; and so on. They then claim that the literal bodily resurrection of Jesus is the best explanation for these facts.

Historical arguments like this aim at providing us with positive reasons for believing that resurrection can and does occur. Philosophical arguments concerning resurrection aim less at showing that resurrection does occur, focusing instead on the possibility or impossibility of resurrection. In what follows we will examine some of the most important philosophical arguments for the claim that resurrection is not possible after all.

If resurrection occurs, it occurs in one of three ways: by reassembling at least some of parts from the original body into a new body, or by assembling all new parts into a body that is somehow the same as the original, or, finally, by taking the complete and entire corpse of the original body and "reviving" it. Unfortunately, each of these possibilities is problematic. Let's consider them in turn.

On the first view, resurrection involves reassembly of the parts of the original body. But how many parts of the original? To start we might ask what problems there might be if resurrection required reassembly of *all* the parts. This view faces an objection put rather forcefully by Voltaire:

> A soldier from Brittany goes into Canada; there, by a very common chance, he finds himself short of food, and is forced to eat an Iroquois whom he killed the day before. This Iroquois had fed on Jesuits for two or three months; a great part of his body had become Jesuit. Here, then, the body of a soldier is composed of Iroquois, of Jesuits, and of all that he had eaten before. How is each to take again precisely what belongs to him? And which part belongs to each? (Voltaire, *Questions sur l'encyclopédie*, excerpted in Paul Edwards (ed.), *Immortality*, p. 147)

This is the so-called cannibalism problem. Note that it doesn't depend on the supposition that cannibalism *actually* occurs. Rather, the way to think of the objection is like this: Cannibalism cases of the sort just described *might* occur; and if they did, then God could not resurrect everyone involved in the scenario since there wouldn't be enough parts to go around. (If the Jesuit got all of the Jesuit-parts, then the Iroquois and the Brit would be missing some parts – assuming, as the example does, that the relevant Jesuit parts had become parts of the Iroquois and the Brit, respectively.) But it is absurd to think that God's hands might be tied in such a way. Thus, the doctrine that people survive death by being resurrected by God cannot be true.

So far the argument goes no distance toward showing that resurrection is impossible. Rather, all it seems to show is that there are some practical problems that God would face in trying to bring it about. In particular, God would have to sort out who gets which parts. At any rate, he would have to sort out these problems if resurrection involves, as the example supposes, *reassembly* of the original body. And, as one might expect, this is hardly the only practical problem that would have to be addressed in that case. For example, God will also have to decide whether the parts you had upon death, or upon birth, or on your eighteenth birthday, or at some other time in your life are *the* parts that need to be reassembled in order to resurrect you. Relatedly, God would have to decide at what age to resurrect you. And if you were born with or acquired severe physical defects, or (say) lost limbs or other bodily organs in the course of your life, he would have to decide whether to reproduce these defects upon reassembling you or to correct them. All difficult decisions to be sure. But believers in resurrection have been rightly sanguine about the possibility that an omniscient, omnipotent God just might be able to sort it all out in the end.

Perhaps this view makes resurrection out to be harder than it really is. Perhaps, that is, rather than requiring reassembly of all the parts, resurrection requires only reassembly of *some* parts. While this view might soften the worries raised by the cannibalism problem, it raises another problem: how *many* of the original parts must be used in the reassembly? Presumably if God could resurrect you by reassembling all of them, then he could do so by reassembling all but one tiny atom. So not *all* of the parts are needed. But then *how many*? Or what proportion? Half? Two-thirds? Any answer seems arbitrary.

Since neither of the reassembly options is without difficulty, perhaps we should jettison those views. What if, rather than reassembling old parts, resurrection takes place using entirely new parts? To see the problem with this view it will be useful to digress briefly here to discuss an example from contemporary science fiction. In the *Star Trek* films and television episodes, there is a device known as the "transporter room" which works as follows: You step into the device on your spaceship; your body is completely dismantled; and then your body is reassembled in the location to which the transporter is transporting you. Under one theory of how the transporter operates, all of the original matter in your body is left on the spaceship, and your body is reassembled using new, local matter from the place to which you are transported. If something like this were possible it would also be possible in principle for God to reassemble your body using all new parts.

The problem, however, is that there is good reason to think that the transporter room is *not* possible. To see why, consider the following scenario: Spock steps into the transporter room. He is dismantled. On the surface of the planet below, Spock is reassembled ... thrice over. In other words, the transporter takes local matter and reconstitutes not just one "version" of Spock, but three. We now have a situation very much like the mind-upload scenario described on page 269. We can say that just one of the resulting persons *is* Spock; but that seems arbitrary. There is simply no reason to think that one would be Spock if the others aren't.

We can try to say that all three of the resulting persons are Spock; but that is nonsense. Thus, there is considerable pressure to say that none would be Spock. But if none would be Spock in that case, then we should say that in the case where the transporter reconstitutes just one "version" of Spock, there too the resulting person is not Spock. For whether Spock survives the transporter room and arrives on the planet cannot depend on whether duplicates of Spock are made. To put the point another way: Call the resulting persons in our scenario "Spock 1," "Spock 2," and "Spock 3." The point is that if, say, Spock 1 isn't *Spock*, that fact doesn't depend on the existence of Spock 2 or Spock 3. If Spock 1 isn't Spock, then he wouldn't have been Spock if he had been unaccompanied by the other two. And the same goes for Spock 2 and Spock 3.

In sum, then, to say that God must use all of your original parts – whatever those might be – in reassembling you leads to the cannibalism objection; to say that he must use some but not all forces us to an arbitrary decision about just what proportion is required; and to say that he can reconstitute you using all new parts is untenable, since it leaves open the possibility for duplication (as in the transporter room scenario).

Note too that it won't help matters to insist on some form of dualism, or on some sort of psychological continuity criterion of personal identity over time. The reason is that resurrection occurs *only if* you have numerically the same body in the afterlife as you had when you died – and this regardless of whether *you* are, fundamentally, an immaterial soul or a soul–body composite or the sort of thing whose identity is determined by continuity of psychological states rather than by some sort of material continuity.

In addition to these problems for specific accounts of resurrection, it seems that any account that involves reassembly or reconstitution faces a more general problem: explaining how something once destroyed could somehow be brought back into existence. Peter van Inwagen explains this general problem this way:

> Suppose a certain monastery claims to have in its possession a manuscript written in St Augustine's own hand. And suppose the monks of this monastery further claim that this manuscript was burned by Arians in the year 457. It would immediately occur to me to ask how *this* manuscript, the one I can touch, could be the very manuscript that was burned in 457. Suppose their answer to this question is that God miraculously recreated Augustine's manuscript in 458. I should respond to this answer as follows:

the deed it describes seems quite impossible, even as an accomplishment of omnipotence. God certainly might have created a perfect duplicate of the original manuscript, but it would not be *that* one; its earliest moment of existence would have been after Augustine's death; it would never have known the impress of his hand; it would not have been a part of the furniture of the world when he was alive; and so on.[13]

Likewise, van Inwagen goes on to argue, it is hard to see how a body that has been decomposed could ever be brought back to existence through reassembly or reconstitution – even by an act of God. On the face of it, then, resurrection seems impossible.

As a result, van Inwagen suggests that resurrection is possible *only* if it involves something like the *resuscitation* of a non-decomposed (or not-very-much-decomposed) corpse; and so if God wants to ensure that he will be able to resurrect everyone whom he wants to resurrect, God has to ensure, at least, that none of those people suffer decay after death. How can we take this idea seriously, given the manifest empirical truth that (pretty much) all corpses decay after death? According to van Inwagen, believers in resurrection should take seriously the hypothesis that, upon death, God snatches away the person's body and undetectably replaces it with a simulacrum which then undergoes decay. An omnipotent God surely *could* do this; and if this is what is required for resurrection to be possible, then an omnipotent God who wanted to resurrect some of his creatures surely *would* do this.

It would certainly be odd if resurrection worked this way. But, as has often been pointed out in connection with other philosophical views, oddity is not falsity. Still, if most of our bodies do not in fact decay after death, and if there is a grand cosmic mausoleum somewhere (but where?) that houses all of the corpses of those awaiting resurrection, the universe is a very different place from what we take it to be. Moreover, the view seems still to leave open the possibility that God can't have exactly what he wants. Fred sits on a nuclear warhead and detonates it. Presumably Fred's death will coincide with the rapid scattering of his constituent parts. There will therefore be no corpse here for God to snatch. So what will God do? Snatch Fred alive and then kill him some other way? Or, with regrets, simply allow Fred to lose whatever place he might have had in the general resurrection?

---

[13] "The Possibility of Resurrection," *International Journal for Philosophy of Religion* 9 (1978), pp. 116–17.

Neither alternative is attractive; but if van Inwagen's view is correct, these would seem to be the only options.

Is there any way forward here? Perhaps. The main "problem" with the reconstitution view we looked at above is just that one wants to ask "What would *make it the case* that some newly created body later on is really identical to some earlier body that has since passed out of existence?" As we saw, whatever characteristic one might pick, it looks like a duplicate could have that property as well, and thus there would be two bodies with equal claim to being the original, which is impossible.

One way to think about the question of what could make an original body and a later resurrected body identical would be to ask the more humdrum question: "What makes *your* body now identical to the body that you had when you were five years old?" Your body, after all, has mostly if not entirely different parts than your five-year-old body had; it is a different size and has many other different characteristics. Just as in the case of resurrection, it is hard to give any very good answer to this question. For however your body now happens to be related to that five-year-old body – by similarity relations, spatiotemporal relations, causal relations, and so on – your body could just as easily stand in those very same relations to a wholly distinct five-year-old body. Well, maybe not just as *easily* given our natural laws; but the point is that it is possible for your body to be related to a distinct body in just the ways it is related to itself – *except in this one way*: your body stands to itself in the relation of numerical identity; and it could not bear *that* relation to anything else. But, of course, we can't say that what makes your body identical to your five-year-old body is that the "two" bodies stand in the relation of identity. For that would be circular. In light of this, it seems that what we really ought to say in response to questions like "What makes this body identical to that body?" is "Nothing: they just *are* identical."[14] But if we admit this as an answer, the main problem with the reconstitution view goes away.

Conclusion

In this chapter, we have considered a variety of different conceptions of immortality, and a variety of different arguments for and against belief in

---

[14] This view has been defended by Trenton Merricks, both in the article by him listed in the Further Reading section, as well as in his contribution to Kevin Corcoran's anthology, also listed in that section.

various kinds of immortality. We haven't reached any definitive conc̲
sions about which conception of immortality is *the* correct one; nor have ̲
reached any definitive conclusions about whether life after death actual̲
happens. What we have seen, however, is that those who would argue tha̲
life after death is impossible have their work cut out for them: severa̲
different conceptions of immortality seem viable; and many of the objec̲
tions against belief in different kinds of immortality are readily answerable.

Further reading

Bynum, Caroline Walker, *The Resurrection of the Body* (New York: Columbia University Press, 1995).

Churchland, Paul, *Matter and Consciousness*, revised edition (Cambridge, MA: MIT Press, 1988).

Cooper, John, *Body, Soul and Life Everlasting* (Grand Rapids, MI: Eerdmans, 1989).

Corcoran, Kevin (ed.), *Soul, Body, and Survival* (Ithaca, NY: Cornell University Press, 2001).

Edwards, Paul, (ed.), *Immortality* (New York, NY: Macmillan, 1992).

Merricks, Trenton, "The Resurrection of the Body and the Life Everlasting," in Michael Murray (ed.), *Reason for the Hope Within* (Grand Rapids, MI: Eerdmans, 1999).

Perry, John, *Dialogues on Personal Identity and Immortality* (Indianapolis, IN: Hackett, 1978).

Shoemaker, Sydney and Richard Swinburne, *Personal Identity* (Oxford: Basil Blackwell, 1984).

Swinburne, Richard, *The Evolution of the Soul*, revised edition (Oxford: Clarendon Press, 1997).

Index